Elbert COUNTY GEORGIA

Court *of* Ordinary

Record *of* Apprentices
- 1867-1903 -

(Volume #2)

Compiled by:
Michael A. Ports

Southern Historical Press, Inc.
Greenville, South Carolina

Copyright 2020
By: Michael A. Ports

All rights reserved. No part of this publication may be reproduced, stored in a retrieval system, transmitted in any form, posted on to the web in any form or by any means without the prior written permission of the publisher.

Please direct all correspondence and orders to:

www.southernhistoricalpress.com
or
SOUTHERN HISTORICAL PRESS, Inc.
PO BOX 1267
375 West Broad Street
Greenville, SC   29601
southernhistoricalpress@gmail.com

ISBN #0-89308-552-9

Printed in the United States of America

Introduction

On December 10, 1790, the Georgia General Assembly created Elbert County from a portion of Wilkes County, making Elberton the seat of its new Government. Portions of Elbert County were taken to establish Madison County in 1811 and Hart County in 1853. During the period covered by the following records, the powers of the Court of Ordinary were vested in an Ordinary, who was the ex officio clerk. The court had jurisdiction over all probate matters, including apprenticeships, subject to an appeal to the Superior Court.

The following transcription is taken from the microfilm photographed on March 16, 1960 at the courthouse in Elberton by the Genealogical Society of Salt Lake City, Utah, and available at the Georgia Archives in Morrow, Georgia. The heading on the microfilm reads

Elbert County
State of Georgia

Court of Ordinary
Record of Apprentices
1867 - 1903

Index

The records primarily consist of copies of the indentures of apprenticeship, essentially the contracts binding the apprentice to the master. The indentures provide the date and term of the apprenticeship, and the names of the apprentice, the master, the person authorizing the indenture, usually a parent, guardian, next of kin, the ordinary, or judge, as well as witnesses. The indentures also specify the duties and responsibilities of both the apprentice and master.

The original record volume contains an index arranged alphabetically only the name of the apprentice. A complete full-name index follows the transcription. The reader should know that a lone surname in the index indicates that no first name appears in the record, for example Mr. Smith, Smith & Company, or said Smith. An index entry such as Smith, ___ indicates that a first name was entered, but has been obscured by an ink blot, smear, tear, or other imperfection. Similarly, an index entry such as ___. Cynthia indicates that either no surname was entered, or the surname is obliterated. The pages of the original record volume are numbered. The numbers between brackets, for example [163], are the original page numbers and are placed in the upper right hand corner of each original page. Due to the size of the original record book, the following transcription includes the pages 267 through 558 of the original volume. James J. Burch served as ordinary during the period covered by the transcription. The records apparently contain no original signatures, except of course those of the ordinary.

For the most part, their handwriting is legible, and the quality of the microfilm is good, making the reading and transcription process straightforward and not too difficult, although several of the microfilm images are faint, blurred, or dark. The occasional ink blot, smear, or other imperfection is noted within brackets, for example [blot] or [faint]. The transcription follows Sperry's recommended guidelines for reading early American handwriting.[1] Generally, the transcription maintains the overall format of the minutes, but presents the case citations, jury panels, and other court proceedings in a standard and consistent format. No grammar or spelling errors are corrected in the transcription, although a few commas, semicolons, apostrophes, and periods are added for clarity. The clerks entered a vertical squiggly line to delineate case citations, affidavit and petition headings, and signature citations, replicated by the symbol } in the transcription.

Sometimes the clerk formed the letters "a" and "o" in a very similar manner, making abbreviations like Jas. and Jos. and surnames Bagg and Bogg or Shannan and Shannon difficult to distinguish. At other times, the letters "a" and "u" are too similar to differentiate such names as Barden and Burden or Barnett and Burnett. At still other times, the clerk failed to dot the letter "i," making the name Silman appear to be Selman. In a similar manner, the names Edmond and Edmund can be difficult to distinguish. The formation of the letters "n" and "r" at the end of surnames sometimes appear to be the same. Invariably, the formation of the capital letters "I" and "J" are identical. Determining which letter usually not difficult when the first letter of a name, but almost entirely a guess when an initial. The clerk often crossed the letter "t" by extending the horizontal line across the entire word, making it difficult to distinguish between such surnames as Watters and Walters. Compounding the problem, he sometimes neglected to cross any "t" in a word, making a "t" appear to be an "l," and making it difficult to distinguish Garrett from Garrell, Walter from Waller, or Motes from Moles. The letters "L" and "S" can be difficult to distinguish, confusing such names as Landers and Sanders. Careful researchers will consult the original record or the microfilm copy to either confirm the transcription or formulate an alternative interpretation of the clerk's handwriting.

---

[1] Sperry, Kip, *Reading Early American Handwriting.* Genealogical Publishing Company, Baltimore, Maryland, Sixth Printing, 2008.

The book is dedicated to the memory of William Blake, John and Martha (Moon) Blake, Jacob and Caty Eberhart, David and Susannah (Griffith) Eberhart, James and Isabella (Rhea) McCleskey, William and Sarah Moon, William and Margaret (Harbin) Suttle, Isaac and Sarah Suttle, and Samuel and Elizabeth (Patton) Wood, all early residents of Elbert County and just a few of the author's numerous Georgia ancestors. Many thanks are offered to the kind, patient, and generous staff of the Georgia Archives, for their assistance and suggestions, not only in locating the original records, but in understanding their historical context. Thanks also are offered LaBruce Lucas of the Southern Historical Press for his sage professional advice and counsel. Special thanks are offered to the author's late mother, Ouida J. Ports, who inspired and encouraged her son's interest in history and genealogy.

Record of Apprentices

Georgia   }   [267]
Elbert County   } This Indenture, made and entered into this the 12th day of June in the Year of our Lord eighteen hundred and ninety seven, between Thomas Brawner, of the one part, and Omire Colbert, Mother of Comus Brawner aged 18 years old, of the other part. Witnesseth: that the said Omire Colbert hereby binds and apprentices to the said Thomas Brawner the said Comus Brawner until he shall become twenty one years of age. Upon the following Condition or Terms: said Thomas Brawner agrees to take into his custody said Comus Brawner, to teach him the business of husbandry, furnish him with protection, wholesome food, suitable clothing, necessary medicine and medical attention, teach him habits of industry, honesty, and morality, Cause him to be taught the elementary principals Mathematics and to read English, and shall govern him with humanity, using only the same degree of force to compel his obedience as a father may use with his minor child, and when said Comus Brawner arrives at the age of twenty one years of age, He is to be provided for as by law in such cases provided. In Consideration of all of which, the said Thomas Brawner is to be entitled to the services of the said Comus Brawner until he becomes twenty one years of age. Witness our hands and Seals this the day & year above written.

Signed, sealed, and delivered in the presence of

Ja^s F. Reaves	Thomas + Brawner. his mark
J. J. Burch	Omire + Colbert, her mark
Ordinary E. C.	

Georgia   }   [268]
Elbert County   } This Indenture, made and entered into this the 18th day of June 1897, between E. J. Bell, of the one part, and Kate Thunderburg, the mother of Jep Brawner, the father of the said Jep being dead, now age nineteen years, all of Said County. Witnesseth: that the said Kate Thunderburg hereby binds and apprentices to the said E. J. Bell the said Jep Brawner for the full term and period of one year from the date of these articles, upon the following conditions. Said E. J. Bell agrees to take into his custody the said Jep, to teach him the business of husbandry, furnish him with protection, wholesome food, Suitable clothing, necessary medicine and medical attention, teach him habits of industry, honesty, and morality, and govern him with humanity, using only the same degree of force to compel his obedience as a father may use with his minor child, and the said E.

J. Bell agrees further to pay to the said Jep, or to the said Kate Thunderburg, his Mother, the sum of five and one half dollars per Month during the continuance of the Apprenticeship. In Consideration of all of which, the said E. J. Bell is entitled to the services of the said Jep for the said period of one year from this date. Witness our hands Seals the year and day first above written.

Signed, sealed, and }
Delivered in the presence of }   Kate + Thunderburg, her mark
J. J. Burch }   E. J. Bell
Ordinary C. C. }

Executed in Duplicate.

Filed in office June 18, 1897.

J. J. Burch, Ord

Georgia } [269]
Elbert County } This Indenture, made this 7th day of August 1897, between Mandy Brawner, of said County, for and in behalf of her minor Daughter Alia, being of the age of Alia Three years, of the one part, and Ida Rucker, of the County aforesaid, of the other part. Witnesseth: That the said Mandy Brawner aforesaid does by these presents bind out her said minor daughter Alia, of Said County, as Apprentice to said Ida Rucker in the trade or craft of Servant or as Laborer upon the plantation of the Said Ida Rucker to be taught the Said Craft or trade of servant or Laborer, to live with, continue, and serve the said Ida Rucker as an Apprentice from the date hereof for and during the term of her minority. During all of which time, the said Mandy Brawner, as afore Said, doth covenant with the said Ida Rucker that the said Alia Brawner Shall well and faithfully demean herself as such Apprentice, observing fully the commands of the said Ida Rucker, and in all things, deporting and behaving her self as a faithful Apprentice to the Said Ida Rucker, neither revealing her secrets, nor at any time leaving or neglecting the business of the Said Ida Rucker. And for and in consideration of the Service well and faithfully Rendered by the Said Alia Brawner, of the first part, said Ida Rucker, of the second part, doth covenant, promise, and agree to instruct her said Apprentice, or otherwise cause her to be well and faithfully instructed, in the said trade or craft of Servant or laborer, and also to read the english Language, and shall also allow, furnish, and provide her said Apprentice with meat and drink and clothing during the said term, and all other necessary meet and proper, in sickness and in health. And shall also, at the expiration of the Said term, allow and pay the

Apprentice what is now allowed by the Statute in such cases made and provided. Witness our hands and Seals the day and year first before written.

Executed before me   Mandy + Brawner, her mark
J. J. Burch, Ordinary   Ida Rucker

Filed in office, approve, & Recorded August 7, 1897.

J. J. Burch

Georgia   }   [270]
Elbert County } This Indenture, Made this the 2nd day of August 1897, between Milly Blackwell, of Said County, for and in behalf of Mattie and Lizzie Blackwell, her minor Daughters, being of the age of Mattie 14 & Lizzie 11 years, of the one part, and J. E. Herndon, of the County aforesaid, of the other part. Witnesseth: that the said Milly Blackwell, as aforesaid, does by these presents bind out the Said Mattie and Lizzie, of Said County, as Apprentice to Said J. E. Herndon in the trade or craft of House Servants or as Laborers upon the plantation of the Said J. E. Herndon to be taught the Said Craft or trade of House Servants or Laborer, and to live with, continue, and serve the said J. E. Herndon as an Apprentice from the date hereof for and During the term of two years. During all of which time, the said Milly Blackwell, as aforesaid, doth covenant with the Said J. E. Herndon that the said Mattie & Lizzies shall well and faithfully demean them selves as such Apprentice, observing fully the Command of the Said J. E. Herndon And in all things deporting and behaving them Selves as faithful Apprentices to the Said J. E. Herndon, neither revealing his secrets, nor at any time leaving or neglecting the business of the Said J. E. Herndon.

And for and in consideration of the service well and faithfully rendered by the said Mattie & Lizzie, of the first part, said J. E. Herndon, of the second part, doth covenant, promise, and agree to instruct his said Apprentices, or otherwise cause them to be well and faithfully instructed, in the Said trade or craft of House Servant or laborer, and also to read the English language, and shall also allow, furnish, and provide his said Apprentices with meat and drink and clothing during the said term, and all other necessaries meet and proper, in sickness and in health. And shall also, at the expiration of the said term, allow and pay the Said Apprentice what is now allowed by the Statute in such case made & provided.

Witness our hands & Seals the day and year first before written.

executed before me   Milly + Blackwell, her mark
J. H. Thornton, N. P.   J. E. Herndon

[The Ordinary wrote the following notation vertically in the left margin of the page.]

Filed in office August 3rd and Recorded August 7th 1897.

         J. J. Burch, Ord

Georgia }   [271]
Elbert County } This Indenture, Made this the 3rd day of August 1897, between Sallie Gunter, of Said County, for and in behalf of her Daughters Rosa, Lottie, Antonett and her son Isaac, being of the age Rosa 19, Lottie, 17, Antonett 14, and Isaac 11 years, of the one part, and Isaac Hutson, of the County aforesaid, of the other part. Witnesseth: That the said Sallie Gunter, as aforesaid, does by these presents bind out her Said Daughters, Rosa, Lottie, Antonett, and Isaac, of said County, as apprentice to said Isaac Hutson in the trade or craft of Servants or as labors upon the plantation of the Said Isaac Hutson, to be taught the said craft or trade of Servants or Laborers, and to live with, continue, and serve the said Isaac Hutson as an Apprentice from the date hereof for and during the term of five months or the remainder of the year 1897. During all of which time, the said Sallie Gunter, as aforesaid, doth covenant with the said Isaac Hutson that the said Rosa, Lottie, Antonett, & Isaac Shall well and faithfully demean themselves as such faithful Apprentices, observing fully the commands of the said Isaac Hutson and in all things deporting and behaving themselves as faithful Apprentices to the said Isaac Hutson, neither revealing his secrets, nor at any time leaving or neglecting the business of the said Isaac Hutson.

And for and in consideration of the service well and faithfully rendered by the said Rosa, Lottie, Antonett, and Isaac, of the first part, Said Isaac Hutson, of the second part, doth covenant, promise, and and agree to instruct his said Apprentices, or otherwise cause them to be well and faithfully instructed, in the said trade or craft of Servant or Laborer, and shall also allow, furnish, and provide his said Apprentices with meat and Drink and Clothing for Isaac during the said term, and all other necessaries meet and proper, in sickness and in health. And shall also, at the expiration of the said term, allow and pay the Said Apprentices Sixty Two & $^{80}/_{100}$ Dollars.

Witness our hands & Seals the day and year first before written.

Executed before me   Sallie + Gunter, her mark
J. J. Burch, Ord   Isaac + Hutson, his mark

[The Ordinary wrote the following notation vertically in the left margin of the page.]

Filed in Office August 3rd and Recorded 7th August 1897.

          J. J. Burch, Ord

Georgia }   [272]
Elbert County } This Indenture, Made this the 12th day of August 1897, between Allen Eberhart, of Said County, for and in behalf of his Minor Son Tom Biggs, being of the age Twenty years, of the one part, and J. J. Brown, of the County aforesaid, of the other part. Witnesseth: That the said Allen Eberhart, as aforesaid, does by these presents bind out his said son Tom Biggs, of said County, as Apprentice to Said J. J. Brown in the trade or craft of Servant or as laborer upon the plantation of the Said J. J. Brown, to be taught the said craft or trade of Servant or Laborer, and to live with, Continue, and serve the said J. J. Brown as an Apprentice from the date hereof for and during the term of one year. During all of which time, the said Allen Eberhart, as aforesaid, doth covenant with the Said J. J. Brown that the said Thos Biggs Shall well and faithfully demean him self as such faithful Apprentice, observing fully the commands of the said J. J. Brown, and in all things deporting and behaving him self as a faithful Apprentice to the said J. J. Brown, neither revealing his secrets, nor at any time leaving or neglecting the business of the said J. J. Brown.

And for and in consideration of the Services well and faithfully rendered by the Said Tom Biggs, of the first part, Said J. J. Brown, of the second part, doth covenant with the said Allen Eberhart that the Said Thos Biggs Shall well and faithfully demean him self as such faithful Apprentice, observing fully the commands of the said J. J. Brown, and in all things deporting and behaving him self as a faithful Apprentice to the said J. J. Brown, neither revealing his secrets, nor at any time neglecting or leaving the business of the said J. J. Brown. And for and in consideration of the Service well and faithfully rendered by the said Tom Biggs, of the one part, said J. J. Brown, of the second part, doth covenant, promise, and agree to instruct his said Apprentice, or other wise cause him to be well and faithfully instructed, in the said trade or craft of Servant. and in consideration of the faithful

Service rendered, the said J. J. Brown agrees and promises to pay the [273] Said Allen Eberhart Fifty eight & $^{95}/_{100}$ Dollars. Now should the said Thos Biggs leave the service of the said J. J. Brown before the end of the time above specified, then the said Allen Eberhart, Father of said minor Tom, and his son Freeman agrees to surply whatever time the said Tom Biggs neglect or refuse to work.

Witness our hands & Seals the day and year first before written.

Executed in the presence of	Allen + Eberhart, his mark
J. J. Burch, Ordinary	J. J. Brown

Georgia } [274]
Elbert County } This Indenture, Made this the 25th day of September 1897, between Lewis Parker, of Said County, for and in behalf of him Self, being of the age of 26 years, of the one part, and Ge° A. Lunsford, of the County aforesaid, of the other part. Witnesseth: That the said Lewis Parker, as aforesaid, does by these presents bind out him Self, of said County, as apprentice to said Ge° A. Lunsford in the trade or Craft of Servant or as laborer upon the plantation of the Said Ge° A. Lunsford to be taught the Said Craft or trade of Servant or laborer, and to live with, continue, and serve the said Ge° A. Lunsford as an Apprentice from the date hereof for and during the term of Seven months.

During all of which time, the said Lewis Parker, as aforesaid, doth covenant with the said Ge° A. Lunsford that the Said Lewis Parker Shall well and faithfully demean him self as such faithful Apprentice, observing fully the commands of the said Ge° A. Lunsford and in all things deporting and behaving him self as a faithful Apprentice to the said Ge° A. Lunsford, neither revealing his secrets, nor at any time leaving or neglecting the business of the Said Ge° A. Lunsford.

And for and in consideration of the services well and faithfully rendered by the said Lewis Parker, of the first part, Said Ge° A. Lunsford, of the second part, doth covenant, promise, and agree to instruct his Said Apprentice, or otherwise cause him to be well and faithfully instructed, in the Said trade or craft of Servant or Laborer, and shall also allow, furnish, and provide his Said Apprentice with meat and drink, and shall also, at the expiration of the Said term, allow and pay the said Apprentice Seven dollars per month for the said Seven Months.

Witness our hands and seals the day and year first before written.

Executed before me	Lewis + Parker, his mark
J. J. Burch, Ordinary E. C.	Ge° A. + Lunsford, his mark

[The Ordinary wrote the following notation vertically in the left margin of the page.]

Filed in office Sep^t 25th 1897.

J. J. Burch

Georgia   }   [275]
Elbert County } This Indenture, Made this the 4th day of October 1897, between Elias Brawner, of Said County, for and in behalf of Junius Moseby, being of the age of Fifteen years, of the one part, and B. A. Neal, of the County aforesaid, of the other part. Witnesseth: That the said Elias Brawner, as aforesaid, does by these presents bind out said Junius Moseby, of said County, as apprentice to said B. A. Neal in the trade or craft of laborer upon the plantation of the Said B. A. Neal, to be taught the said Craft or trade of such a farm laborer, and to live with, Continue, and serve the said B. A. Neal as an Apprentice from the date hereof for and during the term of Five years.

During all of which time, said Elias Brawner doth covenant with the said B. A. Neal that the Said Junius Moseby shall well and faithfully demean him self as such faithful Apprentice, observing fully the commands of the Said B. A. Neal and in all things deporting and behaving him self as a faithful Apprentice to the said B. A. Neal, neither revealing his Secrets, nor at any time leaving or neglecting the business of the Said B. A. Neal. And for and in Consideration of the services well and faithfully rendered by the said Junius Moseby, of the first part, Said B. A. Neal, of the second part, doth covenant, promise, and agree to instruct his said Apprentice, or otherwise cause him to be well and faithfully instructed, in the said trade or craft of farm laborer, and shall also allow, furnish, and provide his said Apprentice with meat and drink & clothing, and all other necessary meet and proper, in sickness and in health, and shall also, at the expiration of the said term, allow and pay the said Apprentice what is now allowed by the statute in such case made & provided.

Witness our hands and seals the day and year first before written.

Executed Before us	Elias + Brawner, his mark
D. F. Hudgens	B. A. Neal
J. J. Burch, Ord E. C.	

Georgia   }   [276]
Elbert County } This Indenture, Made this the 20th day of October 1897, between Ansberry Eberhart, of Said County, for and in behalf of Charley Eberhart, being of the age of Fifteen years, of the one part, and J. F. Olbon, of the County aforesaid, of the other part. Witnesseth: That the said Ansberry Eberhart, as aforesaid, does by these presents bind out said Charley Eberhart, of Said County,

as apprentice to said J. F. Olbon in the trade or Craft of Servant or laborer upon the plantation of the Said J. F. Olbon, to be taught the Said Craft or trade of servant or laborer, and to live with, Continue, and serve the said J. F. Olbon as an Apprentice from the date hereof for and during the term of nine months. During all of which time, said Asberry Eberhart doth Covenant with the said J. F. Olbon that the said Charley Eberhart shall well and faithfully demean him self as such faithful Apprentice, observing fully the commands of the said J. F. Olbon, and in all things deporting & behaving him self as a faithful Apprentice to the said J. F. Olbon, neither revealing his Secrets, nor at any time leaving or neglecting the business of the Said J. F. Olbon. And for and in Consideration of the services well and faithfully rendered by the said Charley Eberhart, of the first part, Said J. F. Olbon, of the second part, doth covenant, promise, and agree to instruct his said Apprentice, or otherwise cause him to be well and faithfully instructed, in the said trade or craft of servant or laborer, and shall also allow, furnish, and provide his said Apprentice with meat and drink, and shall also, at the expiration of the said term, allow and pay the said Apprentice Fifty seven Dollars. Witness Our hands and Seals the day and year before written.

Executed in presence   Asberry + Eberhart, his mark
J. H. H. Mewborn   J. F. Olbon
J. J. Burch, Ordinary E. C.

Georgia   }   [277]
Elbert County } This Indenture, made this the 20th day of Octr 1897, between Asberry Eberhart, of Said County, for and in behalf of Judge Eberhart, being of the age of Nineteen years, of the one part, and A. T. Mewborn, of the County aforesaid, of the other part. Witnesseth: That the said Asberry Eberhart, as aforesaid, does by these presents bind out said Judge Eberhart, of Said County, as apprentice to said A. T. Mewborn in the trade or Craft of Servant or laborer upon the plantation of the Said A. T. Mewborn, to be taught the said Craft or trade of Servant or laborer, and to live with, continue, and serve the said A. T. Mewborn as an Apprentice from the date hereof for and during the term of Six months. During all of which time, said Asberry Eberhart doth covenant with the said A. T. Mewborn that the said Judge Eberhart shall well and faithfully demean him self as such faithful Apprentice, observing fully the commands of the said A. T. Mewborn and in all things deporting and behaving him self as a faithful Apprentice to the said A. T. Mewborn, neither revealing his secrets, or at any time leaving or neglecting the business of the Said A. T. Mewborn. and for and in consideration of the services well and faithfully rendered by the said Judge Eberhart, of the first part, Said A. T. Mewborn, of the second part, doth covenant,

promise, and agree to instruct his said Apprentice, or otherwise cause him to be well and faithfully instructed, in the said trade or craft of Servant or laborer, and shall also allow, furnish, and provide his said Apprentice meat and drink, and shall also, at the expiration of the said term, allow and pay the Apprentice Thirty Six dollars.

Witness our hands and seals the day & year above written.

J. H. H. Mewborn	Asberry + Eberhart, his mark
J. J. Burch, Ordinary E. C.	A. T. Mewborn

Georgia } [278]
Elbert County } This Indenture, made this the 23rd day of October 1897, between Alex Rock, of Said County, for and in behalf of himself, being of the age of 42 years, of the one part, and W. L. Fleming, of the County aforesaid, of the other part. Witnesseth: that the said Alex Rock, of said County, does by these presents bind out him self as apprentice to said W. L. Fleming in the trade or craft of servant or laborer upon the plantation of said W. L. Fleming to be taught the said Craft or trade of Servant or laborer, and to live with, Continue, and serve the said W. L. Fleming as an apprentice from the first day of June 1898 & during the term of five months. during all of which time, said Alex Rock doth covenant with the said W. L. Fleming that the said Alex Rock shall well and faithfully demean him self as such faithful apprentice, observing fully the commands of the said W. L. Fleming, and in all things deporting and behaving him self as such faithful apprentice to the said W. L. Fleming, of the second part, neither revealing his secrets, nor at any time leaving or neglecting the business of the said W. L. Fleming. and for and in consideration of the services well & faithfully rendered by the said Alex Rock, of the first part, said W. L. Fleming, of the second part, doth covenant, promise, and agree to instruct his said apprentice, or cause him to be well & faithfully instructed, in the craft or trade of servant or laborer, and shall also allow, furnish, and provide said apprentice meat & Drink, and shall also, at the expiration of the said term, allow and pay the said apprentice Twenty seven dollars. and [blurred] Witness Our hands and seals the day & year before written.

T. S. Burch, J^r	Alex + Rock, his mark
J. J. Burch, ordinary E. C.	W. L. Fleming

Georgia } [279]
Elbert County } This Indenture, made this the 27th day of Nov 1897, between Wiley Morrison, of Said County, for and in behalf of him self, being of the age of thirty five years, of the one part, and George Lunsford, of the other part, both of

the county & State aforesaid. Witnesseth: that the said Wiley Morrison does by these presents bind out him self as an apprentice to the said George Lunsford in the trade or craft of servant or laborer upon the plantation of the said George Lunsford, to be taught the said craft or trade of laborer, and to live with, continue for the space of seven months upon the plantation of the said George Lunsford Commencing the first day of January 1898.

During all of which time, said Wiley Morrison doth covenant with the said George Lunsford that the said Wiley Morrison shall well & faithfully demean him self as a faithful Apprentice, observing fully the commands of the said George Lunsford, and in all things deporting & behaving him self as a faithful Apprentice to the said George, neither revealing his secrets, nor at any time leaving or neglecting the business of the said George Lunsford.

And for & in consideration of the services well & faithfully rendered by the said Morrison, of the first part, said George Lunsford, of the second part, doth covenant, promise, and agree to instruct his said apprentice, or otherwise cause him to be well and faithfully instructed, in the said craft or craft of servant or laborer, and shall also furnish and provide said Apprentice meat and drink, and shall also, at the expiration of the said term, allow and pay the said Apprentice Forty Two Dollars.

Witness our hands and seals the day & year before written.

Executed in presence
R. M. Heard George + Lunsford, his mark
J. J. Burch, ordinary E. C. Wiley + Morrison, his mark

Georgia } [280]
Elbert County } This Indenture, made this the 26th day of December 1897, between Sam Jackson, of Hart County, for and in behalf of his son Willie Jackson, being of the age of sixteen years, of the one part, and Wm M. Sanders, of the County of Elbert, of the other part. Witnesseth: that the said Sam Jackson, as aforesaid, does by these presents bind out his said son Willie Jackson, of Said Hart County, as apprentice to said Wm M. Sanders in the trade or craft of Servant or Laborer upon the plantation of the said Wm M. Sanders to be taught the said craft or trade of Servant or Laborer, and to live with, continue, and serve the said Wm M. Sanders as an apprentice from the date hereof for and during the term of nine months. During all of which time, Said Sam Jackson, as aforesaid, doth covenant with the said Wm M. Sanders that the said Willie Jackson shall well and faithfully demean him self as such faithful Apprentice, observing fully the commands of the

said Wm M. Sanders, and in all things deporting & behaving him self as a faithful Apprentice to the said W. M. Sanders, neither revealing his secrets, nor at any time leaving or neglecting the business of the said W. M. Sanders.

And for and in Consideration of the services well and faithfully rendered by the said Willie Jackson, of the first part, said W. M. Sanders, of the second part, doth covenant, promise, and agree to instruct his said apprentice, or otherwise cause him to be well and faithfully instructed, in the said trade or craft of servant or laborer, and shall also allow, furnish, & provide his said Apprentice meat & Drink, during the said term, and all other necessaries meet and proper, in Sickness & in health, & shall also, at the expiration of the said term, allow & pay the said Apprentice Fifty Dollars, and allow him half of any other Saturday. Witness our hands and Seals the day & year before written.

Executed before us
R. M. Cleveland   Sam + Jackson, his mark
J. J. Burch, ordinary E. C.   W. M. Sanders

Georgia   }   [281]
Elbert County } This Indenture, made this the 24 day of December 1897, between Asbel Eberhart, of Hart County, for and in behalf of his son Jessie Eberhart, being of the age of fifteen years, of the one part, and R. S. Gaines, of the County of Elbert, of the other part. Witnesseth: that the said Asbel Eberhart, as aforesaid, does by these presents bind out his said son Jessie Eberhart, of said Hart County, as apprentice to R. S. Gaines in the trade or craft of servant or laborer upon the plantation of the said R. S. Gaines, to be taught the said craft or trade of servant or laborer, and to live with, continue, and serve the said R. S. Gaines as an apprentice from the fifteenth of January 1898 for and during the term of Six months. During all of which time, Said Asbel Eberhart, as aforesaid, doth covenant with the Said R. S. Gaines that the said Jessie Eberhart shall well & faithfully demean him self as such faithful apprentice, observing fully the Commands of the Said R. S. Gaines, and in all things Deporting and behaving him self as a faithful apprentice to the said R. S. Gaines, neither revealing his secrets, nor at any time leaving or neglecting the business of the said R. S. Gaines. And for and in consideration of the services well and faithfully rendered by the said Jessie Eberhart, of the first part, said R. S. Gaines, of the second part, doth Covenant, promise, and agree to instruct his said apprentice, or otherwise cause him to be well and faithfully instructed, in the said trade or craft of servant or laborer, and shall also allow, furnish, and provide his said apprentice with meat & Drink during the said term, and all other necessary meet and proper in health,

and shall also, at the expiration of the said term, allow & pay the said apprentice Thirty five dollars.

Witness our hands and Seals the day & year first before written.

Executed in presence
J. J. Burch, Ordinary   Asbel + Eberhart, his mark
Samuel L. Oliver   R. S. Gaines

Georgia   }   [282]
Elbert County   }   This indenture, made this the 24th day of December 1897, between W. F. Moore and Isham Mattox, the father of jacob Mattox, now aged sixteen years, said Moore of said County and said Isham and Jacob Mattox of Oglethorpe County. Witnesseth: that the said John Mattox hereby binds and apprentices to the said W. F. Moore the Said Jacob Mattox for the year 1899, beginning Jany 1st 1898 and Ending December 31st 189, Subject to the following term. said W. F. Moore agrees to take into his Custody said Jacob Mattox for the time above mentioned and to teach him the business of husbandry in all its details, furnish him with protection, whole some food, Suitable Clothing, necessary Medicine, & medical attention, teach him habits of industry, honesty, and morality, and shall govern him with humanity, using only the same degree of force to compel his obedience as a father may use with his minor child, and when said year shall be ended Said Isham Mattox is to receive as Compensation for Services of said Jacob Mattox Fifty five dollars, and the custody of said Jacob Mattox is to be given back to said Isham Mattox at the expiration of the year 189. In consideration of all of which, Said Wm F. Moore is to be intitled to the service and earnings of said Jacob Mattox for the year 189.

Witness our hands & seals this the 24th day of December 1897.

Signed, sealed, & delivered }
in presence of   }
J. J. Burch, ordinary E. C.   }   Isham + Mattox, his mark
Samuel L. Oliver   }   W. F. Moore

Georgia   }   [283]
Elbert County   }   This indenture, made this the 24th day of December 1897, between W. F. Moore, of Elbert County, and Julian Mattox, of Oglethorpe County. Witnesseth: that the said Julian Mattox, in consideration of the promises and undertakings of said W. F. Moore hereinafter set forth, does hereby bind himself to the said W. F. Moore for the term of one year, beginning January 1st, 189 and Ending December 31st 189. and he hereby agrees and Contracts with said

W. F. Moore to work faithfully under his direction, respect and obey all orders and Commands of said W. F. Moore with reference to the business hereinafter set forth, at all times demean himself orderly and soberly. and the said Julian Mattox further agrees to account to said Moore for all lost time, except in case of temporary sickness, if such sickness should be of longer duration at any one time than six days, then such lost time is to be accounted for at the same rate per day as he is then receiving pay under this contract. and should this Contract be terminated by the death of either of the parties to this indenture, then the compensation of Said Mattox be proratta for the time completed for the year in which the death may occur. And the said W. F. Moore, in Consideration of the promises and undertakings of the said Mattox, agrees & contracts with said Mattox to furnish him with board, lodging, every day necessary apparel, and washing. He further agrees to pay said Mattox on the 26 day of December 189 fifty five dollars. And he further agrees to teach said Mattox the trade of husbandry in all its details. In witness whereof, the said W. F. Moore and the Said Julian Mattox has hereto respectively set their hands & seals the day and year first above written.

Executed in duplicate in presence of
J. J. Burch, Ordinary E. C.   Julian + Mattox, his mark
Samuel L. Oliver   W. F. Moore

Georgia   }   [284]
Elbert County } This Indenture, made this the 15 day of Jany 1898, between Nathan Blackwell and Charlotte Blackwell for and in behalf of their daughters, Lou Hannah and Lavonia Blackwell, being of the age Lou 12 years and Lavonia 10 years, of the one part, and E. J. Bell, of the other part, both of the County and State aforesaid.

Witness: that the said Nathan & Charlotte Blackwell does by these presents bind out their said Daughters, Lou & Lavonia, as Apprentices to the Said E. J. Bell in the trade or craft of laborer or Servant upon the plantation of the said E. J. Bell to be taught the Said Craft or trade of laborer, and to live with and continue for the Space of three years, Commencing whenever called upon by said E. J. Bell.

During all of which time, said Nathan & Charlotte Blackwell doth Covenant with the Said E. J. Bell that the said Lou and Lavonia Blackwell shall well and faithfully demean them Selves as such faithful Apprentices, observing fully the Commands of the Said E. J. Bell, and in all things deporting and behaving them selves as such faithful Apprentices to the Said E. J. Bell, neither revealing his Secrets, nor at any time leaving or neglecting the business of the said E. J. Bell.

And for and in consideration of the services well and faithfully rendered by the Said Lou & Lavonia Blackwell, of the first part, said E. J. Bell, of the Second part, doth covenant, promise, and agree to instruct his said Apprentices, or otherwise cause them to be well and faithfully instructed, in the said craft or trade of Servant or as laborer, and shall allow, furnish, and provide Said Apprentices with meat and drink and clothing, and Shall, at the expiration of the said term, allow & pay the said Apprentices One Hundred Dollars. Witness our hands and Seal This the year and day above before written.

Witness	Nathan + Blackwell, his mark
John M. Brown	Charlotte + Blackwell, her mark
J. J. Burch, ordinary	E. J. Bell

Georgia } [285]
Elbert County } This Indenture, made this 27th day January 1898, between Sam Starke for himself, of said County, being of the age of 38 years, of the one part, and E. J. Bell, of the County aforesaid, of the other part. Witnesseth: That the said Sam Starke, as aforesaid, does by these presents bind himself, the Said Sam Starke, of said County, as apprentice to said E. J. Bell in the trade or craft of servant or as laborer upon the plantation of the said E. J. Bell to be taught the said craft or trade of Servant or farm laborer, and to live with, continue, and serve the said E. J. Bell as an apprentice from the date hereof during the term of one years, beginning Jany first 1899 and ending Jany first 1900. During all of which time, said Sam Starke, as aforesaid, doth Covenant with the Said E. J. Bell that the said Sam Starke himself shall well and faithfully demean himself as such faithful Apprentice, observing fully the Commands of the Said E. J. Bell, and in all things deporting and behaving himself as a faithful apprentice to the said E. J. Bell, neither revealing his Secrets, nor at any time leaving or neglecting the business of the said E. J. Bell. And for and in consideration of the services well and faithfully rendered by the said Sam Starke, of the first part, Said E. J. Bell, of the second part, doth covenant, promise, and agree to instruct his said Apprentice, or otherwise cause him to be well and faithfully instructed, in the said trade or craft Farm Laborer or Laborer, and pay him Sixty dollars, and shall also allow, furnish, and provide his said Apprentice with meat and drink during the said term, and shall also, at the expiration of the said term, pay the Sixty Dollars less what he may owe me.

Witness our hands and seals the day and year first before written.

Executed Before us   Sam + Starke, his mark
W. B. Adams   E. J. Bell
W. A. Adams, N. P.

Filed in Office and Record Feb 4, 1898.

J. J. Burch, Ord

Georgia   }   [286]
Elbert County   }   This Indenture, made and entered into between Bella Hawkins, of the one part, and M. A. Daniel, of the other part. Witnesseth: that the said Bella Hawkins, who is the mother of George White, seven years of aged, and Ann White, two years of aged, her children by a former marriage, all of Said County and State, hereby binds her children above named and hereby apprentices Said Children to the Said M. A. Daniel until they each become of twenty one years old. Said M. A. Daniel agrees to take said children into his custody, teach them the business of husbandry and house service, furnish them with protection, wholesome food, suitable Clothing, necessary medicine and medical attention, teach them habits of industry, honesty, and morality, Cause them to be taught the elementary principals of mathematics and to read english, and shall govern them with humanity, using the same degree of force to compel obedience as a father may use with his minor child, and when they each arrive at the age of twenty one years of age, he is to pay each the sum of fifty Dollars, provided this indenture is faithfully performed upon their part, in consideration of all of which, said M. A. Daniel is to be entitled to the services and earnings, custody, and control of said Children until they each arrive at twenty one years of age. Should the said Bella or Isabella Hawkins pay or cause to be paid said M. A. Daniel one hundred and two dollars and interest at 8 percent from date, then said Daniel agrees to Cancel this Indenture on his part. Witness our hands and seals This Feb [blank] 1898.

Signed, Sealed, and delivered }
in presence of   }   Isabella + Hawkins, her mark
Jo^s N. Worley   }   John + Hawkins, his mark
J. J. Burch, Ordinary   }   M. A. + Daniel, his mark

Filed in Office and recorded Feb 5, 1898.

J. J. Burch

Georgia   }   [287]
Elbert County } This Indenture, made this the 16 day February 1898, Between J. D. Maxwell, of said County, for and in behalf of him self, being of the age of 24 years, of the one part, and W. J. Ayers, of the County aforesaid, of the other part. Witnesseth: That the said J. D. Maxwell, as aforesaid, does by these presents bind himself, the said J. D. Maxwell, of said County, as apprentice to said W. J. Ayers in the trade or craft of Laborer upon the plantation of the said W. J. Ayers, to be taught the said craft or trade of Laborer, and to live with, continue, and serve the said W. J. Ayers as an apprentice from the date hereof for and during the term of Eighteen months. During all of which time, said J. D. Maxwell, as aforesaid, doth covenant with the Said W. J. Ayers that he, the said J. D. Maxwell shall well and faithfully demean himself as such faithful Apprentice, Observing fully the Commands of the Said W. J. Ayers, and in all things deporting and behaving him self as a faithful Apprentice to the said W. J. Ayers, neither revealing his secrets, nor at any time leaving or neglecting the business of the said W. J. Ayers.

And for and in Consideration of the services well and faithfully rendered by the said J. D. Maxwell, of the first part, Said W. J. Ayers, of the second part, doth Covenant, promise, and agree to instruct his said Apprentice, or otherwise Cause him to be well and faithfully instructed, in the trade or Craft of Laborer, and shall also allow, furnish, and provide his said Apprentice with meat and Drink and clothing, and all other Necessaries meet and proper, in sickness and in health, and shall also, at the expiration of the term, allow and pay the said Apprentice Fifty seven & $^{75}/_{100}$ Dollars.

Witness our hands and seals the day and year first before written.

Executed before us
H. A. Fortson   J. D. + Maxwell, his mark
J. J. Burch, Ordinary E. C.   W. J. + Ayers, his mark

Georgia   }   [288]
Elbert County } This Indenture, made this the 16th day of February 1898, Between William Maxwell, of said County, for and in behalf of him self, being of the age of 56 years, of the one part, and W. J. Ayers, of the County aforesaid, of the other part. Witnesseth: That the said William Maxwell, as aforesaid, does by these presents bind himself, the said William Maxwell, of said County, as Apprentice to said W. J. Ayers in the trade or Craft of Laborer, and to live with, Continue, and serve the said W. J. Ayers as an apprentice from the date hereof for and during the term of Eighteen Months. During all of which time, said William Maxwell, as aforesaid, doth Covenant with the Said W. J. Ayers that he, the said

William Maxwell shall well and faithfully demean him self as such faithful Apprentice, observing fully the Commands of the Said W. J. Ayers, and in all things deporting and behaving himself as a faithful Apprentice to the said W. J. Ayers, neither revealing his secrets, nor at any time leaving or neglecting the business of the said W. J. Ayers. And for and in consideration of the services well and faithfully rendered by the said J. D. Maxwell, who this day has apprenticed himself to the said W. J. Ayers for the term of Eighteen months. And now should the said J. D. Maxwell, his Son aforesaid, refuse or neglect to Carry out the specification in his Said Indenture, then the father, the said William Maxwell, agrees to take his, the said J. D. Maxwell, place and faithfully perform and Labor and make good on the said time that the Said Son, J. D. Maxwell, fails or refuses to perform. And in consideration of the said faithful service rendered by the said William Maxwell, he is to receive prorata the amount promised & paid up to his said Son J. D. Maxwell, Towit, fifty Seven & $^{75}/_{100}$ Dollars. In witness Whereof, We have hereunto set our hands and seals the date first before written.

Executed before us
W. J. Smith   William + Maxwell, his mark
J. J. Burch, Ordinary E. C.   W. J. + Ayers, his mark

Georgia   }   [289]
Elbert County } This Indenture, made this the 16 day of June 1898, between Claiborn Rucker, of said County, for and in behalf of his minor son, Robert Rucker, being of the age of 16 years, of the one part, and E. J. Bell, of the County aforesaid, of the other part. Witnesseth: That the said Claiborn Rucker, as aforesaid, does by these presents bind out Said Minor son, Robert Rucker, of said County, as Apprentice to Said E. J. Bell in the trade or craft of Husbandry or as Laborer upon the plantation of the Said E. J. Bell, to be taught the said craft or trade of Husbandry or Laborer, and to live with, Continue, and serve the said E. J. Bell as an apprentice from the date hereof during the period of twelve months, or such time as it may require to pay the debt of Thirty Three & $^{48}/_{100}$ Dollars at six dollars and Twenty five Cents per month. Said amount having been furnished Said Claiborn Rucker in the way of supplies for the present year 1898. During all of which time, Said Claiborn Rucker doth covenant with the said E. J. Bell that the said Robert Rucker, as aforesaid, shall well and faithfully demean himself as such faithful Apprentice, observing fully the commands of the Said E. J. Bell, And in all things deporting and behaving himself as a faithful apprentice to the said E. J. Bell.

And for and in consideration of the services well and faithfully rendered by the said Robert Rucker, of the first part, And E. J. Bell, of the second part, doth

Covenant, promise, and agree to allow his said Apprentice good and sufficient food and pay to Said Claiborn Rucker the sum of Six and $^{25}/_{100}$ Dollars until debt aforesaid is paid. In witness our hands and seals the day and year above written.

Witness
J. J. Burch, Ordinary
Abda Oglesby

Claiborn + Rucker, his mark
E. J. Bell

Georgia } [290]
Elbert County } This Indenture, made this the 6th day of July 1898, between Ann Bell, of said County, for and in behalf of her minor son, Willie Bell, being of the age of nine years, of the one part, and James Y. Swift, of the County aforesaid, of the other part. Witnesseth: That the said Anna Bell, as aforesaid, does by these presents bind out her said minor son, Willie Bell, of Said County, as Apprentice to said James Y. Swift in the trade or craft of Servant or Laborer upon the plantation of the Said Ja^s Y. Swift, to be taught the Said Craft of Servant or Laborer, and to live with, continue, and Serve the Said J. Y. Swift as an Apprentice from the date here of during the period of Five years. Now should the said Anna Bell, as aforesaid, pay to the said J. Y. Swift the sum of Twenty five dollars by October 15th 1898, Then this contract to be void, else in full force. Now, in consideration of the faithful service rendered by the said Apprentice, Willie Bell, the Said J. Y. Swift agrees to furnish him with good & sufficient food and clothing, And agrees further to use only such force as a father would to his minor child in compelling obedience. And Should the said Anna Bell, as aforesaid, fail or refuse to pay said amount of twenty five dollars, Then the Said J. Y. Swift will pay to Said Apprentice what the law requires in such cases made and provided. Witness our hands and seals the day and year first before written.

Witness
D. R. Blackwell
J. J. Burch, ordinary

Anna + Bell, her mark
J. Y. Swift

Georgia } [291]
Elbert County } This Indenture, made this 17th day of September 1898, between Amy Morrison, of said County, for and in behalf of Moses Morrison, being of the age of Two years, of the one, and William P. Rucker, of the County aforesaid, of the other part. Witnesseth: That the said Amy Morrison, as aforesaid, does by these presents bind out the said Moses Morrison, her minor son, of said County, as apprentice to said W. P. Rucker in the trade or craft of Laborer upon the plantation of the said W. P. Rucker to be taught the said craft or trade of Laborer, and to live with, continue, and serve the said W. P. Rucker as an apprentice from

the date hereof for and during the term of his minority or until he becomes twenty one years of age. During all of which time, Said Amy Morrison, as aforesaid, doth covenant with the said W. P. Rucker that the said Moses Morrison, minor son aforesaid, shall well and faithfully demean himself as such faithful Apprentice, Observing fully the Commands of the said W. P. Rucker, and in things deporting and behaving him self as a faithful Apprentice to the said W. P. Rucker, neither revealing his secrets, nor at any time leaving or neglecting the business of the said W. P. Rucker. And for and in Consideration of the service well and faithfully rendered by the said Moses Morrison, of the first part, Said W. P. Rucker, of the second part, doth covenant, promise, and agree to instruct his said Apprentice, or otherwise cause him to be well and faithfully instructed, in the said trade or Craft of Laborer, and to read the English language, and shall also allow, furnish, and provide his Apprentice with meat and Drink proper, in sickness and in health, and shall also, at the expiration of the said term, allow and pay the said Apprentice what is now allowed by the Statute in such case made and provided.

Witness our hands & seals the day and year first before written.

Executed before us
W. D. Tutt, J^r   }   Amy + Morrison, her mark
J. J. Burch, Ordinary }   William P. + Rucker, his mark

Georgia   }   [292]
Elbert County } This Indenture, Made this the [blank] day of October 1898, between George Haygood and Martha Haygood, of said County, for and in behalf of Fletcher Rucker, being of the age of 15 years, on the one part, and W. N. Auld, of the County aforesaid, of the other part. Witnesseth: that the said George & Martha Haygood, parents of said Fletcher does by these presents bind out Fletcher Rucker, of said County, as apprentice to said W. N. Auld in the trade or craft of Laborer upon the plan of the said Auld to be taught the Said Craft or trade of Laborer, and to live with, Continue, and serve the Said W. N. Auld as an apprentice from the date hereof for and during the term of his minority.

During all of which time, said George & Martha Haygood, as aforesaid, doth covenant with the Said W. N. Auld that the said Fletcher shall well and faithfully demean himself as a faithful Apprentice to the said W. N. Auld, neither revealing his secrets, nor at any time leaving or neglecting the business of the said W. N. Auld. And for and in Consideration of the services well and faithfully rendered by the said Fletcher, of the first part, Said W. N. Auld, of the second part, doth Covenant, promise, and agree to instruct his said apprentice, or otherwise cause him to be well and faithfully instructed, in the trade or Craft of Laborer, and also to read the English language, and shall also allow, furnish, and provide his said apprentice with meat and drink and clothing during the said term, and all other necessaries meet and proper, in Sickness and in health, and shall also, at the expiration of the term, allow and pay the Said Apprentice what is now allowed by the Statute in such case made and provided.

Witness our hands and seals the day and year first before written. In duplicate.

Executed Before us	George + Haygood, his mark
Z. B. Rogers	Martha + Haygood, her mark
Fred W. Auld, N. P.	W. N. Auld

Georgia   }   [293]
Elbert County } This Indenture, made this the 2nd day of November 1898, between Adam Roebuck, for and in behalf of his minor son, Jim Roebuck, being of the age of Fifteen years, of the one part, and R. S. Gaines, of the County aforesaid, of the other part. Witnesseth: that the said Adam Roebuck does by these presents bind out his said minor Son Jim Roebuck, of said County, as apprentice to said R. S. Gaines in the trade or craft of farm Laborer upon the plantation of the said R. S. Gaines to be taught the said Craft or trade of servant or Laborer, and to live with, Continue, and serve the said R. S. Gaines as an Apprentice from the first day of January 1899 for and during the term of Two years. During all of which time, said Adam Roebuck doth covenant with the said R. S. Gaines that the said Jim Roebuck shall well and faithfully demean him self as such faithful apprentice to the said R. S. Gaines, observing fully the Commands of the said R. S. Gaines, and in all things deporting and behaving him self as a faithful Apprentice to the said R. S. Gaines, neither revealing his secrets, nor at any time leaving or neglecting the business of the said R. S. Gaines. And in consideration of the services well and faithfully rendered by the said Jim Roebuck, of the first part, said R. S. Gaines, of the second part, doth Covenant, promise, and agree to instruct his said Apprentice, or otherwise Cause him to be well and faithfully instructed, in the said trade or craft of Farm Labor, and shall allow, furnish, and provide his said Apprentice with meat and drink, and shall also, at the expiration of the said term, allow and pay the said Apprentice Sixty nine dollars and fifty Cents.

Witness our hands and seals the day and year first before written.

Executed Before us }
J. N. Wall } Adam + Roebuck, his mark
J. J. Burch. Ordinary } R. S. Gaines

Georgia } [294]
Elbert County } This Indenture, made this the 9th day of November 1898, between Armstead Isam, of said County, for and in behalf of his minor son Sam Isam, being of the age of 13 years, on the one part, and M. R. Jones, of the County aforesaid, of the other part. Witnesseth: that the said Armstead Isam, Father aforesaid, does by these presents bind out his said minor son Sam Isam, of said County, as apprentice to said M. R. Jones in the trade or craft of Husbandry or as Laborer upon the plantation of the said M. R. Jones, to be taught the said Craft or trade of Husbandry or Laborer, and to live with, continue, and serve the Said M. R. Jones as an apprentice from the date hereof for and during the term of Two years, commencing first day of January 1899.

During all of which time, said Armstead Isam, father aforesaid, doth covenant with the Said M. R. Jones that the Said Sam Isam shall well and faithfully demean him self as such faithful Apprentice to the M. R. Jones, neither revealing his secrets, nor at any time leaving or neglecting the business of the said M. R. Jones. And the Said Armstead Isam aforesaid further agrees and binds himself to make up to said M. R. Jones any lost time of the aforesaid Apprentice Fam Isam from sickness, death, or any other Cause whatever. And for and in Consideration of the services well and faithfully rendered by the said Sam Isam, of the first part, said M. R. Jones, of the second part, doth covenant, promise, and agree to instruct his said Apprentice, or otherwise cause him to be well and faithfully instructed, in the trade or craft of Husbandry or laborer, and provide his said Apprentice with meat and drink during the said term, and shall allow and pay the Said Apprentice fifty eight dollars, which he has agreed to take in a Black man named Bill, about ten or twelve years old, now in possession of said Armstead Isam, the aforesaid.

Witness our hands and seals the day and year first before written.

Executed Before us
A. E. Howard Armstead + Isam, his mark
J. J. Burch, ordinary M. R. Jones

Georgia } [295]
Elbert County } This Indenture, made this the 17 day of November 1898, between Wilborn Jones, of said County, for and in behalf of his minor Son Willis

G. Jones, being of the age of 12 years, on the one part, and J. W. Rucker, of the County aforesaid, of the other part. Witnesseth: that Said Wilborn Jones, as aforesaid, does by these presents bind out his said minor son W. G. Jones, of said County, as Apprentice to Said J. W. Rucker in the trade or Craft of Husbandry or as Laborer upon the plantation of the said J. W. Rucker, to be taught the said Craft or trade of Husbandry or Laborer, and to live with, Continue, and serve the said J. W. Rucker as an Apprentice from the date hereof for and during the term of 4 years. During all of which time, said Wilborn Jones, as aforesaid, doth Covenant with the said J. W. Rucker that the said Willis G. Jones shall well and faithfully demean him self as such faithful Apprentice, observing fully the commands of the said J. W. Rucker, and in all things deporting and behaving him self as such faithful Apprentice to the said J. W. Rucker, neither revealing his secrets, nor at any time leaving or neglecting the business of the Said J. W. Rucker.

And for and in consideration of the Services well and faithfully rendered by the Said W. G. Jones, of the first part, said J. W. Rucker, of the Second part, doth covenant, promise, and agree to instruct his said Apprentice, or otherwise cause him to be well and faithfully instructed, in the said trade or craft of Husbandry or laborer, and also to read the English language, and shall also allow, furnish, and provide his said Apprentice with meat & drink & clothing during the said term, and all other necessaries meet and proper, in Sickness & in health, & shall also, at the expiration of said term, allow & pay the said Apprentice Sixty Dollars, part of which is already paid, the remainder fifteen dollars per year. Witness our hands & seals the day & year first before written. The above interlining was made & before Signing.

Executed Before us }
T. J. Campbell }   Wilborn + Jones, his mark
J. J. Burch, Ordinary }   J. W. Rucker

Georgia } [296]
Elbert County } This Indenture, Made this Sixth day December 1898, between Ansbury Eberhart, of said County, for and in behalf of his minor Son Jim Eberhart, being of the age of twenty years, of the one part, and G. N. Burden, of the County aforesaid, of the other part. Witnesseth: That the said Ansbury Eberhart, as aforesaid, does by these presents bind out his said son Jim Eberhart, of said County, as Apprentice to said G. N. Burden in the trade or craft of Servant or as Laborer upon the plantation of the said G. N. Burden, to be taught the said Craft or trade of servant or labor, and to live with, Continue, and serve the said G. N. Burden as an Apprentice from the first day of January 1899 and during the term of Six Months. During all of which time, said Ansbury Eberhart aforesaid doth

Covenant with the said G. N. Burden that the said Jim Eberhart shall well and faithfully demean his self as such faithful Apprentice, observing fully the commands of the said G. N. Burden, and in all things deporting and behaving his self as such faithful Apprentice to the said G. N. Burden, neither revealing his secrets, nor at any time leaving or neglecting the business of the said G. N. Burden. And for and in Consideration of the service well and faithfully rendered by the Said Jim Eberhart, of the first part, said G. N. Burden, of the second part, doth covenant, promise, and agree to instruct his said Apprentice, or otherwise Cause him to be well and faithfully instructed, in the said trade or craft of Servant or laborer, and shall also allow, furnish, and provide his said Apprentice with meat and drink during the said term, and shall also, at the expiration of said term, allow and pay the Apprentice Thirty Dollars. Witness our hands and seals the day and year first before written.

Executed Before us
Clark Mattox   }   Ansbury + Eberhart, his mark
J. J. Burch, Ordinary }   G. N. Burden

Georgia   }   [297]
Elbert County } This Indenture, Made this the six day of December 1898, between Dora Richardson, of said County, for and in behalf of her minor son Charley Richardson, being of the age of 11 years, of the one part, and C. T. Bond, of the County aforesaid, of the other part. Witnesseth: That the said Dora Richardson, as aforesaid, does by these presents bind out her said son Charley Richardson, of said County, as apprentice to said C. T. Bond, to be taught the said Craft or trade of servant or laborer, and to live with, Continue, and serve the said C. T. Bond as an apprentice from the date hereof for and during the term of ten years. During all of which time, said Dora Richardson as aforesaid doth covenant with the said C. T. Bond that the said Charley Richardson shall well and faithfully demean him self as such faithful Apprentice, observing fully the Commands of the said C. T. Bond, and in all things deporting and behaving him self as a faithful Apprentice to the said C. T. Bond, neither revealing his secrets, nor at any time leaving or neglecting the business of the said C. T. Bond. And for and in Consideration of the services well and faithfully rendered by the said Charley Richardson, of the first, said C. T. Bond, of the second part, doth Covenant, promise, and agree to instruct his said Apprentice, or otherwise Cause him to be well and faithfully instructed, in the said trade or craft of Servant or laborer, and also to read the English language, and shall also allow, furnish, and provide him, said Apprentice, with meat and drink and Clothing during the said term, and all other necessaries meet And proper, in sickness and in health, and shall also, at the

expiration of said term, allow and pay the said Apprentice what is now allowed by the Statute in such case made and provided. Witness our hands and Seals the day and year first before written.

Executed Before us }
Clark Mattox }   Dora + Richardson, her mark
J. J. Burch, Ordinary }   C. T. Bond

Georgia }   [298]
Elbert County }   This Indenture, Made this the 14 day of December 1898, between John C. Chapman, of said County, for & in behalf of his minor son John C. Chapman, Jr, being of the age of 4 years, of the one part, and L. M. Fortson, of the County aforesaid, of the other part. Witnesseth: That the John C. Chapman, as aforesaid, does by these presents bind out his said son John C. Chapman, Jr, of said County, as Apprentice to said L. M. Fortson in the trade or craft of Farming or as laborer upon the plantation of the said L. M. Fortson, to be taught the said Craft or trade of Farming or laborer, & to live with, continue, & serve the Said L. M. Fortson as an apprentice from the date hereof for and during the term of 17 years or during his minority. During all of which time, said John C. Chapman, as aforesaid, doth covenant with the said L. M. Fortson that the said John C. Chapman shall well & faithfully demean him self as such faithful Apprentice, observing fully the Commands of the said L. M. Fortson, & in all things deporting and behaving him self as a faithful Apprentice to the said L. M. Fortson, neither revealing his secrets, nor at any time leaving or neglecting the business of the said L. M. Fortson. And for & in consideration of the services well and faithfully rendered by the said John C. Chapman, of the first part, said L. M. Fortson, of the second part, doth covenant, promise, & agree to instruct his said Apprentice, or otherwise Cause him to be well & faithfully instructed, in the said trade or craft of Farming or laborer, & also to read the English language, & shall also allow, furnish, & provide his said Apprentice with meat & drink & Clothing during the said term, & all other necessaries meet & proper, in sickness & in health, & shall also, at the expiration of Said term, allow & pay the Apprentice what is now allowed by the Statute in such case made and provided.

Witness our hands & seals the day & year first before written.

Executed before us }
R. M. Willis }   John C. Chapman
J. J. Burch, Ordinary }   Launs M. Fortson

[The Ordinary wrote the following notation vertically in the left margin of the page.]

The written apprentice indenture this day disolved by mutual Consent This February 1st 1905.

J. J. Burch, Ordinary

Georgia } [299]
Elbert County } This Indenture, Made this the 22nd day December 1898, between Jack Moon, of said County, for and in behalf of his minor sons Freddie, Arthur, and Ollie Moon, being of the age of 16, 14, & 13 years, of the one part, and Arnold & Cº, of the county aforesaid, of the other part. Witnesseth: That the said Jack Moon, as aforesaid, does by these presents bind out his said minor sons Freddie, Arthur, and Ollie Moon, of said County, as Apprentice to said Arnold & Cº in the trade or craft of Servant or laborer upon the plantation of the said Arnold & Cº, to be taught the said craft or trade of Servant or laborer, and to live with, Continue, and serve the said Arnold & Cº as an Apprentice from the first day of January 1899 for the term of one year. During all of which time, said Jack Moon, as aforesaid, doth covenant with the said Arnold & Cº that the said Freddie, Arthur, & Ollie Moon shall well & faithfully demean them selves as such faithful Apprentices, observing fully the commands of the said Arnold & Cº, and in all things deporting and behaving them selves as faithful Apprentices to the said Arnold & Cº, neither revealing their secrets, nor at any time leaving or neglecting the business of the said Arnold & Cº. And for and in consideration of the services well and faithfully rendered by the said Freddie, Arthur, & Ollie Moon, of the first part, said Arnold & Cº, of the second part, doth covenant, promise, & agree to instruct their said Apprentices, or otherwise cause them to be well and faithfully instructed, in the said trade or craft of Servant or laborer, and also to read the English language, & shall, at the expiration of said term, allow & pay the said Apprentices Sixty Dollars.

Witness our hands and seals the day and year first before written.

Executed Before us }
Benj H. Kay } Jack + Moon, his mark
J. J. Burch, Ordinary E. C. } Arnold & Cº

Georgia } [300]
Elbert County } This Indenture, made this 10 day of January 1899, between Ben Allen, of said County, for and in behalf of his minor daughter Georgia Allen, being of the age of 10 years, of the one part, and James Y. Swift, of the County

aforesaid, of the other part. Witnesseth: that the Said Ben Allen, as aforesaid, does by these presents bind out his said minor Daughter Georgia Allen, of said County, as Apprentice to Said Ja^s Y. Swift in the trade or craft of House Servant or Laborer upon the plantation of the said Ja^s Y. Swift as an Apprentice from the date hereof for and during the term of 8 years.

During all of which time, Said Ben Allen, as aforesaid, doth covenant with the said J. Y. Swift that the said Georgia Allen shall well & faithfully demean her self as such faithful Apprentice, observing fully the Commands of the said J. Y. Swift, and in all things deporting and behaving her self as a faithful Apprentice to the said J. Y. Swift, neither revealing his secrets, nor at any time leaving or neglecting the business of the said J. Y. Swift. And for & in Consideration of the services well & faithfully rendered by the said Georgia Allen, of the first part, said J. Y. Swift, of the second part, doth covenant, promise, & agree to instruct his said Apprentice, or otherwise cause her to be well & faithfully instructed, in the said trade or craft of House Servant or laborer, & also to read the English language, & shall also allow, furnish, & provide his said Apprentice with meat & drink & clothing during the said term, and all other necessaries meet & proper, in sickness & in health, & shall also pay to said Ben Allen Ten Dollars per year. Witness our hands & seals the day & year first before written.

Executed Before us }
Abda Oglesby } Ben + Allen, his mark
J. J. Burch, Ordinary E. C. } J. Y. Swift

Georgia } [301]
Elbert County } This Indenture, Made this the 13th day of January 1899, between Singleton Blackwell, of Said County, for and in behalf of George Blackwell, being of the age of 17 years, of the one part, and John C. Brown, of the County aforesaid, of the other part. Witnesseth: that the Said Sing Blackwell, as aforesaid, does by these presents bind out George Blackwell, of said County, as Apprentice to said John C. Brown in the trade or craft of house Servant or as Laborer upon the plantation of the said John C. Brown to be taught the said craft or trade of house servant or laborer, and to live with, continue, and serve the said John C. Brown as an Apprentice from the 16th January 1899 for and during the term of Four years. During all of which time, said Sing Blackwell, as aforesaid, doth covenant with the said John C. Brown that the said George Blackwell shall well and faithfully demean him self as such faithful Apprentice, Observing fully the commands of the said John C. Brown, and in all things deporting and behaving him self as a faithful Apprentice to the said John C. Brown, neither revealing his Secrets, nor at any time leaving or neglecting the business of the said John C. Brown. And for

and in Consideration of the services well and faithfully rendered by the said George Blackwell, of the first part, Said John C. Brown, of the Second part, doth covenant, promise, and agree to instruct his Said Apprentice, or otherwise Cause him to be well and faithfully instructed, in the trade or craft of house Servant or laborer, and shall also allow, furnish, and provide his said said Apprentice with meat and drink and clothing during the said term, and all other necessaries meet and proper, in sickness & in health.

Witness our hands and Seals the day and year first before written.

Executed Before us }
S. E. Gaines } Singleton + Blackwell, his mark
J. J. Burch, Ordinary } Jnº C. Brown

[The Ordinary wrote the following notation vertically in the left margin of the page.]

This Apprenticeship has been Superceeded by an Other Contract. J. J. Burch, Ord

Georgia } [302]
Elbert County } This Indenture, Made this the 18 day of January 1899, between Armstead Isham, of said County, for and in behalf his minor Children, Sam, Corn, and Sallie Isham, being of the age of 14, 12, & 13 years, of the one part, and L. G. Fambrough, of the County aforesaid, of the other part. Witnesseth: that the said Armstead Isham, as aforesaid, does by these presents bind out Sam, Corn, and Sallie Isham, of Said County, as Apprentice to said L. G. Fambrough in the trade or craft of Hand Servants or as laborers upon the plantation of the said L. G. Fambrough, to be taught the said Craft or trade of Hand Servants or laborers, and to live with, continue, and serve the said L. G. Fambrough as an Apprentice from the date hereof for and during the term of 7, 9, & 8 years, or until they reach their majority. during all of which time, Said Armstead Isham aforesaid doth covenant with the said L. G. Fambrough that the said Sam, Corn, and Sallie Isham shall well and faithfully demean them selves as such faithful Apprentice, observing fully the Command of the said L. G. Fambrough, and in all things deporting and behaving them selves as faithful Apprentices to the said L. G. Fambrough, neither revealing his Secrets, nor at any time leaving or neglecting the business of the said L. G. Fambrough. And for and in Consideration of the service well and faithfully rendered by the said Sam, Corn, and Sallie Isham, of the first, said L. G. Fambrough, of the Second part, doth Covenant, promise, and agree to instruct his said Apprentices, or otherwise Cause them to be well and faithfully instructed, in

the trade or Craft of hand Servants or laborer, and shall also allow, furnish, and provide his said Apprentices with meat and drink and clothing during the said term, and all other necessaries meet and proper, in sickness & in health, and shall also, at the expiration of the term, allow and pay the Said Apprentice One hundred and Twenty Two Dollars, with interest on same from date.

Witness our hands and Seals the day and year first before written.

Executed Before us }
T. A. Willis   }   Armstead + Isham, his mark
J. J. Burch, Ordinary }   L. G. Fambrough

Georgia   }   [303]
Elbert County } This Indenture, made this 25 Jan 1899, between William Pass, of said County, for and in behalf of his son Edmond Pass, being of the age of 17 years, of the one part, and W. S. Grimes, of the County aforesaid, of the other part. Witnesseth: That the said William Pass, as aforesaid, does by these presents bind out his said son Edmond Pass, of said County, as Apprentice to said W. S. Grimes in the trade or Craft of Servant or as laborer upon the plantation of the said W. S. Grimes, to be taught the said Craft or trade of Servant or laborer, and to live with, continue, and serve the said W. S. Grimes as an Apprentice from the 1st of February 1899 for and during the term of one year, or until a debt of $56.00 is Liquidated at four and one Six Dollars per month. During all of which time, said William Pass, as aforesaid, doth covenant with the said W. S. Grimes that the said Edmond Pass shall well and faithfully demean his self as such faithful Apprentice, observing fully the Command of the said W. S. Grimes, and in all things deporting and behaving his self as a faithful Apprentice to the said W. S. Grimes, neither revealing his secrets, nor at any time leaving or neglecting the business of the said W. S. Grimes. And for and in Consideration of the service well and faithfully rendered by the Said Edmond Pass, of the first part, said W. S. Grimes, of the Second part, doth Covenant, promise, and agree to instruct his said Apprentice, or otherwise Cause him to be well and faithfully instructed, in the said trade or Craft of Servant or laborer, and shall also allow, furnish, and provide his Said Apprentice with meat and drink and Clothing during the said term, and all other necessaries meet and proper, in sickness and in health, and shall also, at the expiration of the said term, allow and pay the Said Apprentice four and one Six Dollars per month.

Witness our hands and Seals the day and year first before written.

Executed Before us }
B. H. Goss }
J. J. Burch, ordinary }

William + Pass, his mark
W. S. Grimes

Georgia } [304]
Elbert County } This Indenture, made this the 30th day of January 1899, between Ben Joe Heard, of Said County, for and in behalf of him self & his minor children, to wit, Joe, John, Gate, & Lavonia Heard, being of the age of 35, 18, 12, 19, & 11 years, of the one part, and J. W. Norman, of the County aforesaid, of the other part. Witnesseth: That the Said Ben Joe Heard, as aforesaid, does by these presents bind out himself & his minor children, Joe, John, Gate, & Lavonia Heard, of said County, as Apprentice to said J. W. Norman in the trade or craft of Hand Servant or as Laborer upon the plantation of the said J. W. Norman to be taught the said Craft or trade of Hand Servant or laborer, & to live with, Continue, & Serve the Said J. W. Norman as Apprentice from the date hereof for & during the term of Three years. During all of which time, said Ben Joe Heard, as aforesaid, doth Covenant with the said J. W. Norman that the said Ben Joe, Joe, John, Gate, & Lavonia Heard shall well & faithfully demean them selves as such faithful Apprentice, observing fully the Command of the said J. W. Norman, and in all things deporting & behaving them selves as faithful Apprentices to the said J. W. Norman, neither revealing his Secrets, nor at any time leaving or neglecting the business of the said J. W. Norman. And for & in Consideration of the services well and faithfully rendered by the Said Ben Joe, Joe, John, Gate, & Lavonia Heard, of the first part, said J. W. Norman, of the second part, doth Covenant, promise, & agree to instruct his said Apprentices, or otherwise Cause them to be well & faithfully instructed, in the said trade or craft of Hand Servant or Laborer, and Shall also allow, furnish, & provide his Said Apprentice with meat & drink & clothing during the Said term, & all other necessaries meet & proper, in sickness and in health, & Shall also, at the expiration of the Said term, allow & pay the said Apprentices Twelve Dollars per month, or Seven hundred & Twenty Dollars.

Witness our hands & Seals the day & year first before written.

Executed Before us
J. H. Stovall
J. J. Burch, ordinary

Ben Joe + Heard his mark
J. W. Norman

Georgia } [305]
Elbert County } This Indenture, Made this the first day of February 1899,

between Jep Brawner, of Said County, for and in behalf of Joe Henry Brawner, being of the age of 12 years, of the one part, and H. P. Norman, of the County aforesaid, of the other part. Witnesseth: That the Said Jep Norman, as aforesaid, does by these presents bind out his said son Joe Henry Brawner, of Said County, as Apprentice to Said H. P. Norman in the trade or Craft of Hand Servant or laborer upon the plantation of the said H. P. Norman, to be taught the Said Craft or trade of Hand Servant or laborer, and to live with, Continue, and Serve the Said H. P. Norman as an Apprentice from the date hereof for and during the term of Two years. During all of which time, Said Jep Brawner, as aforesaid, doth Covenant with the said H. P. Norman that the said Joe Henry Brawner Shall well and faithfully demean him self as such faithful Apprentice, observing fully the Command of the Said H. P. Norman, and in all things deporting and behaving him self as a faithful Apprentice to the Said H. P. Norman, neither revealing his secrets, nor at any time leaving or neglecting the business of the Said H. P. Norman. And for and in Consideration of the Service well and faithfully rendered by the Said Joe H. Brawner, of the first part, Said H. P. Norman, of the Second part, doth Covenant, promise, and agree to instruct his Said Apprentice, or otherwise Cause him to be well and faithfully instructed, in the Said trade or Craft of Hand Servant or laborer, and shall also Allow, furnish, and provide his Said Apprentice with meat and drink and Clothing during the said term, and all other necessaries meet and proper, in Sickness and in health, and Shall also, at the expiration of the said term, allow & pay the Said Apprentice Five Dollars per year or ten Dollars in advance. Witness our hands & seals the day & year first before written.

Executed Before us }
C. P. Carrooth }   Jep + Brawner, his mark
J. J. Burch, ordinary }   H. P. Norman

Georgia } [306]
Elbert County } This Indenture, Made this the 1st day of February 1899, between Jep Brawner, of Said County, for and in behalf of Joe Henry Brawner, being of the age of 12 years, of the one part, & H. P. Norman, of the County aforesaid, of the other part. Witnesseth: That the Said Jep Brawner, as aforesaid, does by these presents bind out his said son Joe Henry Brawner, of Said County, as Apprentice to Said H. P. Norman in the trade or craft of Hand servant or as laborer upon the plantation of the said H. P. Norman, to be taught the said Craft or trade of Hand Servant or laborer, and to live with, Continue, & serve the said H. P. Norman as an Apprentice from the date hereof for and during the term of Two years.

During all of which time, said Jep Brawner, as aforesaid, doth covenant with the said H. P. Norman that the said Joe Henry Brawner shall well & faithfully demean him self as such faithful Apprentice, observing fully the Command of the Said H. P. Norman, and in all things deporting and behaving him self as a faithful Apprentice to the said H. P. Norman, neither revealing his secrets, nor at any time leaving or neglecting the business of the Said H. P. Norman.

And for and in consideration of the service well & faithfully rendered by the said Joe Henry Brawner, of the first part, said H. P. Norman, of the second part, doth covenant, promise, & agree to instruct his said Apprentice, or otherwise Cause him to be well & faithfully instructed, in the said trade or craft of Hand Servant or laborer, and shall also allow, furnish, & provide his said Apprentice with meat & drink & Clothing during the said term, and all other necessaries meet & proper, in sickness & in health, and Shall also, at the expiration of the said term, allow & pay the said Apprentice ten Dollars per year.

Witness our hands & Seals the day & year first before written.

Executed Before us
C. P. Carruth   Jep + Brawner, his mark
J. J. Burch, ordinary   H. P. Norman

Georgia   }   [307]
Elbert County } This Indenture, Made this the Sixth day of February 1899, between Calvin Brawner, of Said County, for & in behalf of Tom & Mathew Brawner, being of the age of Tom 15 & Mathew 11 years, of the one part, and McAlpin Arnold, of the County aforesaid, of the other part. Witnesseth: That the Said Calvin Brawner, as aforesaid, does by these presents bind out his said sons Tom & Mathew Brawner, of Said County, as Apprentice to Said McAlpin Arnold in the trade or Craft of Hand Servants or as Laborers upon the plantation of the said McAlpin Arnold, to be taught the said Craft or trade of Hand Servants or laborers, and to live with, Continue, & Serve the Said McAlpin Arnold as an Apprentice from the date hereof for & during the term of Three years. During all of which time, said Calvin Brawner, as aforesaid, doth Covenant with the said McAlpin Arnold that the said Tom & Mathew Brawner Shall well & faithfully demean the Selves as such faithful Apprentice, observing fully the Command of the Said McAlpin Arnold, and in all things deporting & behaving them Selves as faithful Apprentices to the Said McAlpin Arnold, neither revealing his Secrets, nor at any time leaving or neglecting the business of the Said McAlpin Arnold. And for & in Consideration of the Service well & faithfully rendered by the Said Tom & Mathew Brawner, of the first part, said McAlpin Arnold, of the Second

part, doth Covenant, promise, & agree to instruct Said Apprentices, or otherwise Cause them to be well and faithfully instructed, in the said trade or Craft Hand Servants or laborers, and shall also allow, furnish, & provide his Said Apprentice with Meat & Drink & Clothing during the said term, & all other necessaries meet & proper, in Sickness & in health, & Shall also, at the expiration of the Said term, allow and pay the Said Apprentices One hundred and Twenty nine & $^{97}/_{100}$ Dollars.

Witness Our hands & Seals the day & year first before written.

Executed Before us
T. J. Campbell   Calvin + Brawner, his mark
J. J. Burch, ordinary   McAlpin Arnold

Georgia   }   [308]
Elbert County   } This Indenture, Made this the first day of February 1899, between Jordan Heard, of Said County, for and in behalf of his sons Oscar & Simond Heard, being of the age of Oscar 18 years & Simond 15 years, of the one part, and J. W. Norman, of the County aforesaid, of the other part. Witnesseth: That the Said Jordan Heard, as aforesaid, does by these presents bind out his sons Oscar & Simond Heard, of Said County, as Apprentice to Said J. W. Norman in the trade or Craft of Hand Servant or as laborers upon the plantation of the said J. W. Norman, to be taught the said Craft or trade of Hand Servant or laborers, and to live with, Continue, & serve the said J. W. Norman as an apprentice from the date hereof for and during the term of Eleven months. During all of which time, said Jordan Heard, as aforesaid, doth covenant with the said J. W. Norman that the said Oscar & Simond Heard Shall well & faithfully demean them selves as a faithful apprentice, observing fully the Commands of the Said J. W. Norman, And in all things deporting & behaving them selves as a faithful Apprentice to the Said J. W. Norman, neither revealing his secrets, nor at any time leaving or neglecting the business of the said J. W. Norman. And for and in consideration of the Services well & faithfully rendered by the said Oscar & Simond Heard, of the first part, said J. W. Norman, of the Second part, doth Covenant, promise, & agree to instruct his Said Apprentices, or otherwise cause them to be well & faithfully instructed, in the Said trade or Craft of House Servants or laborers, & Shall also allow, furnish, & provide his said Apprentices with meat & drink & clothing during the said term, & all other necessaries meet & proper, in Sickness & in health, & shall also, at the expiration of the Said term, allow & pay the Said Apprentices Twenty five Dollars each.

Witness our hands & Seals the day & year first before written.

Executed Before us }
Abda Oglesby } Jordan + Heard, his mark
J. J. Burch, ordinary E. C. } J. W. Norman

Georgia } [309]
Elbert County } This Indenture, Made this the 28th day of February 1899, between Willis Herndon, of Said County, for and in behalf of him self, being of the age of 28 years, of the one part, and G. P. Norman, of the County aforesaid, of the other part. Witnesseth: That the said Willis Herndon, as aforesaid, does by these presents bind out him self, of said County, as Apprentice to said G. P. Norman in the trade or craft of Hand Servant or as Laborer upon the plantation of the said G. P. Norman, to be taught the said craft or trade of Hand Servant or laborer, & to live with, Continue, & Serve the said G. P. Norman as an Apprentice from the first day of January 1900 for & during the term of one year. During all of which time, said Willis Herndon, as aforesaid, doth Covenant with the said G. P. Norman that he, the said Willis Herndon, shall well & faithfully demean him self as such faithful Apprentice, observing fully the commands of the Said G. P. Norman, & in all things deporting & behaving him self as a faithful Apprentice to the said G. P. Norman, neither revealing his secrets, nor at any time leaving or neglecting the business of the said G. P. Norman. And for & in Consideration of the Service well & faithfully rendered by the said Willis Herndon, of the first part, said G. P. Norman, of the second part, doth Covenant, promise, & agree to instruct his said Apprentice, or otherwise cause him to be well & faithfully instructed, in the said trade or Craft of Hand Servant or laborer, & shall also allow, furnish, & provide his said Apprentice with meat and drink & clothing during the said term, & all other necessaries meet & proper, in sickness & in health, & shall also, at the expiration of the said term, allow & pay the Said Apprentice Seventy five Dollars.

Witness our hands & Seals the day & year first before written.

Executed Before us }
J. Y. Arnold } Willis + Herndon, his mark
J. J. Burch, ordinary } G. P. Norman

Georgia } [310]
Elbert County } This Indenture, Made this the Eight day of April 1899, between Allen Eberhart, of Said County, for and in behalf of John Eberhart, being of the age of 14 years, of the one part, and John C. Brown, of the County aforesaid, of the other part. Witnesseth: That the Said Allen Eberhart, as aforesaid, does by

these presents bind out John Eberhart, of said County, as Apprentice to said John C. Brown in the trade or craft of hand Servant or laborer, & to live with, continue, & Serve the said John C. Brown as an apprentice from the date hereof for and during the term of Seven years. During all of which time, said Allen Eberhart, as aforesaid, doth Covenant with the Said John C. Brown that the said John Eberhart shall well & faithfully demean him Self as such faithful Apprentice, observing fully the Command of the said John C. Brown, and in all things deporting and behaving him self as a faithful Apprentice to the Said John C. Brown, neither revealing his secrets, nor at any time leaving or neglecting the business of the Said John C. Brown. And for and in Consideration of the Service well & faithfully rendered by the said John Eberhart, of the first part, said John C. Brown, of the second part, doth Covenant, promise, and agree to instruct his said Apprentice, or otherwise Cause him to be well & faithfully instructed, in the said trade or craft of hand Servant or laborer, & also to read the English language, & shall also allow, furnish, & provide his said Apprentice with meat & drink & Clothing during the said term, & all other necessaries meet & proper, in sickness & in health, and shall also, at the expiration of the said term, allow & pay the said Apprentice what now allowed by the Statute in such case made & provided.

Witness our hands & seals the day & year first before written.

Executed   }
James McIntire   }   Allen + Eberhart, his mark
J. J. Burch, Ordinary }   John C. Brown

Georgia   }   [311]
Elbert County } This Indenture, Made this the 15 day of April 1899, between Oliver Allen, of said County, for and in behalf of Alfred Allen and Willis Allen, being of the age of 18 & 4 years, of the one part, and J. W. Rucker, of the County aforesaid, of the other part. Witnesseth: That the Said Oliver Allen, as aforesaid, does by these presents bind out Alfred and Willis Allen, of Said County, as apprentice to said J. W. Rucker in the trade or Craft of Hand servant or as Laborers upon the plantation of the said J. W. Rucker, to be taught the said Craft or trade of Hand Servants or laborers, and to live with, continue, and serve the said J. W. Rucker as apprentice from the first of January 1900 for and during the term of 3 and 15 years for Willis Allen. During all of which time, said Oliver Allen, as aforesaid, doth Covenant with the said J. W. Rucker that the said Alfred & Willis Allen Shall well and faithfully demean them self as such faithful Apprentice, observing fully the command of the said J. W. Rucker, and in all things deporting and behaving themselves as faithful Apprentices to the said J. W. Rucker, neither revealing his secrets, nor at any time leaving or neglecting the business of the said

J. W. Rucker. And for and in Consideration of the Service well & faithfully rendered by the Said Alfred & Willis Allen, of the first part, said J. W. Ruck, of the second part, doth Covenant, promise, & agree to instruct his said Apprentice, or otherwise Cause them to be well & faithfully instructed, in the said trade or Craft of hand Servant or laborer, & also to read the English language, and shall also allow, furnish, & provide his said Apprentices with meat & drink & clothing during the said term, & all other necessaries meet & proper, in sickness & in health, & shall also, at the expiration of the said term, allow & pay the Said Apprentices what is now allowed by the statute in such case made & provided.

Witness our hand & seals the day & year first before written.

Executed Before us
T. F. Rouzie
J. J. Burch, ordinary

Oliver + Allen, his mark
J. W. Rucker

Georgia } [312]
Elbert County } This Indenture, Made this the 1st day of June 1899, between Elias Brawner, of said County, for and in behalf of Albert Brawner, being of the age of 12 years, of the one part, and Oliver & Eberhart, of the County aforesaid, of the other part. Witnesseth: That the said Elias Brawner, as aforesaid, does by these presents bind out Albert Brawner, of Said County, as Apprentice to said Oliver & Eberhart in the trade or Craft of Farm Laborer or Laborer upon the plantation of the said Oliver & Eberhart to be taught the said Craft or trade of Farm Labor or Laborer, and to live with, Continue, & serve the Said Oliver & Eberhart as an apprentice from the date hereof for and during the term of Five years. During all of which time, Said Elias Brawner, as aforesaid, doth Covenant with the said Oliver & Eberhart that the said Albert Brawner Shall well and faithfully demean him Self as such faithful Apprentice, observing fully the Command of the Said Oliver & Eberhart, or their Agents, and in all things deporting & behaving him Self as a faithful Apprentice to the Said Oliver & Eberhart, neither revealing their secrets, nor at any time leaving or neglecting the business of the said Oliver & Eberhart.

And for and in Consideration of the service well & faithfully rendered by the said Albert Brawner, of the first part, said Oliver & Eberhart, of the second part, doth Covenant, promise, & agree to instruct his Said Apprentice, or otherwise cause him to be well & faithfully instructed, in the said trade or craft of Farm Labor or Laborer, & also to read the English language, & shall also allow, furnish, & provide his said Apprentice with meat & Drink & Clothing during the said term, & all other necessaries meet & proper, in Sickness & in health, & shall also, at the expiration of the said term, allow & pay the Said Apprentice what is now allowed by the Statute in such case made & provided. Witness our hands & seals the day & year first before written.

Executed Before us }
L. N. Alexander } Elias + Brawner, his mark
J. J. Burch, Ordinary } Oliver & Eberhart

Georgia } [313]
Elbert County } This Indenture, Made this the 5th day of June 1899, between Joe Holley, of Said County, for and in behalf of Earley Holley, being of the age of 17 years, of the one part, and William Hester, of the County aforesaid, of the other part. Witnesseth: That That Joe Holley, as aforesaid, does by these presents bind out Earley Holley, of said County, as Apprentice to said William Hester in the trade or craft of Farm laborer or Laborer upon the plantation of the said William Hester, to be taught the said craft or trade of Farm laborer or Laborer, and to live with, continue, and serve the said William Hester as an apprentice from the date hereof for and during the term of Six months. During all of which time, Said Joe Holley, as aforesaid, doth covenant with the said William Hester that the said Earley Holley shall well and faithfully demean him self as such faithful Apprentice, observing fully the Command of the said William Hester, and in all things deporting and behaving him self as a faithful Apprentice to the said William Hester, neither revealing his secrets, nor at any time leaving or neglecting the business of the said William Hester. And for and in consideration of the service well and faithfully rendered by the said Earley Holley, of the first part, said William Hester, of the second part, doth covenant, promise, and agree to instruct his Apprentice, or otherwise cause him to be well and faithfully instructed, in the said trade or craft of Farm laborer or Laborer, and also to read the English language, and shall also allow, furnish, and provide his said Apprentice with meat and drink and Clothing during the said term, and all other necessaries meet and proper, in sickness and in health, and shall also, at the expiration of the said term, allow and pay the said Apprentice Twenty four Dollars or four Dollars per month.

Witness our hands and seals the day and year first before written.

Executed Before us
Abda Oglesby } Joe + Holley, his mark
J. J. Burch, ordinary E. C. } William Hester

Georgia } [314]
Elbert County } This Indenture, made this the 13 Day June 1899, between

Pearce Davis, of Said County, for & in behalf of him Self & Reubin Davis, being of the age of Pearce 33 years & Reubin 10 years, of the one part, and F. B. Fortson, of the County aforesaid, of the other part. Witnesseth: That the said Pearce Davis, as aforesaid, does by these presents bind out him self and Reubin Davis, of said County, as Apprentices to said F. B. Fortson in the trade or craft of Hand Servants or Laborers upon the plantation of the said F. B. Fortson, to be taught the said craft or trade of Hand Servants or Laborers, and to live with, Continue, & serve the said F. B. Fortson as apprentices from the date hereof for and during 5 years & Reubin 4 years Pearce and 4 years for Reubin. During all of which time, the Said Pearce Davis, as aforesaid, doth Covenant with the said F. B. Fortson that the said Pearce & Reubin Davis Shall well & faithfully demean them selves as faithful Apprentices to the said F. B. Fortson, neither revealing his secrets, nor at any time leaving or neglecting the business of the said F. B. Fortson. And for and in consideration of the service well & faithfully rendered by the said Pearce & Reubin Davis, of the first part, said F. B. Fortson, of the second part, doth covenant, promise, & agree to instruct them, said Apprentices, or otherwise cause them to be well & faithfully instructed, in the Said trade or Craft of Hand Servants or laborers, and also to read the English language, & Shall also allow & furnish & provide them, Said Apprentices, with meat & drink & clothing during the Said term, and all other necessaries meet & proper, in Sickness & in health, & shall also, at the expiration of the Said term, allow & pay the said Apprentices Twenty five Dollars. Witness our hands and seals the day & year first before written.

Executed Before us
T. A. Willis   Pearce + Davis, his mark
J. J. Burch, ordinary   F. B. Fortson

Georgia   }   [315]
Elbert County } This Indenture, Made this the 17 day of July 1899, between Jane McIntosh, of said County, for and in behalf of Alfred McIntosh, being of the age of 13 years, of the one part, and Oliver & Eberhart, of the County aforesaid, of the other part. Witnesseth: That the Said Jane McIntosh, as aforesaid, does by these presents bind out Alfred McIntosh, of said County, as Apprentice to said Oliver & Eberhart in the trade or craft of Farm Laborer or Laborer upon the plantation of the said Oliver & Eberhart to be taught the Said Craft or trade of Farm Laborer or Laborer, & to live with, Continue, & serve the Said Oliver & Eberhart as an apprentice from the date hereof for and during the term of two months.

During all of which time, said Jane McIntosh, as aforesaid, doth Covenant with the Said Oliver & Eberhart that the said Alfred McIntosh shall well & faithfully demean him self as such faithful Apprentice, observing fully the Command of the said Oliver & Eberhart, neither revealing their secrets, nor at any time leaving or neglecting the business of the said Oliver & Eberhart. And for and in consideration of the Services well & faithfully rendered by the said Alfred McIntosh, of the first part, said Oliver & Eberhart, of the second part, doth covenant, promise, & agree to instruct him, said Apprentice, or otherwise Cause him to be well & faithfully instructed, in the Said trade or Craft of Farm Laborer or Laborer, & also to read the English language, & Shall also allow, furnish, & provide him, said Apprentice, with meat & drink & clothing during the said term, and all other necessaries meet & proper, in Sickness & in health, and shall also, at the expiration of the said term, allow allow & pay the said Apprentice what is now allowed by the Statute in such case made & provided.

Witness our hands & Seals the day & year first before written.

Executed Before us }
D. B. Alexander }
J. J. Burch, ordinary }

Jane + McIntosh, her mark
Oliver & Eberhart

Georgia } [316]
Elbert County } This Indenture, made this the 20th day of July 1899, between Wash Christian, of Said County, for and in behalf of himself, being of the age of 21 years, of the one part, and E. V. McLanahan, of the County aforesaid, of the other part. Witnesseth: That the said Wash Christian, as aforesaid, does by these presents bind out him Self, of Said County, as apprentice to said E. V. McLanahan in the trade or craft of Farm Laborer or Laborer upon the plantation of the said E. V. McLanahan, to be taught the Said Craft or trade of Farm Laborer or as Laborer, and to live with, Continue, & serve the said E. V. McLanahan as an Apprentice from the 1st of September 1899 for and during the term of 5 months.

During all of which time, said Wash Christian, as aforesaid, doth Covenant with the Said E. V. McLanahan that the said Wash Christian shall well & faithfully demean him self as such faithful Apprentice, observing fully the Command of the said E. V. McLanahan, and in all things deporting & behaving him self as a faithful Apprentice to the said E. V. McLanahan, neither revealing his secrets, nor at any time leaving or neglecting the business of the said E. V. McLanahan. And for and in consideration of the Services well & faithfully rendered by the said Wash Christian, of the first part, said E. V. McLanahan, of the second part, doth Covenant, promise, & agree to instruct his said Apprentice, or otherwise Cause him to be well & faithfully instructed, in the said trade or Craft of Farm Laborer or laborer, and shall also allow, furnish, & provide his Said Apprentice with meat

& drink & Clothing during the Said term, & all other necessaries meet & proper, in sickness & in health, & shall also, at the expiration of the term, allow & pay the said Apprentice Seven Dollars per month.

Witness our hands and Seals the day & year first before written.

Executed Before us }
D. B. Alexander }
J. J. Burch, ordinary }

Wash + Christian, his mark
E. V. McLanahan

Georgia } [317]
Elbert County } This Indenture, Made this 21st day of July 1899, between John Burton, S^r, of Said County, for and in behalf of John Burton, J^r, being of the age of 16 years, of the one part, and Oliver & Eberhardt, of the County aforesaid, of the other part. Witnesseth: That the said John Burton, S^r, as aforesaid, does by these presents bind out John Burton, J^r, of said County, as Apprentice to Said Oliver & Eberhardt in the trade or craft of Farm laborer or as Laborer upon the plantation of the said Oliver & Eberhardt, to be taught the said Craft or trade of Said Laborer or Laborer, and to live with, continue, & Serve the said Oliver & Eberhardt as an apprentice from the date hereof for and during the term of three months. During all of which time, Said John Burton, S^r, as aforesaid, doth Covenant with the Said Oliver & Eberhardt that the said John Burton, J^r shall well & faithfully demean him self as such faithful Apprentice, observing fully the Command of the said Oliver & Eberhardt, and in all things deporting & behaving him self as a faithful Apprentice to the said Oliver & Eberhart, neither revealing their secrets, nor at any time leaving or neglecting the business of the Said Oliver & Eberhardt.

And for & in consideration of the Service well & faithfully rendered by Said John Burton, J^r, of the first part, Said Oliver & Eberhardt, of the Second part, doth Covenant, promise, & agree to instruct him, Said Apprentice, or otherwise Cause him to be well & faithfully instructed, in the trade or craft of Farm laborer or Laborer, & also to read the English language, & shall also allow, furnish, & provide him, Said Apprentice, with meat & drink & clothing during the Said term, & all other necessaries meet & proper, in sickness & in health, & shall also, at the expiration of the said term, allow & pay the Said Apprentice what is now allowed by the Statute in such case made & provided.

Witness our hands & seals the day & year first before written.

Executed before us }
J. E. Thornton, N. P. }   John + Burton, S^r, his mark
W. T. Arnold }   Oliver & Eberhardt

State of Georgia }   [318]
Elbert County }   This Indenture, made this July the 24th 1899, Between Harrison Ham, of Elbert County Said State, And Oliver & Eberhardt, of Elbert County said. Witnesseth: that said Harrison Ham, in consideration of the promises and undertakings of said Oliver & Eberhardt hereinafter set forth, does hereby bind him self to the said Oliver & Eberhardt for the full term of one year, from January the 1st 1900, and he hereby agrees and Contracts with said Oliver & Eberhardt to work faithfully under their direction at such place and at such Labor as said Oliver & Eberhardt may desire & direct, & to respect & obey all orders & Commands of said Oliver & Eberhardt, & at all times to demean him self orderly & soberly. & the said Harrison Ham further agrees to account to the said Oliver & Eberhardt for all lost time, except in Case of temporary sickness not exceeding three days, the Sum to be deducted from the wages hereinafter set forth & at the same rate. And the said Oliver & Eberhardt, in consideration of the promises & undertakings of said Harrison Ham, agree & Contract with said Harrison Ham to furnish him with food, lodging, & suitable Clothing. They further agree to pay Harrison Ham wages by the year, as follows, on December the 31st 1900 $40.00. It is further agreed that, should this Contract be terminated by the death of either party during said year, said Harrison Ham should be paid prorata for the time he served during said year at the price fixed for Said year. Said Oliver & Eberhardt further agree to teach said Harrison Ham the trade of Farm Laborer in all its details. In witness whereof, Said Harrison Ham and Oliver & Eberhardt have hereunto set their hands the day & year first above written. Signed, sealed, delivered, & executed in Duplicate in presence of

J. E. Thornton, N. P. }   Harrison Ham
A. S. Oliver, J^r }   Oliver & Eberhardt

State of Georgia }   [319]
Elbert County }   This Indenture, made this May the 10th 1899, between Sam Edmonds, of Elbert County Said State, ~~Witnesseth: that the said~~ and Oliver & Eberhardt, a firm composed of A. S. Oliver & L. P. Eberhardt, of Elbert County said State. Witnesseth: that the Said Sam Edmonds, in consideration of the promises & undertakings of the said Oliver & Eberhardt for the full term of one year, from January the 1st 1900. and he hereby Agrees & Contracts with said

Oliver & Eberhardt to work faithfully under their direction at such place and at such labor as said Oliver & Eberhardt may desire & direct, & to respect & obey all orders & Commands of said Oliver & Eberhardt, & at all times to demean him self orderly & soberly. And the said Sam Edmonds further agrees to account to the said Oliver & Eberhardt for all lost time, except in Cases of temporary Sickness not exceeding three days, the sum to be deducted from the wages hereinafter set forth & at the same rate.

And the said Oliver & Eberhardt, in Consideration of the promises & undertakings of the said Sam Edmonds, agrees & contracts with Said Sam Edmonds to furnish him with board, lodging, & suitable Clothing. They further Agree to pay said Sam Edmonds wages by the year, as follows, on December the 25th 1900 fifty Dollars. It is further agreed that, should this Contract be terminated by the death of either party during either of Said years, Said Sam Edmonds shall be paid pro rata for the time he served during said year at the price fixed for said year. Said Oliver & Eberhardt further agree to teach said Sam Edmonds the trade of Farm Laborer in all its details. In Witness Whereof, the said Sam Edmonds and Oliver & Eberhardt have hereunto Set their hands & seals the day & year first above written. Erasure made before Signing

            Sam + Edmonds, his mark
            Oliver & Eberhardt

Signed, Sealed, delivered, & executed }
in duplicate in presence of   }
T. A. Willis, N. P.   }
L. G. Fambrough   }

State of Georgia   }   [320]
Elbert County   } This Indenture, made this Aug the 8 1899, between William Pulliam, of Elbert County Said State, and Oliver & Eberhardt, of Elbert County Said State. Witnesseth: that the said William Pulliam, in Consideration of the promises and undertakings of the Said Oliver & Eberhardt hereinafter set forth, does hereby bind himself to the Said Oliver & Eberhardt for the full term of two years, from January the 1st 1900, and he hereby agrees & Contracts with Said Oliver & Eberhardt to work faithfully under their direction at such place and at such labor as Said Oliver & Eberhardt may desire & direct, & to respect & obey all orders & commands of Said Oliver & Eberhardt, & at all times to demean him self orderly & soberly. And the Said William Pulliam further agrees to account to the Said Oliver & Eberhardt for all lost time, except in Cases of temporary Sickness not exceeding three days, the Same to be deducted from

the wages hereinafter set forth & at the Same rate. And the Said Oliver & Eberhardt, in Consideration of the promises & undertakings of the Said William Pulliam, agrees and contracts with Said William Pulliam to furnish him with board, lodging, & suitable Clothing. They further agrees to pay William Pulliam wages by the year, as follows, on December the 25th 1900 $25.00 Dollars, on December the 25th 1901 $35.00 Dollars. It is further agreed that, Should this Contract be terminated by the death of either party during either of said years, Said William Pulliam shall be paid pro rata for the time he served during Said year at the price fixed for said year. Said Oliver & Eberhardt further agrees to teach Said William Pulliam the trade of Farm Laborer in all its details. In witness whereof, the said William Pulliam and Oliver & Eberhardt have hereunto set their hands & Seals the day and year first above written.

Signed, Sealed, delivered, & Executed }
in Duplicate in presence of   }
J. E. Thornton, N. P.   }   William + Pulliam, his mark
J. W. King   }   Oliver & Eberhardt

Georgia   }   [321]
Elbert County } This Indenture, Made this the 8 day of August 1899, between Rose Tate Davis, of Said County, for and in behalf of Gordon Tate, being of the age of twelve years, of the one part, and Oliver & Eberhardt, of the County aforesaid, of the other part. Witnesseth: That the said Rose Tate Davis, as aforesaid, does by these presents bind out Gordon Tate, of Said County, as Apprentice to Said Oliver & Eberhardt in the trade or craft of Farm laborer or as Laborer upon the plantation of the said Oliver & Eberhardt to be taught the said Craft or trade of Farm Laborer or Laborer, and to live with, Continue, and Serve the said Oliver & Eberhardt as an apprentice from the date hereof for and during the term of Five years.

During all of which time, Said Rose Tate Davis, as aforesaid, doth Covenant with the said Oliver & Eberhardt that the said Gordon Tate shall well and faithfully demean him self as such faithful Apprentice, observing fully the Command of the said Oliver & Eberhardt, and in all things deporting & behaving him self as a faithful Apprentice to the said Oliver & Eberhart, neither revealing their Secrets, nor at any time leaving or neglecting the business of the said Oliver & Eberhardt.

And for and in Consideration of the Service well and faithfully rendered by the said Gordon Tate, of the first part, Said Oliver & Eberhardt, of the second part, doth Covenant, promise, & agree to instruct him, Said Apprentice, or otherwise Cause him to be well and faithfully instructed, in the said trade or Craft of Farm laborer or laborer, & also to read the English language, & shall also allow, furnish, & provide him, said Apprentice, with meat & drink & Clothing during the said term, & all other necessaries meet & proper, in sickness & in health, & shall also, at the expiration of the Said term, allow & pay the Said Apprentice what is now allowed by the Statute in such case made and provided. Witness our hands and seals the day & year first before written.

Executed before us   }
J. E. Thornton, N. P. }
J. L. Wilhite   }   Rose Tate + Davis, her mark
                                             Oliver & Eberhardt

State of Georgia }   [322]
Elbert County   } This Indenture, made this August the 12th 1899, between Jim Brown, of Elbert County said State, and Oliver & Eberhardt, of Elbert County said State. Witnesseth: that the said Jim Brown, in consideration of the promises and undertakings of the Said Oliver & Eberhardt for full term of Four years, from January the 1st 1900. And he hereby agrees and Contracts with said Oliver & Eberhardt to work faithfully under their direction at such place and at such labor as Said Oliver & Eberhardt may desire and direct, and to respect and obey all orders and Commands of Said Oliver & Eberhardt, and at all times to demean him self orderly and soberly. And the Said Jim Brown further agrees to account to Said Oliver & Eberhardt for all lost time, except in cases of temporary sickness not exceeding three days, the same to be deducted from the wages hereinafter set forth And at Same rate.

And the Said Oliver & Eberhardt, in Consideration of the promises and undertakings of the Said Jim Brown, agrees and Contracts with Said Jim Brown to furnish him with board, lodging, and Suitable Clothing. The further agrees to pay Said Jim Brown wages by the year, as follows, on December the 25th 1900 $35.00 Dollars, on December the 25th 1901 $35.00 Dollars, on December the 25th 1902 [blank] Dollars, on December the 25th 1903 [blank] Dollars. It is further agreed that, should this Contract be terminated by the death of either party during either of Said years, said Jim Brown shall be paid pro rata for the time he served during said year at the price fixed for said year. Said Oliver & Eberhardt further agrees to teach Said Jim Brown the trade of Farm laborer in all its details.

In witness whereof, the said Jim Brown and Oliver & Eberhardt have hereunto set their hands and Seals the day and year first above written.

Signed, Sealed, delivered, & Executed in Duplicate in presence of

J. E. Thornton, N. P.   Jim + Brown, his mark
J. W. Summons   Oliver & Eberhardt

Georgia   }   [323]
Elbert County } This Indenture, Made this the 2nd day of September 1899, between Elbert Brawner, of said County, for & in behalf of Robert Brawner and Lu Brawner, being of the age of Robert 13 and Lu 12 years, of the one part, and R. E. Hudgens, of the County aforesaid, of the other part. Witnesseth: That the said Elbert Brawner, as aforesaid, does by these presents bind out Robert Brawner & Lu Braw, of said County, as apprentice to said R. E. Hudgens in the trade or craft of Farm Laborer or as Laborer upon the plantation of the said R. E. Hudgens, to be taught the said Craft or trade of Farm Laborer or Laborer, and to live with, Continue, & serve the said R. E. Hudgens as Apprentices from the date hereof for and during the term of 6½ years. During all of which time, said Elbert Brawner, as aforesaid, doth covenant with the said R. E. Hudgens that the Said Robert and Lu Brawner shall well & faithfully demean them selves as such faithful Apprentices, observing fully the Command of the said R. E. Hudgens, and in all things deporting & behaving them selves as faithful Apprentices to the said R. E. Hudgens, neither revealing his Secrets, nor at any time leaving or neglecting the business of the said R. E. Hudgens.

And for and in Consideration of the service well & faithfully rendered by the said Robert & Lu Brawner, of the first part, said R. E. Hudgens, of the second part, doth Covenant, promise, & agree to instruct his said Apprentices, or otherwise Cause them to be well & faithfully instructed, in the said trade or craft of Farm Laborers or laborers, & also to read the English language, and shall also allow, furnish, & provide his said Apprentices with meat & drink & clothing during the said term, & all other necessaries meet & proper, in sickness & in health, & shall also, at the expiration of the said term, allow & pay the Said Apprentices One hundred and fifty Dollars. Witness our hands & Seals the day & year first before written.

Executed before us
T. A. Willis   Elbert + Brawner. his mark
J. J. Burch, Ordinary   R. E. Hudgens

Georgia   }   [324]
Elbert County } This Indenture, Made this the 11th day of September 1899, between Sarah Rucker, of said County, of the one part, an C. T. Bond, of the

County aforesaid, of the other part. Witnesseth: That the said Sarah Rucker, as aforesaid, does by these presents bind her Self, of Said County, as Apprentice to said C. T. Bond in the trade or Craft of Husbandry or as Laborer upon the plantation of the Said C. T. Bond, to be taught the Said craft or trade of Husbandry or Laborer, and to live with, Continue, & serve the Said C. T. Bond as Apprentice for and during the term of five years, Beginning Jan 1st 1900, Ending Dec 25th 1905. During all of which time, said Sarah Rucker, as aforesaid, doth covenant with the said C. T. Bond that the said Sarah Rucker shall well & faithfully demean her self as a faithful Apprentice to the said C. T. Bond, observing fully the Command of the said C. T. Bond, & in all things deporting & behaving her self as a faithful Apprentice to the said C. T. Bond, neither revealing his secrets, nor at any time leaving or neglecting the business of the said C. T. Bond. And for and in Consideration of the Service well & faithfully rendered by the Said Sarah Rucker, of the first part, Said C. T. Bond, of the second part, doth Covenant, promise, & agree to instruct his said Apprentice, or otherwise Cause her to be well & faithfully instructed, in the said trade or craft of Husbandry or laborer, & shall also allow, furnish, & provide his said Apprentice with meat & drink & clothing during the said term, and all other necessaries meet & proper, in sickness & in health, & shall also, at the expiration of said term, allow & pay the Said Apprentice what is now allowed by the Statute in Such Case made & provided. Inter lined before signing. Witness our hands & seals the day & year first before written.

Executed Before us
L. C. Edward, J. P.   Sarah + Rucker, her mark
Sam L. Oliver   C. T. Bond

Georgia   }   [325]
Elbert County } This Indenture, Made this the 10th day of Sept 1899, between Hettie Rucker, of said County, of the one part, and C. T. Bond, of the County aforesaid, of the other part. Witnesseth: That the said Hettie Rucker, as aforesaid, does by these presents bind herself, of said County, as Apprentice to C. T. Bond in the trade or craft of Husbandry or as Laborer upon the plantation of the said C. T. Bond, to be taught the said craft or trade of Husbandry or laborer, & to live with, Continue, & serve the said C. T. Bond as an Apprentice for and during the term of five years, Beginning Jan 1st 1900, Ending Dec 25, 1905. During all of which time, said Hettie Rucker, as aforesaid, doth Covenant with the said C. T. Bond that the said Hettie Rucker shall well & faithfully demean herself as such faithful Apprentice, observing fully the Command of the said C. T. Bond, and in all things deporting & behaving her self as a faithful Apprentice to the said C. T.

Bond, neither revealing his secrets, nor at any time leaving or neglecting the business of the said C. T. Bond. And for & in Consideration of the service well & faithfully rendered by the said Hettie Rucker, of the first part, said C. T. Bond, of the second part, doth Covenant, promise, & agree to instruct his said Apprentice, or otherwise cause her to be well & faithfully instructed, in the said trade or craft of Husbandry or Laborer, and shall also allow, furnish, & provide his Said Apprentice with meat & drink & clothing during the Said term, and all other necessaries meet & proper, in sickness and in health, and shall also, at the expiration of the said term, allow & pay the said Apprentice what is now allowed by the statute in such case made & provided. Interlined before Signing.

Witness our hands and Seals the day and year first before written.

Executed Before us
L. C. Edwards, J. P.   Hettie + Rucker, her mark
Sam L. Oliver   C. T. Bond

State of Georgia }   [326]
Elbert County   }   This Indenture, made August 25th 1899, between Henry Thompson, of Elbert County said state, and Oliver & Eberhardt, of Elbert County said state. Witnesseth: that the said Henry Thompson, in consideration of the promises and undertakings of the said Oliver & Eberhardt hereinafter set forth, does hereby bind himself to the said Oliver & Eberhardt for full term of Five years, from January 1st 1900. And he hereby agrees & Contracts with said Oliver & Eberhardt to work faithfully under their direction at such place & at such labor as said Oliver & Eberhardt may desire & direct, & to respect & obey all orders and Commands of said Oliver & Eberhardt, And at all times to demean himself orderly & soberly. And the said Henry Thompson further agrees to account to said Oliver & Eberhardt for all lost time, except in cases of Temporary sickness not exceeding three days, the same to be deducted from the wages hereinafter set forth and at same rate. And the said Oliver & Eberhardt, in Consideration of the promises & undertakings of the said Henry Thompson, agrees & contracts with said Henry Thompson to furnish him with board, lodging, and Suitable Clothing. They further agree to pay said Henry Thompson wages by the year, as follows.

On December the 25th 1900 Twenty Five Dollars

On December the 25th 1901 Twenty Five Dollars

On December the 25th 1902 Twenty Five Dollars

On December the 25th 1903 Twenty Five Dollars

On December the 25th 1904 Twenty Five Dollars

It is further agreed that, should this Contract be terminated by the death of either party during Either of said years, said Henry Thompson shall be paid prorata for the time he served during said year at the price fixed for said year. said Oliver & Eberhardt further agrees to teach said Henry Thompson the trade of Farm laborer in all its details.

In Witness whereof, the said Henry Thompson & Oliver & Eberhardt have hereunto set their hands & seals the day & year first above written.

Signed, Sealed, delivered, & executed in duplicate in presence of

J. E. Thornton, N. P. } Henry + Thompson, his mark
W. B. Vail   } Oliver & Eberhardt

State of Georgia } [327]
Elbert County } This Indenture, made this August the 12th 1899, between John Jackson, of Elbert County said state, & Oliver & Eberhardt, of Elbert County said state. Witnesseth: that the said John Jackson, in Consideration of the promises & undertakings of the said Oliver & Eberhardt hereinafter set forth, does hereby bind himself to the said Oliver & Eberhardt for the full term of three years, from January 1st 1900. And he hereby agrees & contracts with said Oliver & Eberhardt to work faithfully under their direction at such place & at such labor as said Oliver & Eberhardt may desire & direct, & to respect & obey all orders and Commands of said Oliver & Eberhardt, And at all times to demean himself orderly & soberly.

And the said John Jackson further agrees to account to the said Oliver & Eberhardt for all lost time, except in cases of temporary sickness not exceeding three days, the same to be deducted from the wages hereinafter set forth and at the same rates. And the said Oliver & Eberhardt, in consideration of the promises & undertakings of the said John Jackson, agrees & contracts with said John Jackson to furnish him with board, lodging, and suitable clothing. They further agree to pay said John Jackson wages by the year, as follows.

On December the 25th 1900 $25.00 Twenty Five Dollars

On December the 25th 1901 $25.00 Twenty Five Dollars

On December the 25th 1902 $25.00 Twenty Five Dollars

It is further agreed that, should this Contract be terminated by the death of either party during Either of said years, said John Jackson shall be paid pro rata for the time he served during said year at the price fixed for said year. Said Oliver & Eberhardt further agrees to teach said John Jackson the trade of Farm laborer in all its details.

In Witness Whereof, the said John Jackson & Oliver & Eberhardt have hereunto set their hands & seals the day & year first above written.

Signed, Sealed, delivered, & executed }
in Duplicate in presence of   }
J. E. Thornton, N. P.   }   John + Jackson, his mark
J. H. Seymore   }   Oliver & Eberhardt

Georgia   }   [328]
Elbert County } This Indenture, Made this the 5th day of April 1899, between Ron Huff, of said County, father of Lella Huff aged 13 years & Grandfather Lula Huff being of the age of 13 years, of the one part, and H. M. Seymore, of the County aforesaid, of the other part. Witnesseth: That the Ron Huff does by these presents bind out the said Lella Huff & Lula Huff, of Said County, as Apprentices to said H. M. Seymore in the trade or craft of Husbandry or as Laborers upon the plantation of the said H. M. Seymore, to be taught the said craft or trade of Husbandry or Laborer, and to live with, Continue, & Serve the said H. M. Seymore as Apprentices from the date hereof for and during the term of their minority, til said Lula & Lella are twenty one years of age.

During all of which time, said Ron Huff, as aforesaid, doth Covenant with the said H. M. Seymore that the said Lella & Lula Shall well & faithfully demean them Selves as such faithful Apprentices, observing fully the Command of the said Seymore, and in all things deporting & behaving them selves as faithful Apprentices to the said H. M. Seymore, neither revealing his secrets, nor at any time leaving or neglecting the business of the Said H. M. Seymore. And for and in consideration of the service well & faithfully rendered by the said Ron Huff, of the first part, said H. M. Seymore, of the second part, doth Covenant, promise, & agree to instruct them, said Apprentices, or otherwise cause them to be well & faithfully instructed, in the said trade or craft Husbandry or Laborer, & also to read the English Language, & Shall also allow, furnish, & provide them, Said Apprentice, with meat & drink & Clothing during the said term, & all other necessaries meet & proper, in Sickness & in health, & shall also, at the expiration of the said term, allow & pay the said Apprentices what is now allowed by the Statute in such case made & provided.

Witness our hands & Seals the day & year first before written. Interlined before Signing.

Executed Before us
D. B. Alexander
J. J. Burch, Ordinary

Ron + Huff, his mark
H. M. Seymore

Georgia } [329]
Elbert County } This Indenture, made this the 12th day of October 1899, between Wade Dickerson, of Said County, for and in behalf of Will Dickerson, his son, being of the age of 12 years, of the one part, and J. W. Whorton, of the County aforesaid, of the other part. Witnesseth: that the said Wade Dickerson, father of Will Dickerson, does by these presents bind out Will Dickerson, of said County, as Apprentice to said J. W. Whorton in the trade or craft of farming or as Laborer upon the plantation of the said J. W. Whorton, to be taught the said craft or trade of farming or Laborer, and to live with, continue, & Serve the said J. W. Whorton as an Apprentice from January the 1st 1900, for and during the term of Two years. During all of which time, said Wade Dickerson, father of Will Dickerson, doth Covenant with the said J. W. Whorton that the said Will Dickenson shall well & faithfully demean him self as such faithful Apprentice, observing fully the Command of the said J. W. Whorton, and in all things deporting & behaving him self as a faithful Apprentice to the said J. W. Whorton, neither revealing his Secrets, nor at any time leaving or neglecting the business of the said J. W. Whorton. And for & in Consideration of the service well & faithfully rendered by the Said Will Dickerson, of the first part, said J. W. Whorton, of the second part, doth Covenant, promise, and agree to instruct his said Apprentice, or otherwise Cause him to be well & faithfully instructed, in the said trade or Craft of farming or Laborer, & also to read the English Language, & shall also allow, furnish, and provide his said Apprentice with meat & Drink & Clothing during the said term, and all other necessaries meet and proper, in Sickness & in health.

Witness our hands & seals the day & year first before written.

Executed Before us
J. C. Vanduzer
J. J. Burch, Ordinary

Wade + Dickerson, his mark
J. W. Whorton

Georgia } [330]
Elbert County } This Indenture, made the 15th day of April 1898, between Lindsay Gray and Jno W. McCalla, both of Said County and State. Witnesseth: That the Said Lindsay Gray hereby apprentices to the Said McCalla his minor son

Elie Gray until he becomes Twenty one (21) years old. The Said boy being now about twelve years old. The Said McCalla is to treat said boy humanely and Kindly, furnish proper and sufficient food & Clothing, all necessary medical attention, such Education as can be had in the Common Schools of the County, and cause him to be instructed in the art or Craft of husbandry or farming.

Made in duplicate. Read in presence of both parties. Signed, Sealed, & delivered in presence of

J. B. Jones, J^r, N. P. Exoffic J. P. } Lindsay + Gray, his mark
T. J. Brownlee   } J. W. McCalla

Georgia   }   [331]
Elbert County } This Indenture, Made this the 9th day of November 1899, between Thomas Fortson, of said County, for and in behalf of his son, Jessie Fortson, being of the age of 10 years, of the one part, and G. P. Hall, of the County aforesaid, of the other part. Witnesseth: That the Said Thomas Fortson, as aforesaid, does by these presents bind out his said son Jessie Fortson, of said County, as Apprentice to said G. P. Hall in the trade or craft of Farm Laborer or as Laborer upon the plantation of the said G. P. Hall, to be taught the said Craft or trade of Farm Laborer or Laborer, and to live with, Continue, and Serve the said G. P. Hall as an Apprentice from the date hereof for and during the term of Eleven years or during his minority. During all of which time, said Thomas Fortson, as aforesaid, doth Covenant with the said G. P. Hall that the said Jesse Fortson shall well and faithfully demean him self as such faithful Apprentice, observing fully the Command of the Said G. P. Hall, and in all things deporting and behaving him self as a faithful Apprentice to the said G. P. Hall, neither revealing his Secrets, nor at any time leaving or neglecting the business of the said G. P. Hall. And for and in Consideration of the service well and faithfully rendered by the said Jessie Fortson, of the first part, said G. P. Hall, of the second part, doth Covenant, promise, and agree to instruct his said Apprentice, or otherwise Cause him to be well & faithfully instructed, in the said trade or Craft of Farm Laborer or Laborer, and also to read the English language, and shall also allow, furnish, & provide his said Apprentice with meat & Drink & Clothing during the said term, & all other necessaries meet & proper, in sickness and in health, and shall also, at the expiration of the said term, allow and pay the said Apprentice what is now allowed by the Statute in such case made and provided. All interlinations made before Signing.

Witness our hands & seals the day & year first before written.

Executed Before us }
A. S. J. Stovall }
J. J. Burch, Ordinary }

Thomas + Fortson, his mark
G. P. Hall

Georgia } [332]
Elbert County } This Indenture, Made this the 4th day of November 1899, between Harriet Rucker, of said County, for & in behalf of Lizzie, Ada, George, Hattie, Samie, & Minnie Rucker, being of the age of 15, 14, 10, 6, 4, 1 years, of the one part, and Hunter Rucker, jr, of the County aforesaid, of the other part. Witnesseth: That the said Harriet Rucker, as aforesaid, does by these presents bind out Lizzie, Ada, George, Hattie, Samie, and Minnie Rucker, of Said County, as Apprentice to said Hunter Rucker, jr in the trade or Craft of Farm Laborers or as Laborers upon the plantation of the said Hunter Rucker, Jr, to be taught the Said Craft or trade of Farm Laborer or Laborers, and to live with, Continue, & serve the Hunter Rucker, Jr as Apprentices from the date hereof for and during the term of their Minority. During all of which time, said Harriet Rucker, as aforesaid, doth covenant with the said Hunter Rucker that the said Lizzie, Ada, George, Hattie, Samie, and Minnie Rucker shall well & faithfully demean them selves as such faithful Apprentices, observing fully the Command of the said Hunter Rucker, Jr and in all things deporting & behaving them selves as faithful Apprentices to the said Hunter Rucker, Jr, neither revealing his secrets, nor at any time leaving or neglecting the business of the said Hunter Rucker, Jr. And for & in Consideration of the service well and faithfully rendered by the said Lizzie, Ada, George, Hattie, Samie, & Minnie Rucker, of the first part, said Hunter Rucker, Jr, of the second part, doth Covenant, promise, & agree to instruct his said Apprentices, or otherwise Cause them to be well & faithfully instructed, in the said trade or Craft of farm labor or laborers, and to read English Language, and shall also allow, furnish, & provide his said Apprentices with meat and drink & Clothing during the said Term, and all other necessaries meet & proper, in sickness & in health, and shall also, at the expiration of the said term, allow & pay the said apprentices what is now allowed by the Statute made and provided. Witness our hands & Seals.

T. A. Willis
J. J. Burch, Ordinary

Harriet + Rucker, her mark
Hunter + Rucker, his mark

Georgia } [333]
Elbert County } This Indenture, made this the 15th day of November 1899, between Dick Banks and Lizzie Banks, of said County, parents, for and in behalf

of them selves and their Son Dunsie McCalla, being of the age of 19 years, of the one part, and Ge⁰ P. Norman, of the County aforesaid, of the other part. Witnesseth: That the Said Dick & Lizzie Banks, as aforesaid, does by these presents bind out them selves and their son Dunsie McCalla, of said County, as Apprentices to said Ge⁰ P. Norman in the trade or craft of Farm Laborer or as Laborer upon the plantation of the said Ge⁰ P. Norman, to be taught the said Craft or trade of Farm Laborers or Laborers, & to live with, Continue, & serve the said George P. Norman as apprentices from the date hereof for and during the term of one year.

During all of which time, Said Dick & Lizzie Banks, as aforesaid, doth Covenant with the said Ge⁰ P. Norman that the said Dick & Lizzie Banks & Dunsie McCalla Shall well & faithfully demean them selves as such faithful apprentices, observing fully the Command of the said Ge⁰ P. Norman, and in all things deporting & behaving them selves as such faithful Apprentices to the said Ge⁰ P. Norman, neither revealing his secrets, nor at any time leaving or neglecting the business of the Said Ge⁰ P. Norman. And for and in Consideration of the service well and faithfully rendered by the said Dick & Lizzie Banks and Dunsie McCalla, of the first part, said Ge⁰ P. Norman, of the second part, doth Covenant, promise, and agree to instruct his said Apprentices, or otherwise Cause them to be well & faithfully instructed, in the said trade or craft of Farm Laborers or Laborers, and also to read the English Language, & shall also allow, furnish, & provide his said Apprentices with meat & drink & Clothing during the said term, and all other necessaries meet & proper, in sickness and in health, & shall also, at the expiration of the Said term, allow & pay the said Apprentices Sixty Dollars.

Witness our hands & seals the day & year first before written.

Executed Before us }	Dick Banks
A. M. Shumate }	Lizzie + Banks, her mark
J. J. Burch, Ordinary }	G. P. Norman

State of Georgia }   [334]
Elbert County   } This Contract, made and entered into between D. E. Brownlee, of the first part, and Lewellyn Tate and his wife Emma Tate and Jerry Dubose and his wife Edna Dubose and Luvina Dubose, minor Daughter of Jerry Dubose, of the second part. witnesseth: that Said parties of the second part agree (Jerry Dubose agreeing on the part of his said Daughter) to work for D. E. Brownlee for and during the term of twelve months, beginning on the 19th day of November 1899 and ending Nov 19th 1900, as farm laborer on his lands owned and rented and Cultivated by D. E. Brownlee during said term, doing all things in a good and

faithful manner when, where, and as directed by Said Brownlee or her Agents, doing good and faithful work during Said term, and not leaving the employ of said Brownlee during Said term.

In Consideration of the above, Said Brownlee agrees to pay Lewelling Tate one hundred and Seventy dollars, including the bord and Clothing of himself and wife, and to pay said Jerry Dubose one hundred and Eighty dollars, including the bord Clothing of him self, his said wife, and said minor daughter. So that whatever is taken up in board and Clothing by Said parties of the second part does not exceed the amount agreed to be paid each party of the second part. Parties of the second agree to make good all lost time at the rate of forty Cents per day for each day lost, but by each of the parties of the second part, each party making good his own lost time.

Witness our hands and seals this the 16 day of Nov 1899.

Test. James McIntosh }   Jerry Dubose
J. J. Burch, ordinary }   Emma Dubose
                                 Lewellyn + Tate, his mark
                                 Edna + Tate, her mark
                                 Luvina Dubose
                                 by Jerry + Dubose, his mark

Georgia   }   [335]
Elbert County } This Indenture, made this the 16th day of November 1899, between Ike Rucker, of said County, for and in behalf of his minor children, Lewellyn Rucker, Tinsley Rucker, and Caroline Rucker, being of the age of 17, 12, 14 years, of the one part, and Jnº C. Brown, of the County aforesaid, of the other part. Witnesseth: That the said Ike Rucker, as aforesaid, does by these presents bind out his said children, Lewellyn, Tinsley, & Caroline Rucker, of said County, as Apprentices to said John C. Brown in the trade or Craft of Farm Laborers or as Laborers upon the plantation of the said John C. Brown, to be taught the said Craft or trade of Farm Laborers or Laborers, and to live with, Continue, and Serve the said John C. Brown as apprentices from the date hereof for and during the term of their minority. During all of which time, Said Ike Rucker, as aforesaid, doth Covenant with the said John C. Brown that the said Lewellyn, Tinsley, & Caroline Shall well and faithfully demean them selves as such faithful apprentices, observing fully the Command of the said John C. Brown, and in all things deporting & behaving them selves as such faithful apprentices to the said John C. Brown, neither revealing his secrets, nor at any time leaving or neglecting the business of the said John C. Brown. And for & in

Consideration of the service well and faithfully rendered by the said Lewellyn, Tinsley, & Caroline, of the first part, said John C. Brown, of the second part, doth Covenant, promise, & agree to instruct his said Apprentices, or otherwise Cause them to be well & faithfully instructed, in the said trade or craft of Farm Laborers or Laborers, and also to read the English Language, and shall also allow, furnish, & provide his said Apprentices with meat and drink and Clothing during the said term, and all other necessaries meet & proper, in Sickness and in health, & Shall also, at the expiration of the said term, allow & pay the said Apprentices what is now allowed by the statute in such case made & provided.

Witness our hands and Seals the day & year first before written.

Executed before us }
J. J. Chandler   }   Ike + Rucker, his mark
J. J. Burch, Ordinary }   Jnº C. Brown

Georgia   }   [336]
Elbert County } This Indenture, made this the 13th day of November 1899, between Wade Dickerson & Lizzie Dickerson, of said County, parents, for and in behalf of their children, Tom, Sallie, May, Willis, Tinsley, Ella, Lullu, and an infant unnamed, being of the age of 13, 11, 10, 127, 3, & 1 years, of the one part, and John W. McCalla, of the County aforesaid, of the other part. Witnesseth: That the said Wade & Lizzie Dickerson, parents as aforesaid, does by these presents bind out Said Children, of said County, as Apprentices to Said John W. McCalla in the trade or Craft of Husbandry or as Laborers upon the plantation of the Said John W. McCalla, to be taught the said Craft or trade of Husbandry or Laborer, and to live with, Continue, and serve the said John W. McCalla as Apprentices from the date hereof for and during the term of their minority. During all of which time, said Wade & Lizzie Dickerson, parents as aforesaid, doth Covenant with the Said J. W. McCalla that the said named Children shall well and faithfully demean them Selves as faithful Apprentices to the said John W. McCalla, and in all things deporting & behaving them selves as such faithful apprentices to the said John W. McCalla, neither revealing his secrets, nor at any time leaving or neglecting the business of the said John W. McCalla. And for and in consideration of the service well and faithfully rendered by the said Children, of the first part, Said John W. McCalla, of the second part, doth covenant, promise, & agree to instruct his said Apprentices, or otherwise cause them to be well & faithfully instructed, in the said trade or craft of Husbandry or Laborers, & also to read the English Language, & shall also allow, furnish, & provide his said apprentices with meat & drink & Clothing during the said term, & all other necessaries meet & proper, in sickness

& in health, & shall also, at the expiration of the said term, allow & pay the said Apprentices what is now allowed by the Statute in such case made and provided.

Witness our hands & Seals the day & year first before written.

Executed Before us }
James Wharton }
J. J. Burch, Ordinary }

Wade + Dickerson, his mark
Lizzie + Dickerson, her mark
John W. McCalla

Georgia } [337]
Elbert County }   This Indenture, Made this the 25 day of November 1899, between John Allen, of said County, for and in behalf of Oscar, Erskin, & Ernest, his minor sons, being of the age of 12, 11, 9 years respectively, of the one part, & Mrs Martha E. Tinsly, of the County aforesaid, of the other part. Witnesseth: That the said John Allen, as aforesaid, does by these presents bind out his said minor Sons, of Said County, as apprentices to said Mrs Martha E. Tinsly in the trade or Craft of house Servants or as Laborers upon the plantation of the said Mrs Martha E. Tinsly, to be taught the said Craft or trade of house Servants or Laborers, and to live with, Continue, & serve the said Mrs Martha E. Tinsly as apprentices from the date hereof for and during the term of five years. During all of which time, Said John Allen, as aforesaid, doth covenant with the said Mrs Martha E. Tinsly that the said Oscar, Erskin, & Ernest Shall well and faithfully demean them selves as such faithful apprentices, observing fully the Command of the said Mrs Tinsly, & in all things deporting & behaving them selves as faithful apprentices to the said Mrs Tinsly, neither revealing her secrets, nor at any time leaving or neglecting the business of the said Mrs Martha E. Tinsly. And for & in Consideration of the service well & faithfully rendered by the Said Minors, of the first part, said Mrs Tinsly, of the second part, doth Covenant, promise, & agree to instruct her said Apprentices, or otherwise Cause them to be well and faithfully instructed, in the said trade or craft of house service or laborers, & Also to read the English language, & shall also allow, furnish, & provide her Said Apprentices with meat & drink & clothing during the said term, & all other necessaries meet & proper, in sickness & in health, & shall also, at the expiration of said term, allow & pay the Said Apprentices what is now allowed by the Statute in such Case made & provided. Witness our hands and Seals the day & year first before written.

Executed Before Us
H. J. Brewer
J. J. Burch, ordinary

John + Allen, his mark
M. E. Tinsley

State of Georgia } [338]
Elbert County } This Indenture, made this December 16th 1899, between Oliver & Eberhardt, of Elbert County said State, and Allen Stark, of Elbert County said State. Witnesseth: that the said Allen Stark, in Consideration of the promises & undertakings of the said Oliver & Eberhardt hereinafter set forth, does hereby bind himself to the said Oliver & Eberhardt for the full term of five years, from January 1st 1900. And he hereby agrees & contracts with said Oliver & Eberhardt to work faithfully under their direction at such place and at such labor as said Oliver & Eberhardt may desire & direct, & to respect & obey all orders & Commands of said Oliver & Eberhardt, & at all times to demean himself orderly & Soberly. And the said Allen Stark further agrees to account to said Oliver & Eberhardt for all lost time, except in Cases of temporary sickness not exceeding three days, the same to be deducted from said hereinafter set forth & at the same rates.

And the said Oliver & Eberhardt, in Consideration of the promises & undertakings of the said Allen Stark, agrees and Contracts with said Allen Stark to furnish him with board, lodging, suitable Clothing. They further agree to pay said Allen Stark wages by the year, as follows. On Jany 1st 1901 Thirty five Dollars, on Jany 1st 1902 Thirty five Dollars, on Jany 1st 1903 Thirty five Dollars, on Jany 1st 1904 Thirty five Dollars, on Jany 1st 1905 Thirty five Dollars. It is further agreed that, should this Contract be terminated by the death of either party during either of said years, Said Allen Stark shall be paid pro rata for the time he served during said year at the price fixed for said year. Said Oliver & Eberhardt further agrees to teach said Allen Stark the trade of Farm laborer in all its details. In witness whereof, the said Oliver & Eberhardt & Allen Stark have hereunto set their hands & seals the day & year first above written. Entered and interlined before signing.

Signed, Sealed, & Executed in Duplicate in presence of

J. E. Thornton, N. P.   Oliver & Eberhardt
B. H. Thornton   Allen + Stark, his mark

State of Georgia } [339]
Elbert County } This Indenture, made this oct 10th 1899, between Oliver & Eberhardt, of Elbert County said state, & Elijah Edwards, of Elbert County said state. Witnesseth: that the said Elijah Edwards, in Consideration of the promises & undertakings of the said Oliver & Eberhardt hereinafter set forth, does hereby bind himself to the said Oliver & Eberhardt for the full term of Five years, from January the 1st 1900. And he hereby agrees & contracts with said Oliver & Eberhardt to work faithfully under direction at such place & at such labor as said

Oliver & Eberhardt may desire & direct, and to respect & obey all orders & commands of said Oliver & Eberhardt, & at all times to demean himself orderly & soberly. And the Said Elijah Edwards further agrees to account to said Oliver & Eberhardt for all lost time, except in case of temporary sickness not exceeding three days, the same to be deducted from wages hereinafter set forth and at the same rates.

And the said Oliver & Eberhardt, in Consideration of the promises & undertakings of the said Elijah Edwards, agrees and Contracts with said Elijah Edwards to furnish him with board, lodging, & suitable clothing.

They further agree to pay said Elijah Edwards wages by the year, as follows. On January the 1st 1900 Twenty five Dollars, on January the 1st 1902 Twenty five Dollars, on January the 1st 1903 Twenty five Dollars, on January the 1st 1904 Twenty five Dollars, on January 1st 1905 Twenty five Dollars. It is further agreed that, should this Contract be terminated by the death of either party during either of said years, said Elijah Edwards shall be paid prorata for the time he served during Said year at the price fixed for said year. Said Oliver & Eberhardt further agrees to teach said Elijah Edwards the trade Farm Laborer in all its details. In witness whereof, the said Oliver & Eberhardt & Elijah Edwards have hereunto set their hands & Seals the day & year first above written.

           Elijah + Edwards, his mark
           Oliver & Eberhardt

Signed, Sealed, delivered, & Executed in duplicate in the presence of

J. E. Thornton, N. P.
T. S. Gaines

Georgia   }   [340]
Elbert County } This Indenture, made this the 20th day of December 1899, between Barney Jones & Cary Jones, of said County, for and in behalf of Andrew Jones, their son, being of the age of 19 years, of the one part, & C. H. Allen, of the County aforesaid, of the other part. Witnesseth: That the said Barney & Cary Jones, as aforesaid, does by these presents bind out their said son Andrew Jones, of Said County, as Apprentice to said C. H. Allen in the trade or Craft of Farm Laborer or as Laborer upon the plantation of the said C. H. Allen, to be taught the said Craft or trade of Farm Laborer or laborer, & to live with, Continue, & serve the said C. H. Allen as an Apprentice from the first day January 1900 for & during the term of one year. During all of which time, said Barney & Cary Jones, as aforesaid, doth Covenant with the said C. H. Allen that the said Andrew Jones

shall well and faithfully demean him self as such faithful Apprentice, observing fully the Command of the said C. H. Allen, & in all things deporting & behaving him self as a faithful Apprentice to the said C. H. Allen, neither revealing his secrets, nor at any time leaving or neglecting the business of the said C. H. Allen. And for & in Consideration of the service well & faithfully rendered by the said Andrew Jones, of the first part, said C. H. Allen, of the second part, doth covenant, promise, & agree to instruct his said Apprentice, or otherwise Cause him to be well and faithfully instructed, in the said trade or craft of Farm Laborer or laborer, and also to read the English language, & shall also allow, furnish, & provide his said Apprentice with meat & drink & Clothing during the said term, & all other necessaries meet & proper, in sickness and in health, & shall also, at the expiration of said term, allow & pay the said Apprentice what is now allowed by the statute in such case made & provided.

Witness our hands & seals the day & year first before written.

Executed Before Us }   Barney + Jones, his mark
R. M. Heard   }   Cary + Jones, her mark
J. J. Burch, ordinary }   C. H. Allen

Georgia   }   [341]
Elbert County } This Indenture, Made this the 14th Day December 1899, between Abe Hudson, of said County, for and in behalf of his son Charley Hudson, being of the age of 17 years, of the one part, & J. A. McLanahan, of the County aforesaid, of the other part. Witnesseth: That the said Abe Hudson, as aforesaid, does by these presents bind out his said Son Charley, of said County, as Apprentice to said J. A. McLanahan in the trade or craft of Farm Laborer or as Laborer upon the plantation of the said J. A. McLanahan, to be taught the said Craft or trade of Farm Laborer or Laborer, and to live with, Continue, & Serve the said J. A. McLanahan as an Apprentice from the date hereof for & during the term of One year. During all of which time, said Abe Hudson, as aforesaid, doth Covenant with the said J. A. McLanahan that the said Charley Hudson shall well & faithfully demean his self as such faithful Apprentice, observing fully the Command of the said J. A. McLanahan, & in all things deporting & behaving his Self as a faithful Apprentice to the said J. A. McLanahan, neither revealing his secrets, nor at any time leaving or neglecting the business of the said J. A. McLanahan. And for & in Consideration of the service well & faithfully rendered by the said Charley Hudson, of the first part, said J. A. McLanahan, of the second part, doth Covenant, promise, & agree to instruct his said Apprentice, or otherwise Cause him to be well & faithfully instructed, in the said trade or craft of Farm Laborer or laborer, & also to read the English language, & shall also allow,

furnish, & provide his said Apprentice with meat & drink & Clothing during the said term, and all other necessaries meet & proper, in sickness & in health, and shall also, at the expiration of said term, allow & pay the Said Apprentice Ten Dollars.

Witness our hands & seals the day & year first before written.

Executed Before Us
D. B. Alexander   Abe + Hudson, his mark
J. J. Burch, Ordinary   J. A. McLanahan

Georgia   }   [342]
Elbert County   }   This Indenture, made this the 20th day of December 1899, between Beckie Cauthen, of Said County, for & in behalf of her sons George Scales & Billie Scales, being of the age of 10 & 8 years, of the one part, & William Hester, of the County aforesaid, of the other part. Witnesseth: That the said Beckie Cauthen, as aforesaid, does by these presents bind out her said Sons George & Billie Scales, of Said County, as Apprentices to said William Hester in the trade or Craft of Farm Laborers or as Laborers upon the plantation of the said William Hester, to be taught the said Craft or trade of farm laborer or laborers, & to live with, Continue, & serve the said William Hester as Apprentices from the date hereof for and during the term of five years.

During all of which time, said Beckie Cauthen, as aforesaid, doth covenant with the said William Hester that the said George & Billie Scales shall well and faithfully demean them self as such faithful Apprentices, observing fully the command of the said William Hester, & in all things deporting & behaving them selves as faithful Apprentices to the said William Hester, neither revealing his secrets, nor at any time leaving or neglecting the business of the said William Hester. And for & in Consideration of the services well & faithfully rendered by the said George & Billie Scales, of the first part, said William Hester, of the second part, doth covenant, promise, & agree to instruct his said Apprentices, or otherwise them to be well & faithfully instructed, in the said trade or craft of Farm Laborer or Laborers, & also to read the English language, & shall also allow, furnish, & provide his said Apprentices with meat & drink & clothing during the said term, & all other necessaries meet & proper, in sickness & in health, & shall also, at the expiration of said term, allow & pay the said Apprentices what is now allowed by the statute in such case made & provided.

Witness our hands & seals the day & year first before written.

Executed Before Us }
E. T. Adams }
J. J. Burch, ordinary }

Beckie + Cauthen, her mark
W. A. Hester

Georgia } [343]
Elbert County } This Indenture, Executed this 19th day December 1899, between Clyde Thompson, of the first part, and A. A. Seymore, of second part. now, therefore, the said Clide Thompson, being a man of twenty four years old, does hereby bind and apprentice himself to the said A. A. Seymore from the date hereof until December 19th 1901, thereby intitling the said A. A. Seymore to the reasonable labor of said Clide Thompson during said period, subject however to the following terms & Conditions. Said A. A. Seymore shall teach the said Clide Thompson the business of husbandry, shall maintain and protect him, shall furnish him with wholesome food, suitable clothing, and necessary medical attention, shall teach him habits of industry, honesty, and morality, both by precept and example, shall govern him with humanity, using only the same degree of force to Compel obedience as a father may use with his minor Child. In Witness whereof, the said Contracting parties have hereto set their hands and affixed their seals the day & year above written. Signed, sealed, & delivered in presence of

T. L. Adams }
M. F. Adams, J. P. }

C
Clide + Thompson, his mark
[blank]

Georgia } [344]
Elbert County } This Indenture, Executed this the 19th day December 1899, between Millard Thompson, of the first part, & A. A. Seymore, of second part, of the same County & State. Witnesseth: That whereas, said Millard Thompson, as father of Ora Thompson, a minor of the age (18) Eighteen years old, does hereby bind and apprentice the said Ora Thompson to the said A. A. Seymore from the date hereof until the 19 day December 1901, thereby intitling the said A. A. Seymore to the reasonable labor of said minor during said period, Subject however to the following Terms & conditions. Said minor shall always, during said period, receive at the hands of the said A. A. Seymore maintenance, protection, & human treatment. Said A. A. Seymore shall teach the said Ora Thompson the business of Farming, shall maintain and protect him, shall furnish him with wholesome food, Suitable Clothing, & necessary medicine and medical attention, shall teach him habits of industry, honesty, and morality, both by precept and example, shall govern him with humanity, using only the same degree

of force to compel obedience as a father may use with his minor Child. In witness whereof, the said Contracting parties have hereto set their hands & affixed their seals the day & year above written. Signed, sealed, & delivered in presence of

T. L. Adams
M. F. Adams, N. P. & J. P.

Millard + Thompson, his mark
A. A. Seymore

Georgia } [345]
Elbert County } This Indenture, Made this the 22nd day December 1899, between Corry Spurlock, of Said County, for & in behalf of her son Arthur Spurlock, being of the age of 12 years, of the one part. Witnesseth: That the said Corry Spurlock, as aforesaid, does by these presents bind out her said son Arthur, of said County, as Apprentice to said Felix Mattox in the trade or Craft of Farm Laborer or as Laborer upon the plantation of the said Felix Mattox, to be taught the said Craft or trade of Farm Laborer or Laborer, & to live with, Continue, & serve the said Felix Mattox as Apprentice from the date hereof for and during the term of Two years. During all of which time, Said Corry Spurlock, as aforesaid, doth Covenant with the said Felix Mattox that the said Arthur Spurlock shall well & faithfully demean his self as such faithful Apprentice, observing fully the command of the said Felix Mattox, & in all things deporting & behaving his self as a faithful Apprentice to the said Felix Mattox, neither revealing his secrets, nor at any time leaving or neglecting the business of the said Felix Mattox. And for & in Consideration of the service well & faithfully rendered by the said Arthur Spurlock, of the first part, Said Felix Mattox, of the second part, doth Covenant, promise, & agree to instruct his said Apprentice, or otherwise Cause him to be well & faithfully instructed, in the said trade or craft of Farm Laborer or Laborer, & also to read the English language, & shall also allow, furnish, & provide his said Apprentice with meat & drink & clothing during the said term, & all other necessaries meet & proper, in sickness & in health, & shall also, at the expiration of the said term, allow & pay the said Apprentices Sixty five Dollars.

Witness our hands & seals the day & year first above written.

Executed Before Us
T. C. Upshaw
J. J. Burch, Ordinary

Corry + Spurlock, her mark
Felix + Mattox, his mark

Georgia } [346]
Elbert County } This Indenture, Made this the 29th day of December 1899, between Charles Rucker, of Said County, for & in behalf of Jeptha Rucker and Tinney Rucker, being of the age of 15 & 16 years, of the one part, and W. O. Jones

& Cº, of the County aforesaid, of the other part. Witnesseth: That the said Charles Rucker, as aforesaid, does by these presents bind out his said Sons Jeptha & Tinney Rucker, of Said County, as Apprentices to said W. O. Jones & Cº in the trade or Craft of Farm Laborers or Laborers upon the plantation of the said W. O. Jones & Cº, to be taught the said Craft or trade of Farm Laborers or Laborers, and to live with, Continue, & Serve the Said W. O. Jones & Cº as Apprentices from the date hereof for and during the term of five years. During all of Which time, Said Charles Rucker, as aforesaid, doth covenant with the said W. O. Jones & Cº that the Said Jeptha & Tinney Rucker shall well and faithfully demean them selves as such faithful Apprentices, observing fully the command of the said W. O. Jones & Cº, and in all things deporting & behaving them selves as faithful Apprentices to the said W. O. Jones & Cº, neither revealing their Secrets, nor at any time leaving or neglecting the business of the said W. O. Jones & Cº. And for and in Consideration of the Service well & faithfully rendered by the said Jeptha & Tinney Rucker, of the first part, Said W. O. Jones & Cº, of the second part, doth Covenant, promise, & agree to instruct them, said Apprentices, or otherwise Cause them to be well & faithfully instructed, in the said trade or craft of Farm Laborers or Laborers, & also to read the English language, & shall also allow, furnish, & provide them, said Apprentices, with meat & drink & clothing during the Said term, & all other necessaries meet & proper, in sickness & in health, & shall also, at the expiration of said term, allow & pay the Said Apprentices what is now allowed by the Statute in such Case made & provided. Witness our hands & seals the day & year first before written.

Executed Before Us }
J. A. Blackwell   }   Charles + Rucker, his mark
J. J. Burch, ordinary }   W. O. Jones & Cº

Georgia   }   [347]
Elbert County } This Indenture, Executed the 19th day December 1899, between Millard Thompson, of the first part, and J. M. Pulliam, of the second part. Witness that Whereas, Millard Thompson, The Father of Kye Thompson and Gordan Thompson, of the ages as follows, Kye age (19) Nineteen years, Gordan age (16) Sixteen years old, does bind and apprentice said Kye & Gordan Thompson and My Self unto the said J. M. Pulliam from the date hereof until December 19th 1901, hereby intitling the said J. M. Pulliam to the Reasonable labor of said minors and my Self during Said period, subject however to the following Conditions and terms. Said Minors shall always during Said period receive at the hands of the Said J. M. Pulliam Maintenance, protection, and humane treatment. Said J. M. Pulliam Shall teach the said Kye and Gordan the

business of husbandry, Shall maintain and protect them, furnish them with wholesome food, Suitable Clothing, and necessary Medicine and Medical attention, Shall tech them habits of industry, honesty, and morality, both by precept and example, shall govern them with humanity, using only the same degree of force to Compel obedience as a father may use with his minor children. In Witness Whereof, the said Contracting parties have hereto set their hands and affixed their Seals the day & year above written.

Signed, sealed, and delivered in presence of

T. L. Adams
M. F. Adams, N. P. & J. P.

Millard + Thompson, his mark
J. M. Pulliam

Georgia }
Elbert County } This Indenture, Made this the 6th day of January 1900, between Joe Cleveland, of said County, for & in behalf of his minor sons Stark and L. M. Cleveland, being of the age of 15 & 14 years, of the one part, and J. A. Clinkscales, of Abbeville County, S. C., of the other part. Witnesseth: That the said Joe Cleveland, as aforesaid, does by these presents bind out his said sons Stark & L. M. Cleveland, of Said County, as Apprentices to said J. A. Clinkscales in the trade or Craft of Farm Laborers or Laborers upon the plantation of the Said J. A. Clinkscales, to be taught the said Craft or trade of Farm Laborers or Laborers, to live with, Continue, & serve the Said J. A. Clinkscales as Apprentices from the date hereof for and during the term of one year. [348]

During all of which time, said Joe Cleveland, as aforesaid, doth covenant with the said J. A. Clinkscales that the said Stark & L. M. Cleveland shall well and faithfully demean them selves as such faithful Apprentices, observing fully the Command of the said J. A. Clinkscales, and in all things deporting & behaving them selves as faithful apprentices to the said J. A. Clinkscales, neither revealing his secrets, nor at any time leaving or neglecting the business of the said J. A. Clinkscales.

And for and in Consideration of the service well and faithfully rendered by the said Stark & L. M. Cleveland, of the first part, Said J. A. Clinkscales, of the Second part, doth Covenant, promise, & agree to instruct his said said Apprentices, or otherwise Cause them to be well & faithfully instructed, in the said trade or craft of farm Laborers or Laborers, & to read the English language, & shall also allow, furnish, & provide his said Apprentices with meat & drink & clothing during the said term, & all other necessaries meet & proper, in sickness

& in health, & shall also, at the expiration of said term, allow & pay the said Apprentices Sixty dollars.

Witness our hands & seals the day & year first before written.

Jackson Moss
J. J. Burch, ordinary

Joe Cleveland
J. A. Clinkscales
per Moss

Georgia } [349]
Elbert County } This Indenture, Made this the 6th day of January 1900, between Charles Rucker, of said County, for & in behalf of his minor sons Jeptha & Tinny Rucker, being of the age of 15 & 16 years, of the one part, and W. J. Jones, of the County aforesaid, of the other part. Witnesseth: That the said Charles Rucker, as aforesaid, does by these presents bind out his said minor sons Jeptha & Tinney Rucker, of Said County, as Apprentices to said W. J. Jones in the trade or Craft of Farm Laborers or Laborers upon the plantation of the said W. J. Jones, to be taught the Said Craft or trade of Farm Laborers or laborers, and to live with, Continue, & serve the said W. J. Jones as Apprentices from the date hereof for & during the term of five years. During all of which time, said Charles Rucker, as aforesaid, doth covenant with the said W. J. Jones that the said Jeptha & Tinny Rucker shall well & faithfully demean them selves as such faithful Apprentices, observing fully the Command of the said W. J. Jones, And in all things deporting & behaving them selves as faithful apprentices to the said W. J. Jones, neither revealing his secrets, nor at any time leaving or neglecting the business of the said W. J. Jones. (~~neither revealing his secrets, nor at any time leaving or neglecting the business of the said W. J. Jones~~)

And for & in Consideration of the service well & faithfully rendered by the said Jeptha & Tinney Rucker, of the first part, said W. J. Jones, of the second part, doth Covenant, promise, & agree to instruct his Said Apprentices, or otherwise Cause them to be well & faithfully instructed, in the said trade or craft of Farm Laborers or laborers, & also to read the English language, and shall also allow, furnish, & provide his said Apprentices with meat & drink & clothing during the said term, & all other necessaries meet & proper, in sickness & in health, & shall also, at the expiration of said term, allow & pay the said Apprentices what is now allowed by the statute in such case made & provided.

Witness our hands & seals the day & year first before written.

Executed Before us
Jnº T. Heard
J. J. Burch, ordinary

Charles + Rucker, his mark
W. J. Jones

Georgia } [350]
Elbert County } This Indenture, Made this the 20th day of January 1900, between Ben A. Rucker, of Elbert County, for & in behalf of his minor sons Jnº Jackson & Albert Rucker, being of the age of 15 & 8 years, of the one part, and Arnold and Cº, of the ~~other part~~ County aforesaid, of the other part. Witnesseth: That the Ben A. Rucker, as aforesaid, does by these presents bind out Jnº Jackson and Albert Rucker, of Said County, as Apprentices to said Arnold & Cº in the trade or craft of Farm Labor or laborer upon the plantation of the said Arnold & Cº, to be taught the said Craft or trade of Farm Labor or laborers, and to live with, Continue, & Serve the said ~~Craft or trade~~ Arnold & Cº as apprentices from the date hereof for & during the term of 6 years.

During all of which time, said Ben A. Rucker, as aforesaid, doth covenant with the said Arnold & Cº that the said Jnº Jackson & Albert Rucker shall well and faithfully demean them selves as such faithful Apprentices, observing fully the Commands of the said Arnold & Cº, and in all things deporting & behaving them Selves as faithful apprentices to the said Arnold & Cº, neither revealing their secrets, nor at any time leaving or neglecting the business of the said Arnold & Cº. And for and during in Consideration of the service well & faithfully rendered by the said Jnº Jackson & Albert Rucker, of the first part, said Arnold & Cº, of the second part, doth Covenant, promise, & agree to instruct said Apprentices, or otherwise cause them to be well & faithfully instructed, in the said trade or craft of Farm Laborers or laborers, and also to read the English language, & shall also allow, furnish, & provide said Apprentices with meat & drink & clothing during the said term, & all other necessaries meet & proper, in sickness & in health, & shall also, at the expiration of said term, allow & pay the said Apprentices what is now allowed by the statute in Such case made & provided. Witness our hands & Seals the day & year first before written.

Executed before us
J. E. Thornton, N. P.
J. Y. Arnold

Ben^{jn} + Rucker, his mark
Arnold & Cº

Georgia } [349]
Elbert County } This Indenture, Made this the 25th day of January 1900, between

Carter Cade, of said County, for and in behalf of his minor sons Jim Cade & Frank Cade, being of the age of 18, 15 years, of the one part, and Brown Bros., of the County aforesaid, of the other part. Witnesseth: That the said Carter Cade, as aforesaid, does by these presents bind out his said sons Jim & Frank Cade, of said County, as Apprentices to said Brown Bros. in the trade or Craft of Farm Laborers or Laborer upon the plantation of the said Brown Bros., to be taught the Said Craft or trade of Farm Laborers or Laborers, and to live with, Continue, & serve the said Brown Bros. as Apprentices from the first January 1900 for and during the term of one Year. During all of which time, said Carter Cade, as aforesaid, doth Covenant with the said Brown Bros. that the said Jim & Frank Cade shall well & faithfully demean them selves as such faithful Apprentices, observing fully the Commands of the said Brown Bros., and in all things deporting & behaving them selves as faithful apprentices to the Said Brown Bros., neither revealing their secrets, nor at any time leaving or neglecting the business of the said Brown Bros. And for & in Consideration of the service well & faithfully rendered by the said Jim & Frank Cade, of the first part, Said Brown Bros., of the Second part, doth Covenant, promise, & agree to instruct their Said Apprentices, or otherwise Cause them to be well & faithfully instructed, in the said trade or craft of Farm Laborers or Laborers, & also to read the English Language, & shall also allow, furnish, & provide their said Apprentices with meat & drink & clothing during the said term, and all other necessaries meet & proper, in sickness & in health, and shall also, at the expiration of the said term, allow & pay the said Apprentices what is now allowed by the statute in such case made & provided.

Witness our hands & Seals the day & year first before written.

Executed Before us
T. A. Willis   Carter + Cade, his mark
J. J. Burch, ordinary   Brown Bros.

Georgia   }   [352]
Elbert County } This Indenture, Made this the 27th day of January 1900, between John Fortson, of said County, for and in behalf of him self, being of the age of 21 years, of the one part, and Mack McLanahan, of the County aforesaid, of the other part. Witnesseth: That the said John Fortson, as aforesaid, does by these presents bind out him self, of said County, as Apprentice to said Mack McLanahan in the trade or Craft of Farm Laborer or laborer upon the plantation of the said Mack McLanahan, to be taught the said Craft or trade of Farm laborer or laborer, & to live with, Continue, & serve the said Mc McLanahan as an Apprentice from the date hereof for & during the term of 8 Months. During all of which time, said John Fortson, as aforesaid, doth covenant with the said Mack McLanahan that the

said John Fortson shall well & faithfully demean him self as such faithful Apprentice, observing fully the Command of the said Mack McLanahan, and in all things deporting and behaving him self as a faithful apprentice to the said Mc McLanahan, neither revealing his secrets, nor at any time leaving or neglecting the business of the said Mc McLanahan. And for and in Consideration of the service well and faithfully rendered by the said John Fortson, of the first part, said Mack McLanahan, of the second part, doth Covenant, promise, & agree to instruct his said Apprentice, or otherwise Cause him to be well & faithfully instructed, in the said trade or craft of Farm Laborer or laborer, and shall also allow, furnish, and provide his said Apprentice with meat and drink and clothing during the said term, and all other necessaries meet & proper, in sickness and in health, and shall also, at the expiration of the said term, allow & pay the said Apprentice Forty Dollars or five Dollars per Month.

Witness Our hands and Seals the day and year first before written.

Executed Before us
W. J. Burch   John + Fortson, his mark
J. J. Burch, Ordinary   Mc McLanahan

Georgia   }   [353]
Elbert County } This Indenture, Made this the 8th day of January 1900, between Green Gaines, of said County, for & in behalf of his minor children, Mollie, Francis, Arthur, & Ira Gaines, being of the age of 18, 16, 15, 7 years, of the one part, and G. A. Lunsford, of the County aforesaid, of the other part. Witnesseth: That the said Green Gaines, as aforesaid, does by these presents bind out his said children, Mollie, Francis, Arthur, Ira Gaines, of said County County, as Apprentices to said G. A. Lunsford in the trade or craft of Farm Laborers or as Laborers upon the plantation of the said G. A. Lunsford, to be taught the said craft or trade of Farm Laborers or Laborers, and to live with, Continue, & serve the said G. A. Lunsford as Apprentices from the date hereof for & during the term of their Minority. During all of which time, said Green Gaines, as aforesaid, doth covenant with the said G. A. Lunsford that the said Mollie, Francis, Arthur, & Ira Gaines shall well & faithfully demean them selves as such faithful Apprentices, observing fully the Command of the said G. A. Lunsford, and in all things deporting & behaving them selves as faithful apprentices to the said G. A. Lunsford, neither revealing his secrets, nor at any time leaving or neglecting the business of the said G. A. Lunsford. And for & in Consideration of the service well & faithfully rendered by the said Mollie, Francis, Arthur, & Ira Gaines, of the first part, said G. A. Lunsford, of the second part, doth Covenant, promise, & agree to instruct his said Apprentices, or otherwise Cause them to be well &

faithfully instructed, in the said trade or craft of Farm Laborers or laborers, and also to read the English language, and shall also allow, furnish, & provide his said Apprentices with meat & drink & clothing during the said term, & all other necessaries meet & proper, in sickness & in health, & shall also, at the expiration of the said term, allow and pay the said Apprentices what is now allowed by the statute in such case made & provided.

Witness our hands & Seals the day & year first before written.

Executed Before Us
P. A. Cleveland   }   Green + Gaines, his mark
G. W. Haley, Notary Public }   G. A. Lunsford

Georgia   }   [354]
Elbert County }   This Indenture, Made this the 17th day of February 1900, between Stephen Dean, of said County, for and in behalf of his minor son, Ora Dean, being of the age of 10 years, of the one part, and D. L. McLanahan, of the County aforesaid, of the other part. Witnesseth: That the said Stephen Dean, as aforesaid, does by these presents bind out his said Son Ora Dean, of Said County, as apprentice to said D. L. McLanahan in the trade or craft of Farm Laborer or as Laborer upon the plantation of the said D. L. McLanahan, to be taught the said craft or trade of Farm Laborer or Laborer, & to live with, Continue, & serve the said D. L. McLanahan as an apprentice from the date hereof for and during the term of Five years. During all of which time, said Stephen Dean, as Aforesaid, doth Covenant with the said D. L. McLanahan that the said Ora Dean Shall well & faithfully demean his self as such faithful Apprentice, observing fully the Command of the said D. L. McLanahan, and in all things deporting & behaving his self as a faithful apprentice to the Said D. L. McLanahan, neither revealing his secrets, nor at any time leaving or neglecting the business of the Said D. L. McLanahan. And for & in consideration of the service well and faithfully rendered by the said Ora Dean, of the first part, said D. L. McLanahan, of the second part, doth Covenant, promise, & agree to instruct his said Apprentice, or otherwise cause him to be well & faithfully instructed, in the said trade or Craft of Farm Laborer or Laborer, & also to read the English language, & shall also allow, furnish, & provide his said Apprentice with meat & drink and clothing during the said term, & all other necessaries meet & proper, in sickness & in health, & shall also, at the expiration of the said term, allow & pay the Said Apprentice what is now allowed by the Statute in such case made & provided.

Witness our hand & Seals the day and year first before written.

Executed Before Us }
A. S. J. Stovall }
J. J. Burch, Ordinary }

Stephen + Dean, his mark
D. L. McLanahan

Georgia } [355]
Elbert County } This Indenture, Made this the 5th day of March 1900, between William Washington, of said County, for and in behalf of his minor son General Washington, being of the age of 14 years, of the one part, and J. A. Cauthen, of the County aforesaid, of the other part. Witnesseth: That the said William Washington, as aforesaid, does by these presents bind out his said son General Washington, of said County, as Apprentice to said J. A. Cauthen in the trade or craft of Farm Laborer or as Laborer upon the plantation of the said J. A. Cauthen, to be taught the said Craft or trade of Farm Laborer or Laborer, and to live with, Continue, and serve the said J. A. Cauthen as an apprentice from the date hereof for & during the term of Eighteen Months. During all of which time, Said William Washington, as aforesaid, doth Covenant with the said J. A. Cauthen that the said General Washington shall well & faithfully demean his self as such faithful Apprentice, observing fully the Command of the said J. A. Cauthen, and in all things deporting & behaving his self as a faithful Apprentice to the said J. A. Cauthen, neither revealing his secrets, nor at any time leaving or neglecting the business of the said J. A. Cauthen.

And for & in Consideration of the service well & faithfully rendered by the said General Washington, of the first part, said J. A. Cauthen, of the second part, doth Covenant, promise, & agree to instruct his said Apprentice, or otherwise Cause him to be well & faithfully instructed, in the said trade or craft of Farm Laborer or Laborer, & also to read the English language, & shall also allow, furnish, & provide his said Apprentice with meat & drink & clothing during the said term, & all other necessaries meet & proper, in sickness & in health, & shall also, at the expiration of the said term, allow & pay the said Apprentice what is now allowed by the statute in such Case made & provided.

Witness our hands and seals the day & year first before written.

Executed Before Us
James McIntosh
J. J. Burch, Ordinary

William + Washington, his mark
J. A. Cauthen
per W.

Georgia } [356]
Elbert County } This Indenture, Made this the 27th day of February 1900, between H. C. Rousey, of said County, for and in behalf of Lula Brown, being of the age of 14 years, of the one part, and Jim Pulliam, of the County aforesaid, of the other part. Witness: That the said H. C. Rousey, as aforesaid, does by these presents bind out Lula Brown, of said County, as apprentice to said Jim Pulliam in the trade or craft of House Servant or as Laborer upon the plantation of the said Jim Pulliam, to be taught the said craft or trade of House Servant or laborer, and to live with, Continue, & serve the said Jim Pulliam as an Apprentice from the date hereof for and during the term of 7 years. During all of which time, Said H. C. Rousey, as aforesaid, doth Covenant with the Said Jim Pulliam that the said Lula Brown Shall well & faithfully demean her Self as Such faithful Apprentice, observing fully the Command of the said Jim Pulliam, And in All things deporting & behaving her Self as a faithful apprentice to the said Jim Pulliam, neither revealing his secrets, nor at any time leaving or neglecting the business of the Said Jim Pulliam.

And for & in Consideration of the service well and faithfully rendered by the said Lula Brown, of the first part, said Jim Pulliam, of the second part, doth Covenant, promise, & agree to instruct his said Apprentice, or otherwise Cause her to be well & faithfully instructed, in the said trade or craft of House Servant or laborer, and also to read the English language, & shall also allow, furnish, & provide his said Apprentice with meat & drink & clothing during the said term, & all other necessaries meet & proper, in sickness & in health, & shall also, at the expiration of the said term, allow & pay the Said Apprentice what is now allowed by the Statute in such Case made & provided

Witness our hands & seals the day and year first before written.

Executed Before us }
James McIntosh } H. C. Rousey
J. J. Burch, Ordinary } Jim Pulliam

Georgia } [357]
Elbert County } This Indenture, made this the 16 day of March 1900, between Danis McCalla, Dick Banks, & Lizzie Banks, of said County, all being of full age, of the one part, and Geo P. Norman, of the County aforesaid, of the other part. Witnesseth: That the said Danis McCalla, Dick Banks, and Lizzie Banks, as aforesaid, does by these presents bind them selves as apprentices to said Geo P. Norman in the trade or craft of Farm Laborers or as Laborers upon the plantation of the said Geo P. Norman, to be taught the said Craft or trade of Farm Laborers

or Laborers, & to live with, Continue, & serve the said Geº P. Norman as Apprentices from the date hereof for and during the term of two years, or until a debt of Seventy five Dollars is paid at the rate of Ten Dollars per month. During all of which time, said Danis McCalla, Dick Banks, & Lizzie Banks, as aforesaid, doth Covenant with the said G. P. Norman that they, the aforesaid Danis McCalla, Dick Banks, & Lizzie Banks, will well & faithfully demean them Selves as Such faithful Apprentices, neither revealing his secrets, nor at any time leaving or neglecting the business of the said Geº P. Norman. And to make good any time lost by Sickness or death at the same rate per month, to wit, Ten dollars.

And for & in consideration of the services well & faithfully performed by the said Danis, Dick, & Lizzie, The said Geº P. Norman, of the second part, doth promise and agree to well & faithfully instruct his aforesaid apprentices in the trade or craft of Farm Laborers or Laborers & shall also allow & furnish & provide his Said apprentices with meat & drink & clothing, during the said term, & all other necessaries meet & proper, in sickness & in health, & shall also, at the expiration of Said term, allow & pay Said apprentices ten Dollars per month. Witness our hands & seals the day and the year first before written. All interlineation made before signing. Executed Before Us.

	Danis + McCalla, his mark
C. T. Bond	Dick + Banks, his mark
J. J. Burch, ordinary	Lizzi + Banks, her mark
	G. P. Norman

Georgia } [358]
Elbert County } This Indenture, Made this the 15th day of March 1900, between John Grimes, of said County, for & in behalf him self, said John Grimes being of the age of 29 years, of the one part, and Geº A. Lunsford, of the County aforesaid, of the other part. Witnesseth: That the said John Grimes, as aforesaid, does by these presents bind out him self, of Said County, as Apprentice to said Geº A. Lunsford in the trade or Craft of Farm Laborer or as Laborer upon the plantation of the said Geº A. Lunsford, to be taught the said Craft or trade of Farm Laborer or Laborer, & to live with, Continue, & serve the said Geº A. Lunsford as an Apprentice from the date hereof for and during the term of Six Months, or until a debt of Twenty one dollars is paid at Six Dollars per month. During all of which time, said John Grimes, as aforesaid, doth covenant with the said Geº A. Lunsford that the said John Grimes shall well & faithfully demean his self as a faithful Apprentice to the said Geº A. Lunsford, neither revealing his secrets, nor at any time leaving or neglecting the business of the said G. A. Lunsford. And for & in consideration of the service well & faithfully rendered by the said John Grimes,

of the first part, said G. A. Lunsford, of the second part, doth Covenant, promise, & agree to instruct his said Apprentice, or otherwise cause him to be well & faithfully instructed, in the said trade or Craft of Farm Laborer or laborer, and also to read the English language, & shall also allow, furnish, & provide his said Apprentice with meat & drink & clothing during the said term, & all other necessaries meet & proper, in sickness & in health, & shall also, at the expiration of the said term, allow & pay the Said Apprentice what is now allowed by the Statute in such Case made & provided

Witness our hands & seals the day & year first before written.

Executed Before Us
C. P. Dodd   John + Grimes, his mark
J. J. Burch, Ordinary   Ge° A. + Lunsford, his mark

Georgia   }   [359]
Elbert County } This Indenture, Made this the 23rd day of March 1900, between John Grimes, Mary Downer, & Doe Tate, of said County, for and in behalf of them Selves, being of the age of 29, 22, & 21 years, of the one part, and W. O. Jones, of the County aforesaid, of the other part. Witnesseth: That the said John Grimes, Mary Downer, & Doe Tate, as aforesaid, does by these presents bind out them Selves, of said County, as apprentices to said W. O. Jones in the trade or Craft of Farm Laborers or laborers upon the plantation of the Said W. O. Jones, to be taught the said Craft or trade of Farm Laborers or Laborers, & to live with, continue, & serve the said W. O. Jones as apprentices from the date hereof for and during the term of one year. During all of which time, said John Grimes, Mary Downer, & Doe Tate, as aforesaid, doth Covenant with the said W. O. Jones that the said John Grimes, Mary Downer, & Doe Tate shall well & faithfully demean them selves as such faithful Apprentices, observing fully the Command of the Said W. O. Jones, & in all things deporting & behaving them selves as faithful Apprentices to the said W. O. Jones, neither revealing his secrets, nor at any time leaving or neglecting the business of the said W. O. Jones.

And for & in consideration of the service well and faithfully rendered by the said John Grimes, Mary Downer, & Doe Tate, of the first part, said W. O. Jones, of the second part, doth Covenant, promise, & agree to instruct his said Apprentices, or otherwise cause them to be well & faithfully instructed, in the said trade or craft of Farm Laborers or laborer, & also to Read the English language, & shall also allow, furnish, & provide his said Apprentice with meat & drink & clothing during the said term, & all other necessaries meet & proper, in sickness & in health, &

shall also, at the expiration of the said term, allow & pay the Said Apprentices what is now allow by the statute in such Case made & provided

Witness our hands & seals the day & year first before written.

Executed Before us
W. H. Irvin
J. J. Burch, ordinary

John + Grimes, his mark
Mary + Downer, her mark
Doe + Tate, her mark
W. O. Jones

Georgia } [360]
Elbert County } This Indenture, made this the 14 day March 1900, between Russel Fleming, of said County, for and in behalf of him self, being of the age of 21 years, of the one part, and T. J. Wall, of the County aforesaid, of the other part. Witnesseth: That the said Russel Fleming, as aforesaid, does by these presents bind out him self, said Russel Fleming, of said County, as Apprentice to said T. J. Wall in the trade or craft of Farm Laborer or laborer upon the plantation of the said T. J. Wall, to be taught the said craft or trade of Farm Laborer or laborer, & to live with, Continue, & serve the said T. J. Wall as an Apprentice from the date hereof for and during the term of five years, or until a debt of one hundred & Thirty Dollars is paid by his bro Will Fleming & his Two sisters Josie & Misoura Fleming, now Apprenticed to said T. J. W. Wall. And I further agree to make good all lost time, either by sickness or the death of either one of my brother or sisters above named. During all of which time, said Russel Fleming, as aforesaid, doth Covenant with the said T. J. Wall that the said Russel Fleming shall well & faithfully demean his self as such faithful apprentice, observing fully the Command of the said T. J. Wall, neither revealing his secrets, nor at any time leaving or neglecting the business of the said T. J. Wall. And for & in Consideration of the services well & faithfully rendered by the said Russel Fleming, of the first part, said T. J. Wall, of the second part, doth promise & agree to furnish & provide said Apprentice with meat & drink & clothing during the said term, & all other necessaries meet & proper, in sickness & in health, & shall also, at the expiration of the said term, & shall allow & pay said Apprentice One hundred & thirty seven Dollars above specified. Witness our hands & Seals the day & year first before written.

Executed Before Us
W. J. B. Jones, J. P.
R. E. Wall
J. E. Hammond

Russel + Fleming his mark
T. J. Wall

Georgia } [361]
Elbert County } This Indenture, made this the 14th day of March 1900, between Charlotte Fleming, of said County, for & in behalf of her minor children, Will, Josie, & Masouria, being of the age of 18, 14, 15 years, of the one part, & T. J. Wall, of the County aforesaid, of the other part. Witnesseth: That the said Charlotte Fleming, as aforesaid, does by these presents bind out her Children, Will, Josie, & Masouria, of said County, as Apprentices to said T. J. Wall in the trade or Craft of Farm Laborers or as Laborers upon the plantation of the Said T. J. Wall, to be taught the said Craft or trade of Farm Laborers or Laborers, & to live with, continue, & serve the said T. J. Wall as apprentices from the date hereof for & during the term of their Minority.

During all of which time, said Charlotte Fleming, as aforesaid, doth Covenant with the said T. J. Wall that the said Will, Jossie, & Masouria Fleming shall well & faithfully demean them selves as such faithful Apprentices, observing fully the Command of the said T. J. Wall, & in all things deporting & behaving them selves as faithful apprentices to the said T. J. Wall, neither revealing his secrets, nor at any time leaving or neglecting the business of the said T. J. Wall. And for & in Consideration of the services well & faithfully rendered by the said Will, Jossie, & Masouria Fleming, of the first part, said T. J. Wall, of the second part, doth Covenant, promise, & agree to instruct his said Apprentices, or otherwise Cause them to be well & faithfully instructed, in the said trade or craft of Farm Laborers or laborers, & also to read the English language, and shall also allow, furnish, & provide his said Apprentices with meat & drink & clothing during the said term, and all other necessaries meet & proper, in sickness & in health, & shall also, at the expiration of the said term, allow & pay the said Apprentices what is now allowed by the Statute in such case made & provided.

Witness our hands & seals the day & year first before written.

Executed Before Us
W. G. B. Jones, J. P.   Charlotte + Fleming, her mark
R. E. Wall   T. J. Wall
J. E. Hammond

Georgia } [362]
Elbert County } This Indenture, made this the 14th day of April 1900, between King Wall, of said County, for and in behalf of Tommie Wall, being of the age of 16 years, of the one part, and T. B. Hall, of the County aforesaid, of the other part. Witnesseth: That the Said King Wall, as aforesaid, does by these presents bind out Tommie Wall, of said County, as Apprentice to said T. B. Hall in the trade or

craft of servant or as Laborer upon the plantation of the said T. B. Hall, to be taught the said Craft or trade of servant or Laborer, and to live with, Continue, & serve the said T. B. Hall as an Apprentice from the date hereof for and during the term of one year. During all of which time, said King Wall, as aforesaid, doth covenant with the said T. B. Hall that the said Tommie Wall shall well & faithfully demean him self as such faithful Apprentice, observing fully the Command of the said T. B. Hall, and in all things deporting & behaving him self as a faithful apprentice to the said T. B. Hall, neither revealing his secrets, nor at any time leaving or neglecting the business of the said T. B. Hall.

And for and in Consideration of the service well & faithfully rendered by the said Tommie Wall, of the first part, said T. B. Hall, of the second part, doth covenant, promise, & agree to instruct his said Apprentice, or otherwise Cause him to be well & faithfully instructed, in the said Trade or craft of servant or Laborer, and also to read the English language, & shall also allow, furnish, & provide his said Apprentice with meat & drink & clothing during the said term, & all other necessaries meet & proper, in sickness & in health, & shall also, at the expiration of the said term, allow & pay the said Apprentice what is now allowed by the statute in such case made & provided

Witness our hands & seals the day & year first before written.

Executed Before Us
J. M. Stovall   King + Wall, his mark
C. A. Edwards, J. P.   T. B. Hall

Georgia   }   [363]
Elbert County } This Indenture, Made this the 12th day of April 1900, between Henry Cummings, of said County, for and in behalf of his minor son Bud Cummings, being of the age of 8 years, of the one part, and J. G. Burris, of the County aforesaid, of the other part. Witnesseth: That the said Henry Cummings, as aforesaid, does by these presents bind out his said Son Bud Cummings, of said County, as Apprentice to said J. G. Burris in the trade or Craft of Farm Laborer or as Laborer upon the plantation of the Said J. G. Burris, to be taught the said Craft or trade of Farm Laborer or Laborer, & to live with, Continue, and serve the said J. G. Burris as an apprentice from the date hereof for and during the term of his minority. During all of which time, said Henry Cummings, as aforesaid, doth covenant with the said J. G. Burris that said Bud Cummings shall well & faithfully demean his self as a faithful Apprentice to said J. G. Burris, neither revealing his secrets, nor at any time leaving or neglecting the business of the said J. G. Burris. And for and in Consideration of the service well and faithfully rendered by the

said Bud Cummings, of the first part, said J. G. Burris, of the second part, doth Covenant, promise, and agree to instruct his said Apprentice, or otherwise Cause him to be well and faithfully instructed, in the said trade or craft of Farm Laborer or Laborer, and also to read the English language, and shall also allow, furnish, and provide his said Apprentice with meat and drink and clothing during the said term, & all other necessaries meet and proper, in sickness & in health, and shall also, at the expiration of the said term, allow and pay the said Apprentice what is now allowed by the statute in such case made and provided.

Witness our hands and Seals the day and year first before written.

Executed Before Us
J. B. Jones, J^r, Ex officio J. P.   Henry + Cummings, his mark
M. D. Alexander   J. G. Burris

Georgia   }   [364]
Elbert County } This Indenture, Made this the 9th day of June 1900, between Jim Thornton, of said County, for and in behalf of him self, being of the age of 19 years, of the one part, and G. A. Lunsford, of the County aforesaid, of the other part. Witnesseth: That the said Jim Thornton, as aforesaid, does by these presents bind out him self, of said County, as Apprentice to said G. A. Lunsford in the trade or Craft of Farm Laborer or as Laborer upon the plantation of the said G. A. Lunsford, to be taught the said Craft or trade of Farm Laborer or Laborer, and to live with, Continue, & Serve the said G. A. Lunsford as an Apprentice from the date hereof for and during the term of four months, or until a debt of $21.00 is paid at $5.00 per month. During all of which time, said Jim Thornton, as aforesaid, doth covenant with the said G. A. Lunsford that the said Jim Thornton shall well & faithfully demean his self as such faithful Apprentice, observing fully the Command of the said G. A. Lunsford, & in all things deporting & behaving his self as a faithful apprentice to the said G. A. Lunsford, neither revealing his secrets, nor at any time leaving or neglecting the business of the said G. A. Lunsford. And for & in consideration of the service well & faithfully rendered by the said Jim Thornton, of the first part, said G. A. Lunsford, of the second part, doth Covenant, promise, & agree to instruct his said Apprentice, or otherwise Cause him to be well & faithfully instructed, in the said trade or Craft of Farm Laborer or Laborer, and shall also allow, furnish, & provide his said Apprentice with meat & drink & Clothing during the said term, & all other necessaries meet & proper, in sickness & in health, & shall also, at the expiration of the said term, allow & pay the said Apprentice what is now allowed by the statute in such case made & provided.

Witness our hands & Seals the day & year first before written.

All interlineations made before Signing.

Executed Before us
M. E. Maxwell   Jim + Thornton, his mark
J. J. Burch, ordinary   G. A. + Lunsford, his mark

Georgia   }   [365]
Elbert County } This Indenture, made this 11th day of June 1900, between Ephrie Spurlock, of said County, for and in behalf of his minor son, Arthur Spurlock, being of the age of 12 years, of the one part, and J. T. Glanton, of the County aforesaid, of the other part. Witnesseth: That the said Ephrie Spurlock, as aforesaid, does by these presents bind out his said son Arthur Spurlock, of said County, as apprentice to said J. T. Glanton in the trade or craft of Farm Laborer or as Laborer upon the plantation of the Said J. T. Glanton, to be taught the said Craft or trade of Farm Laborer or Laborer, & to live with, Continue, & serve the said J. T. Glanton as an apprentice from the date hereof for and during the term of 2 years, or until a debt of Fifty four & $^{20}/_{100}$ Dollars is paid at Two Dollars & fifty Cents per month. During all of which time, said Ephrie Spurlock, as aforesaid, doth Covenant with the said J. T. Glanton that the said Arthur Spurlock shall well & faithfully demean his self as a faithful Apprentice, observing fully the Command of the said J. T. Glanton, & in all things deporting & behaving his self as a faithful Apprentice to the said J. T. Glanton, neither revealing his secrets, nor at any time leaving or neglecting the business of the said J. T. Glanton.

And for & in Consideration of the service well & faithfully rendered by the said Arthur Spurlock, of the first part, Said J. T. Glanton, of the second part, doth Covenant, promise, & agree to instruct his said Apprentice, or otherwise Cause him to be well & faithfully instructed, in the said trade or Craft of Farm Laborer or laborer, & also to read the English language, & shall also allow, furnish, & provide his said Apprentice with meat & drink & clothing during the said term, & all other necessaries meet & proper, in sickness & in health, & shall also, at the expiration of the said term, allow & pay the said Apprentice what is now allowed by the statute in such Case made & provided. Witness our hands & Seals the day & year first before written.

Executed Before Us }
T. A. Willis   }   Ephrie + Spurlock, his mark
J. J. Burch, ordinary }   J. T. Glanton

Georgia } [366]
Elbert County } This Indenture, Made this the 30th day June 1900, between William Maxwell, of said County, for & in behalf of his minor son, Thomas Maxwell, being of the age of 10 years, of the one part, & C. H. Allen, of the County aforesaid, of the other part. Witnesseth: That the said William Maxwell, as aforesaid, does by these presents bind out his said son Thomas Maxwell, of said County, as Apprentice to Said C. H. Allen in the trade or Craft of Farm Laborer or as Laborer upon the plantation of the Said C. H. Allen, to be taught the Said Craft or trade of Farm Laborer or Laborer, and to live with, Continue, & serve the said C. H. Allen as an Apprentice from the date hereof for and during the term of 5 years. During all of which time, said William Maxwell aforesaid doth Covenant with the said C. H. Allen that the said Thomas Maxwell shall well & faithfully demean his self as such faithful Apprentice, observing fully the Command of the said C. H. Allen, and in all things deporting & behaving his self as a faithful Apprentice to the said C. H. Allen, neither revealing his secrets, nor at any time leaving or neglecting the business of the said C. H. Allen.

And for & in consideration of the service well & faithfully rendered by the said Thomas Maxwell, of the first part, said C. H. Allen, of the second part, doth Covenant, promise, & agree to instruct his said Apprentice, or otherwise cause him to be well & faithfully instructed, in the said trade or craft of Farm Laborer or laborer, & also to read the English language, & shall also allow, furnish, & provide his said Apprentice with meat & drink & Clothing during the said term, & all other necessaries meet & proper, in sickness & in health, and shall also, at the expiration of the said Term, allow & pay the said Apprentice what is now allowed by statute in such case made & provided

Witness our hands & seals the day & year first before written.

Executed Before Us
L. C. Edwards }   William + Maxwell, his mark
J. J. Burch, ordinary }   Charles Allen

Georgia } [367]
Elbert County } This Indenture, Made this the 26 day of July 1900, between John Ham, of said County, for and in behalf of William Ham, being of the age of ten years, of the one part, and S. S. Brown, of the County aforesaid, of the other part. Witnesseth: That the said John Ham, as aforesaid, does by these presents bind out William Ham, of said County, as Apprentice to said S. S. Brown in the trade or Craft of Farm Laborer or as Laborer upon the plantation of the said S. S. Brown, to be taught the said Craft or trade of Farm Laborer or Laborer, and to live

with, Continue, and serve the said S. S. Brown as an Apprentice from the 1st day of Jany 1901 for and during the term of Six years. During all of which time, said John Ham, as aforesaid, doth Covenant with the said S. S. Brown that the said William Ham shall well & faithfully demean his self as such faithful Apprentice, observing fully the Command of the said S. S. Brown, & in all things deporting & behaving his self as a faithful Apprentice to the said S. S. Brown, neither revealing his secrets, nor at any time leaving or neglecting the business of the said S. S. Brown. And for & in Consideration of the service well and faithfully rendered by the said William Ham, of the first part, said S. S. Brown, of the Second part, doth Covenant, promise, & agree to instruct his said Apprentice, or otherwise Cause him to be well & faithfully instructed, in the said trade or Craft of Farm Laborer or laborer, & also to read the English language, & shall also allow, furnish, & provide his said Apprentice with meat & drink & Clothing during the said term, & all other necessaries meet & proper, in sickness & in health, & shall also, at the expiration of the said term, allow & pay the Said Apprentice the Sum of one Hundred Dollars.

Witness our hands & seals the day & year first before written.

Executed Before Us. All interlineations made before signing.

Abda Oglesby	John + Ham, his mark
J. J. Burch, Ordinary	S. S. Brown

Georgia } [368]
Elbert County } This Indenture, made this the 14 day of August 1900, between George Smith, of Said County, for and in behalf of his minor Sons Joseph & Clarence Smith, being of the age of 14, 12 years, of the one part, and C. M. Seymore, of the County aforesaid, of the other part. Witnesseth: That the Said George Smith, as aforesaid, does by these presents bind out his said sons Joseph & Clarence, of said County, as Apprentices to said C. M. Seymore in the trade or craft of Farm Laborers or as Laborers upon the plantation of the said C. M. Seymore, to be taught the said craft or trade of Farm Laborers or Laborers, & live with, Continue, & Serve the said C. M. Seymore as Apprentices from the first of Jany 1901 for and during the term of one year. During all of which time, said George Smith, as aforesaid, doth covenant with the said C. M. Seymore that the said Joseph & Clarence Smith shall well and faithfully demean them selves such faithful Apprentices, observing fully the Command of the said C. M. Seymore, and in all things deporting & behaving them selves as faithful Apprentices to the said C. M. Seymore, neither revealing his secrets, nor at any time leaving or neglecting the business of the said C. M. Seymore. And for & in Consideration

of the Service well & faithfully rendered by the said Joseph & Clarence Smith, of the first part, said C. M. Seymore, of the second part, doth Covenant, promise, & agree to instruct his said Apprentices, or otherwise cause them to be well & faithfully instructed, in the said trade or craft of Farm Laborers or Laborers, & also to read the English language, & shall also allow, furnish, & provide his said Apprentices with meat & drink & clothing during the Said term, & all other necessaries meet & proper, in sickness & in health, & shall also, at the expiration of the said term, allow & pay the said Apprentices what is now Allowed by the Statutes in such Case made & provided.

Witness our hands & Seals the day & year first before written.

Executed Before Us }
A. O. Harper }
J. J. Burch, ordinary }

George + Smith, his mark
C. M. Seymore

Georgia } [369]
Elbert County } This Indenture, Made this the 10th day of December 1899, between Abe Hudson, of said County, for & in behalf of him self and wife Ada Hudson, being of the age of 55, 40 years, of the one part, and J. J. Nelms, of the County aforesaid, of the other part. Witnesseth: That the said Abe Hudson, as aforesaid, does by these presents bind out him Self & his wife Ada, of Said County, as Apprentices to said J. J. Nelms in the trade or craft of Farm Laborer or as Laborer upon the plantation of the said J. J. Nelms, to be taught the said craft or trade of Farm Laborers or Laborers, & to live with, Continue, & serve the said J. J. Nelms as Apprentices from the date hereof until Twenty Dollars is paid at a rate understood between the parties.

During all of which time, the said Abe Hudson, as aforesaid, doth Covenant with J. J. Nelms that the said Abe Hudson & his wife Ada shall well & faithfully demean them selves as such faithful Apprentices, observing fully the Command of the said J. J. Nelms, and in all things deporting & behaving them selves as faithful Apprentices to the said J. J. Nelms, neither revealing his secrets, nor at any time leaving or neglecting the business of the said J. J. Nelms. And for and in consideration of the services well & faithfully rendered by the Said Abe Hudson & Ada Hudson, of the first part, J. J. Nelms, of the second part, doth Covenant, promise, & Agree to instruct his said Apprentices, or otherwise Cause them to be well & faithfully instructed, in the said trade or craft of Farm Laborers or laborers, & shall also allow & furnish & provide them, said Apprentices, with meat & drink & Clothing during the said term, & all other necessaries meet & proper, in sickness as in health, & shall also, at the expiration of the said term, allow & pay his Said Apprentices what is now allowed by the statute in such case made & provided.

Witness our hands & seals the day & year first before written. Erasure & interlineation made before Signing.

J. A. McLanahan	Abe + Hudson, his mark
J. J. Burch, ordinary	Ada +, her mark
	J. J. Nelms

Georgia   }   [370]
Elbert County } This Indenture, Made this the 7th day of August 1900, between Henry Parker, of said County, for and in behalf of William Parker, being of the age of the age of 15 years, of the one part, and R. P. Carter, of the County aforesaid, of the other part. Witnesseth: that the said Henry Parker, as aforesaid, does by these presents bind out William Parker, of said County, as Apprentice to said R. P. Carter in the trade or craft of Farm Laborer or as Laborer upon the plantation of the said R. P. Carter, to be taught the said craft or trade of Farm Laborer or Laborer, and to live with, continue, & serve the said R. P. Carter as an apprentice from the first day Jany 1901 for and during the term of one year.

During all of which time, said Henry Parker, as aforesaid, doth covenant with the said R. P. Carter that the said William Parker Shall well & faithfully demean his self as such faithful Apprentice, observing fully the Command of the said R. P. Carter, and in all things deporting and behaving his self as a faithful Apprentice to the said R. P. Carter, neither revealing his secrets, nor at any time leaving or neglecting the business of the said R. P. Carter. And for and in Consideration of the service well & faithfully rendered by the said William Parker, of the first part, said R. P. Carter, of the second part, doth covenant, promise, & agree to instruct his said Apprentice, or otherwise Cause him to be well & faithfully instructed, in the said trade or craft of Farm Laborer or laborer, & also to read the English Language, & shall also allow, furnish, and provide his said Apprentice with meat & drink & Clothing during the Said term, & all other necessaries meet & proper, in sickness & in health, & shall also, at the expiration of the said term, allow & pay the said Apprentice what is now allowed by the Statute in such case made & provided.

Witness our hands & seals the day & year first before written.

Executed Before Us	
D. B. Alexander	Henry + Parker, his mark
J. J. Burch, ordinary	R. P. Carter

Georgia } [371]
Elbert County } This Indenture, made this the 22nd day of August 1900, between Mandy Foster, of said County, for & in behalf of her minor sons William & John Henry Foster, being of the age of 16, 14 years, of the one part, & John C. Brown, of the County aforesaid, of the other part. Witnesseth: that the said Mandy Foster, as aforesaid, does by these presents bind out her said sons William & John Henry Foster, of said County, as Apprentices to said John C. Brown in the trade or craft of Farm Laborers or as Laborers upon the plantation of the said John C. Brown, to be taught the said craft or trade of Farm Laborers or laborers, & to live with, Continue, & serve the said John C. Brown as Apprentices from the date hereof for & during the term of 2 years. During all of which time, said Mandy Foster, as aforesaid, doth Covenant with the said John C. Brown that the said William & John Henry shall well & faithfully demean them selves as such faithful Apprentices, observing fully the Command of the said Jn° C. Brown, & in all things deporting & behaving them selves as faithful Apprentices to the said John C. Brown, neither revealing his secrets, nor at any time leaving or neglecting the business of the said John C. Brown. And for & in Consideration of the services well & faithfully rendered by the said William Foster & John Henry Foster, of the first part, said Jn° C. Brown, of the second part, doth Covenant, promise, & agree to instruct his said Apprentices, or otherwise Cause them to be well & faithfully instructed, in the said trade or craft of Farm Laborers or Laborers, & also to read the English language, & shall also allow, furnish, & provide his said Apprentices with meat & drink & Clothing during the said term, & all other necessaries meet & proper, in sickness & in health, & shall also, at the expiration of the said term, allow & pay the said Apprentices what is now allowed by the Statute in such Case made and provided.

Witness our hands & seals the day & year first before written.

Executed Before Us.
H. J. Brown   Mandy + Foster, her mark
J. J. Burch, Ordinary   Jn° C. Brown

Georgia } [372]
Elbert County } This Indenture, Made this the 4th day of September 1900, between Willis Jones, of said County, for & in behalf of him self, being of the age of 40 years, of the one part, and C. H. Brown, of the County aforesaid, of the other part. Witnesseth: That the Said Willis Jones, as aforesaid, does by these presents bind out him Self, of said County, as Apprentice to said C. H. Brown, to be taught the said craft or trade of trade of Farm laborer or Laborer, & to live with, Continue,

& serve the said C. H. Brown as an Apprentice from the date hereof for and during the Term of one year.

During all of which time, said Willis Jones, as aforesaid, doth Covenant with the Said C. H. Brown that the said Willis Jones shall well and faithfully demean his Self as such faithful Apprentice, observing fully the Command of the said C. H. Brown, and in all things deporting & behaving his Self as a faithful Apprentice to the said C. H. Brown, neither revealing his secrets, nor at any neglecting or leaving the business of the said C. H. Brown.

And for & in Consideration of the service well & faithfully rendered by the said Willis Jones, of the first part, said C. H. Brown, of the Second part, doth Covenant, promise, & agree to instruct his said Apprentice, or otherwise Cause him to be well & faithfully instructed, in the said trade or Craft of Farm Laborer or laborer, & shall also allow, furnish, & provide his said Apprentice with meat & drink & clothing during the said term, & all other necessaries meet & proper, in sickness & in health, & shall also, at the expiration of the said term, allow & pay the Said Apprentice Thirty Three Dollars & ten Cents.

Witness our hands & Seals the day and year first before written.

Executed Before Us
H. A. Fortson   Willis + Jones, his mark
J. J. Burch, ordinary   C. H. Brown

Georgia   }   [373]
Elbert County } This Indenture, made this the first day of September 1900, between Zannie Hudson, of said County, for and in behalf of him Self, being of the age of 21 years, of the one part, & J. E. Herndon, jr, of the County aforesaid, of the other part. Witnesseth: That the said Zannie Hudson, as aforesaid, does by these presents bind out him self, of said County, as Apprentice to said J. E. Herndon, jr in the trade or craft of Farm Laborer or as Laborer upon the plantation of the said J. E. Herndon, J^r, to be taught the said craft or trade of Farm Laborer or Laborer, and to live with, Continue, & serve the said J. E. Herndon, J^r as an apprentice from the 1st of January 1900 for & during the term of one year. During all of which time, said Zannie Hudson, as aforesaid, doth Covenant with the said J. E. Herndon that the said Zannie Hudson shall well & faithfully demean his self as such faithful Apprentice, observing fully the Command of the said J. E. Herndon, jr, & in all things deporting & behaving his self as a faithful Apprentice to the said J. E. Herndon, jr, neither revealing his secrets, nor at any time leaving or neglecting the business of the said J. E. Herndon, J^r. And for & in consideration

of the service well & faithfully rendered by the said Zannie Hudson, of the first part, said J. E. Herndon, J^r, of the second part, doth covenant, promise, & agree to instruct his said Apprentice, or otherwise Cause him to be well & faithfully instructed, in the said trade or craft of Farm Laborer or Laborer, & also to read the english language, & shall also allow, furnish, & provide his said apprentice with meat & drink & clothing during the said term, & all other necessaries meet & proper, in sickness & in health, & shall also, at the expiration of the said term, allow & pay the said Apprentice what is now allowed by the statute in such Case made & provided.

Witness our hands & seals the day & year first before written.

Executed Before Us.
G. T. Bond   Zennie Rucker
J. J. Burch, ordinary   J. E. Herndon, J^r

Georgia   }   [374]
Elbert County   } This Indenture, made this Sep^t 10th day 1900, between Robert Rucker, of said County, being 37 years, of the one part, & W. J. Brown, of the County aforesaid, of the other part. Witnesseth: That the said Robert Rucker, as aforesaid, does by these presents bind him self, of said County, as Apprentice to said W. J. Brown in the trade or craft of Farming or as Laborer upon the plantation of the said W. J. Brown, to be taught the said craft or trade of Farming or Laborer, & to live with, Continue, & serve the said W. J. Brown as an Apprentice from the date hereof for & during the term of Five years.

During all of which time, said Robert Rucker, as aforesaid, doth Covenant with the said W. J. Brown that the said Robert Rucker shall well & faithfully demean him self as such faithful Apprentice, observing fully the Command of the said W. J. Brown, & in all things deporting & behaving him self as a faithful Apprentice to the said W. J. Brown, Neither revealing his secrets, nor at any time leaving or neglecting the business of the said W. J. Brown. And for & in Consideration of the services well & faithfully rendered by the said Robert Rucker, of the first part, said W. J. Brown, of the second part, doth covenant, promise, & agree to instruct his said Apprentice, or otherwise Cause him to be well & faithfully instructed, in the said trade or craft of Farming or Laborer, and shall also allow, furnish, & provide his said Apprentice with meat & drink & clothing during the said term, and all other necessaries meet & proper, in sickness & in health, And shall also, at the expiration of the said term, allow & pay the said Apprentice Fifty dollars each year. All interlineation made before signing within Contract is settled by the parties.

Witness our hands & seals the day and year first before written.

Executed Before Us.
T. L. Adams   Robert Rucker
J. J. Burch, ordinary   W. J. Brown

Georgia   }   [375]
Elbert County   }   This Indenture, Made this the 15th October 1900, between Robert Massey & Mary Massey, of said County, for and in behalf of them selves, being of the age of 30 & 23 years, of the one part, & C. M. Seymore, of the County aforesaid, of the other part. Witnesseth: That the said Robert & Mary Massey, as aforesaid, does by these presents bind out them selves, of said County, as Apprentices to said C. M. Seymore in the trade or craft of Farm Laborers or as Laborers, & to live with, continue, & serve the said C. M. Seymore as Apprentices from the date hereof for & during the term of one year. During all of which time, said Robert & Mary Massey, as aforesaid, doth covenant with the said C. M. Seymore that the said Robert & Mary Massey shall well & faithfully demean them selves as such faithful Apprentices, observing fully the Command of the said C. M. Seymore, and in all things deporting & behaving them selves as faithful Apprentices to the said C. M. Seymore, neither revealing his secrets, nor at any time leaving or neglecting the business of the said C. M. Seymore. And for & in Consideration of the services well & faithfully rendered by the said Robert & Mary Massey, of the first part, said C. M. Seymore, of the part, doth Covenant, promise, & agree to instruct his said Apprentices, or otherwise cause them to be well & faithfully instructed, in the said trade or craft of Farm Laborers or Laborers, and shall also allow, furnish, & provide his said Apprentices with meat & drink & clothing during the said term, & all other necessaries meet & proper, in sickness & in health, & shall also, at the expiration of the said term, allow & pay the said Apprentices what is now allowed by the statute in such case made and provided.

Witness our hands & seals the day & year first before written.

Executed Before Us.
P. M. Hawes   Robert Massey
J. J. Burch, ordinary   C. M. Seymore

Georgia   }   [376]
Elbert County   }   This Indenture, Made this the 27th day of October 1900, between Steve Robson, of said County, for & in behalf of him self, being of the age of 23 years, of the one part, & E. V. McLanahan, of the County aforesaid, of

the other part. Witnesseth: That the said Steve Robson, as aforesaid, does by these presents bind out him self, of said County, as Apprentice to said E. V. McLanahan in the trade or craft of Farm Laborer or as Laborer upon the plantation of the said E. V. McLanahan, to be taught the said Craft or trade of Farm Laborer or Laborer, & to live with, Continue, & Serve the said E. V. McLanahan as an Apprentice from the date hereof for & during the term of one year.

During all of which time, said Steve Robson, as aforesaid, doth Covenant with the said E. V. McLanahan that the said Steve Robson shall well and faithfully demean his self as such faithful Apprentice, observing fully the Command of the said E. V. McLanahan, and in all things deporting & behaving his self as a faithful Apprentice to the said E. V. McLanahan, neither revealing his secrets, nor at any time leaving or neglecting the business of the said E. V. McLanahan.

And for & in Consideration of the services well and faithfully rendered by the said Steve Robson, of the first part, said E. V. McLanahan, of the second part, doth Covenant, promise, & agree to instruct his said Apprentice, or otherwise Cause him to be well & faithfully instructed, in the said trade or craft of Farm Laborer or as Laborer, & shall also allow, furnish, and provide his said Apprentice with meat & drink & clothing during the Said term, & all other necessaries meet & proper, in sickness & in health, & shall also, at the expiration of the said term, allow & pay the said Apprentice what is now allowed by the statute in such case made & provided.

Witness our hands & seals the day & year first before written.

Executed Before Us }
J. L. Shon }   Steve + Robson, his mark
J. J. Burch, ordinary }   E. V. McLanahan

Georgia }   [377]
Elbert County } This Indenture, Made this the 27th day of October 1900, between Mark Gresham, of said County, for & in behalf of him Self, his wife Sue, & his daughter Tame Gresham, being of the age of 35, 30, & 15 years, of the one part, & M. A. McLanahan, of the County aforesaid, of the other part. Witnesseth: That the said Mark Gresham, as aforesaid, does by these presents bind out them selves, of said County, as apprentices to said M. A. McLanahan in the trade or Craft of Farm Laborers or as Laborers upon the plantation of the said M. A. McLanahan, to be taught the said craft or trade of Farm Laborers or Laborers, & to live with, Continue, & serve the said M. A. McLanahan as Apprentices from the date hereof for & during the term of one year. During all of which time, said

Mark, his wife Sue, & Tame Gresham, as aforesaid, doth Covenant with the said M. A. McLanahan that the said Mark, his wife Sue, & Tame Gresham shall well & faithfully demean them selves as such faithful Apprentices, observing fully the Command of the said M. A. McLanahan, & in all things deporting & behaving them selves as faithful Apprentices to the said M. A. McLanahan, neither revealing his secrets, nor at any time leaving or neglecting the business of the said M. A. McLanahan.

And for & in Consideration of the services well & faithfully rendered by the said Mark, Sue, & Tame Gresham, of the first part, said M. A. McLanahan, of the second part, doth covenant, promise, & agree to instruct his said Apprentices, or otherwise Cause them to be well & faithfully instructed, in the said trade or craft of Farm Laborers or Laborers, and shall also allow, furnish, & provide his said Apprentices with meat & drink during the said term, & all other necessaries meet & proper, in sickness & in health, and shall also, at the expiration of the said term, allow & pay the said Apprentices Sixty five Dollars.

Witness our hands & seals the day & year first before written.

Executed Before Us }	Mark + Gresham, his mark
James McIntosh }	Sue + Gresham, her mark
J. J. Burch, ordinary }	M. A. McLanahan

Georgia   }   [378]
Elbert County } This Indenture, Made this the 27 day of October 1900, between Georgia Durrett, of said County, for & in behalf of her daughters Irene & Rose Mary Durrett, being of the age of 4 & 1 years, of the one part, & John Durrett, of the County aforesaid, of the other part. Witnesseth: That the said Georgia Durrett, as aforesaid, does by these presents bind out her minor Daughters Irene & Rose Mary, of said County, as Apprentices to said John Durrett in the trade or craft of House Servants or as Laborers upon the plantation of the said John Durrett, to be taught the said Craft or trade of House Servants or Laborers, & to live with, Continue, & serve the said John Durrett as Apprentices from the date hereof for & during the term of their minority. During all of which time, said Georgia Durrett, as aforesaid, doth Covenant with the said John Durrett that the Said Irene & Rose Mary Durrett shall well & faithfully demean them selves as such faithful apprentices, observing fully the Command of the Said John Durrett, And in all things deporting & behaving them selves as faithful Apprentices to the said John Durrett, neither revealing his secrets, nor at any time leaving or neglecting the business of the said John Durrett. And for & in Consideration of the service well & faithfully rendered by the said Irene & Rose Mary, of the first part, said John

Durrett, of the second part, doth Covenant, promise, & agree to instruct his said Apprentices, or otherwise Cause them to be well & faithfully instructed, in the said trade or Craft of House Servants or Laborers, and also to read the English language, & shall also allow, furnish, & provide his said Apprentices with meat and drink & clothing during the said term, & all other necessaries meet & proper, in sickness & in health, & shall also, at the expiration of the said term, allow & pay the said Apprentices what is now allowed by the statute in such case made & provided.

Witness our hands & seals the day & year first before Written.

Executed Before Us }
J. H. Stovall }   Georgia Durrett
J. J. Burch, Ordinary }   John Durrett

Georgia }   [379]
Elbert County } This Indenture, Made this the 24th day of November 1900, between Jep Brawner, of said County, for & in behalf of his minor son Joe Brawner, being of the age of 13 years, of the one part, & W. T. M. Brown, of the County aforesaid, of the other part. Witnesseth: That the said Jep Brawner, as aforesaid, does by these presents bind out his said son Joe Brawner, of said County, as Apprentice to said W. T. M. Brown in the trade or craft of Farm Laborer or as Laborer upon the plantation of the said W. T. M. Brown, to be taught the said craft or trade of Farm laborer or laborer, & to live with, Continue, & serve the said W. T. M. Brown as an Apprentice from the 25th day of December 1900 for & during the term of 2 years. During all of which time, said Jep Brawner, as aforesaid, doth covenant with the said W. T. M. Brown that the said Joe Brawner shall well & faithfully demean him self such faithful Apprentice, observing fully the command of the said W. T. M. Brown, & in all things deporting & behaving his self as a faithful Apprentice to the said W. T. M. Brown, neither revealing his secrets, nor at any time leaving or neglecting the business of the said W. T. M. Brown. And for & in Consideration of the Services well & faithfully rendered by the said Joe Brawner, of the first part, said W. T. M. Brown, of the second part, doth covenant, promise, & agree to instruct his said Apprentice, or otherwise cause him to be well & faithfully instructed, in the said trade or Craft of Farm Laborer or laborer, & also to read the english language, & shall also allow, furnish, & provide his Said Apprentice with meat & drink ~~& Clothing~~ during the said term, & all other necessaries meet and proper, in Sickness & in health, and shall also, at the expiration of the said Term, allow & pay the said Apprentices Thirty Dollars. All interlineations made before signing.

Witness our hands & Seals the day & year first before written.

Executed Before Us }
M. F. Mewbourn }
J. J. Burch, ordinary }

Jep + Brawner, his mark
W. T. M. Brown

Georgia } [380]
Elbert County } This Indenture, made this the 5th day of December 1900, between Andrew Fortson, of said County, for and in behalf of his minor sons Wyley, Andrew, Robert, and Willie Fortson, being of the age of 17, 16, 14, 12 years, of the one part, & M. E. Maxwell, of the County aforesaid, of the other part. Witnesseth: that the said Andrew Fortson, as aforesaid, does by these presents bind out his said sons Wyley, Andrew, Robert, & Willie Fortson, of said County, as apprentices to said M. E. Maxwell in the trade or craft of Farm laborers or laborers upon the plantation of the said M. E. Maxwell, to be taught the said craft or trade of Farm Laborers or Laborers, and to live with, continue, & serve the said M. E. Maxwell as an Apprentice from the date hereof for and during the term of 4 years. During all of which time, said Andrew Fortson, as aforesaid, doth covenant with the said M. E. Maxwell that the said Wyley, Andrew, Robert, & Willie Fortson shall well & faithfully demean them selves as such faithful Apprentices, observing fully the command of the said M. E. Maxwell, and in all things deporting & behaving them selves as a faithful Apprentice to the said M. E. Maxwell, neither revealing his secrets, nor at any time leaving or neglecting the business of the said M. E. Maxwell. And for & in Consideration of the service well & faithfully rendered by the said Wyley, Andrew, Robert, & Willie Fortson, of the first part, Said M. E. Maxwell, of the second part, doth covenant, promise, & agree to instruct his said Apprentices, or otherwise Cause them to be well & faithfully instructed, in the said trade or craft of Farm Laborers or Laborers, and shall also allow, furnish, & provide his said Apprentices with meat & drink & Clothing during the said term, & all other necessaries meet & proper, in sickness & in health, and shall also, at the expiration of the said term, allow & pay the said Apprentices what is now allowed by the statute in such case made & provided.

Witness our hands & Seals the day & year first before written.

Executed Before Us
S. S. Brown
J. J. Burch, ordinary

Andrew + Fortson, his mark
M. E. Maxwell

Georgia } [381]
Elbert County } This Indenture, made this the 27th day of October 1900, between

Ann Cummings, of said County, for & in behalf of her minor son Bill Cummings, being of the age of 13 years, of the one, & M. Burriss, of the County aforesaid, of the other part. Witnesseth: That the said Ann Cummings, as aforesaid, does by these presents bind out her said Son Bill Cummings, of said County, as apprentice to said M. Burriss in the trade or craft of House Servant or as Laborer upon the plantation of the said M. Burriss, to be taught the said craft or trade of House Servant or laborer, & to live with, Continue, & serve the Said M. Burriss as an apprentice from the date hereof for and during the term of 8 years. During all of which time, said Ann Cumming, as aforesaid, doth Covenant with the said M. Burriss that the said Bill Cummings shall well & faithfully demean his self as such faithful Apprentice, observing fully the Command of the said M. Burriss, and in all things deporting & behaving his self as a faithful Apprentice to the said M. Burriss, neither revealing his secrets, nor at any time leaving or neglecting the business of the said M. Burriss. And for & in consideration of the service well and faithfully rendered by the said Bill Cummings, of the first part, said M. Burriss, of the second part, doth covenant, promise, & agree to instruct his said Apprentice, or otherwise Cause him to be well & faithfully instructed, in the said trade or craft of House Servant or Laborer, and also to read the English language, & shall also allow, furnish, & provide his said Apprentice with meat & drink & clothing during the said term, & all other necessaries meet & proper, in sickness and in health, and shall also, at the expiration of the said term, allow & pay the said Apprentice what is now allowed by the statute in such case made & provided.

Witness our hands & seals the day & year first before written. Executed Before Us

J. B. Jones, J^r, N. P. Ex off J. P.   Ann + Cummings, her mark
C. M. Mattox   M. Burriss

Georgia   }   [382]
Elbert County } This Indenture, made this the 12 day December 1900, between Asbury Eberhart, of said County, for & in behalf of his minor son York Eberhart, being of the age of 15 years, of the one part, and Ja^s W. Bond, jr, of the County aforesaid, of the other part. Witnesseth: That the said Asbury Eberhart, as aforesaid, does by these presents bind out his said son York Eberhart, of said County, as apprentice to said J. W. Bond, jr in the trade or Craft of Farm Laborer or as Laborer upon the plantation of the said Ja^s W. Bond, jr, to be taught the said craft or trade of Farm Laborer or Laborer, & to live with, continue, & serve the said Ja^s W. Bond, jr as an Apprentice from the 15 January 1901 for and during the term of one year, or until a debt of Sixty five Dollars, with interest from date at 8 cent per annum, at the rate of five (5.00) Dollars per month. During all of which

time, said Asbury Eberhart, as afore Said, doth Covenant with the said Ja^s W. Bond, jr that the said York Eberhart shall well & faithfully demean his self as such faithful Apprentice, observing fully the Command of the said Ja^s W. Bond, jr, and in all things deporting & behaving his self as a faithful Apprentice to the said Ja^s W. Bond, jr, neither revealing his secrets, nor at any time leaving or neglecting the business of the said Ja^s W. Bond, jr.

And for & in consideration of the service well and faithfully rendered by the said York Eberhart, of the first part, said Ja^s W. Bond, jr, of the second part, doth covenant, promise, & agree to instruct his said Apprentice, or otherwise cause him to be well & faithfully instructed, in the said trade or Craft of Farm Laborer or Laborer, & shall also allow, furnish, & provide his said Apprentice with meat & drink during the said term, & all other necessaries meet & proper, in sickness & in health, and shall also, at the expiration of the said term, allow & pay the said Apprentice what is now allowed by the state in such case made & provided.

Witness our hands & seals the day & year first before written.

All interlineations made before signing.

Executed Before Us
T. A. Nelms   Asbury + Eberhart, his mark
J. J. Burch, ordinary   J. W. Bond, jr

Georgia   }   [383]
Elbert County } This Indenture, executed this 15 day of December 1900, between J. J. Burch, ordinary of said County, as party of the first part, and Lonnie Haley, of said State and County, as party of the second. Witnesseth: That Whereas said Lonnie Haley did on the 27 day of November 1900 make Application to said ordinary to have bound out to him, the said Lonnie Haley, a Certain minor of Said County, to wit, Lula Huff, whose age at the date of this indenture is thirteen years. which said application, after notice & Citation in terms of the law, were heard & presented by said ordinary. Now, therefore, by virtue of the Statutory Authority in him vested, the said J. J. Burch, ordinary, does hereby bind out and Apprentice the said Lula Huff to the said Lonnie Haley, from the date hereof until the 15th day of December 1901, hereby entitling the said Lonnie Haley to the reasonable labor of said minor during said period, subject however to the following Terms & Conditions. said minor should always during Said period receive at the hands of the Said Haley Maintenance, protection, and humane treatment. Said Haley shall furnish the said Lula Huff with wholesome food, suitable Clothing, and necessary medicine and medical attention, and shall teach her habits of industry, honesty,

and morality, and govern with humanity, using only the same degree of force to compel obedience as a father may use with his minor child.

In Witness Whereof, the said contracting parties have hereto set their hands and affixed their seals the day & year first above written. Signed in Duplicate. Signed, sealed, & delivered in presence of

W. D. Tutt, J^r	J. J. Burch, ordinary
Abda Oglesby, J. P.	Elbert Co., Ga.
	Lonnie + Haley, his mark

Georgia } [384]
Elbert County } This Indenture, made this the 14th day of December 1900, between Charley Heard, of said County, for and in behalf of his minor son Frank Heard, being of the age of 13 years, of the one part, and M. A. McLanahan, of the County aforesaid, of the other part. Witnesseth: that the said Charley Heard, as aforesaid, Does by these presents bind out his said son Frank Heard, of said County, as Apprentice to said M. A. McLanahan in the trade or craft of Farm Laborer or as Laborer upon the plantation of the said M. A. McLanahan, to be taught the said craft or trade of Farm Laborer or Laborer, and to live with, Continue, & Serve the said M. A. McLanahan as an apprentice from the 1st day of March 1901 for and during the Term of Ten months. During all of which time, said Charles Heard, as aforesaid, doth Covenant with the said M. A. McLanahan that the said Frank Heard Shall well & faithfully demean his self as such faithful apprentice, observing fully the Command of the Said M. A. McLanahan, And in all things deporting & behaving his self as a faithful Apprentice to the said M. A. McLanahan, neither revealing his secrets, nor at any time leaving or neglecting the business of the said M. A. McLanahan. And for and in consideration of the service well and faithfully rendered by the said Frank Heard, of the first part, said M. A. McLanahan, of the second part, doth Covenant, promise, & agree to instruct his said Apprentice, or otherwise Cause him to be well & faithfully instructed, in the said trade or craft of Farm Laborer or Laborer, and shall also allow, furnish, & provide his said Apprentice with meat & drink & clothing during the said term, and all other necessaries meet & proper, in sickness and in health, and shall also, at the expiration of the said term, allow & pay the said Apprentice Fifteen ($15.00) Dollars. Now the said Charles Heard agrees to make good all time lost in the event Said Frank is sick or runaway.

Executed Before Us }	
James McIntosh }	Charley + Heard, his mark
J. J. Burch, ordinary }	M. A. McLanahan

Georgia   } [385]
Elbert County } This Indenture, made this the 18 day of December 1900, between Warren Spear, of Said County, for & in behalf of his minor son George Spear, being of the age of 15 years, of the one part, and D. O. Partin, of the County aforesaid, of the other part. Witnesseth: That the said Warren Spear, as aforesaid, does by these presents bind out his said son George Spear, of said County, as apprentice to said D. O. Partin in the trade or Craft of Farm Laborer or as Laborer upon the plantation of the said D. O. Partin, to be taught the said Craft or trade of Farm Laborer or laborer, & to live with, Continue, & Serve the said D. O. Partin as an apprentice from the 1st day of January 1901 for and during the term of Seven months. During all of which time, Said Warren Spear, as aforesaid, doth Covenant with the said D. O. Partin that the said George Spear shall well & faithfully demean his self as such faithful apprentice, observing fully the Command of the said D. O. Partin, and in all things deporting & behaving his self as a faithful Apprentice to the said D. O. Partin, neither revealing his secrets, nor at any time leaving or neglecting the business of the said D. O. Partin. And for & in consideration of the service well & faithfully rendered by the said George Spear, of the first part, said D. O. Partin, of the second part, doth covenant, promise, & agree to instruct his said Apprentice, or otherwise Cause him to be well & faithfully instructed, in the said trade or Craft of Farm Laborer or laborer, and shall also allow, furnish, & provide his said Apprentice with meat & drink during said term, and shall also, at the expiration of the said term, allow & pay the said Apprentice Seven Dollars per month ($49.00).

Witness our hands & Seals the day & year first before written.

Executed Before us
Geº MaGill
J. J. Burch, ordinary

Warren + Spear, his mark
D. O. + Partin, his mark

Georgia   } [386]
Elbert County } This Indenture, made this the 22nd Dec 1900, between Dick Banks, of said County, for & in behalf of him self, being of the age of 32 years, of the one part, and George P. Norman, of the County aforesaid, of the other part. Witnesseth: That the said Dick Banks aforesaid, does by these presents bind out his self, Dick Banks, of said County, as Apprentice to said Geº P. Norman in the trade or craft of Farm Laborer or as Laborer upon the plantation of the said Geº P. Norman, to be taught the said Craft or trade of Farm Laborer or laborer, & to live with, Continue, & serve the said Geº P. Norman as an Apprentice from the 1st day January 1901 for ~~Geº P. Norman as an Apprentice~~ and during the term of one year. During all of which time, said Dick Banks, as aforesaid, doth Covenant with

the said G. P. Norman that the said Dick Banks shall well & faithfully demean his self as such faithful apprentice, observing fully the Command of the Said G. P. Norman, & in all things deporting & behaving his self as a faithful Apprentice to the said Geº P. Norman, neither revealing his secrets, nor at any time leaving or neglecting the business of the said Geº P. Norman. And for & in consideration of the Service well and faithfully rendered by the said Dick Banks, of the first part, said Geº P. Norman, of the second part, doth covenant, promise, & agree to instruct his said Apprentice, or otherwise Cause him to be well & faithfully instructed, in the said trade or craft of Farm Laborer or Laborer, and shall also allow, furnish, & provide his said Apprentice with meat & drink during said term, & all other necessaries meet & proper, in sickness & in health, & shall also, at the expiration of the said term, allow & pay the said apprentice Seventy Two Dollars.

Witness our hands & Seals the day & year first before written.

Executed Before Us }
T. M. Shumate }
J. J. Burch, ordinary }

Dick + Banks, his mark
Geº P. Norman

Georgia } [387]
Elbert County } This Indenture, Made this the 31st day of December 1900, between Ephraim McCalla, of said County, for & in behalf of his minor daughter Martha McCalla, being of the age of 13 years, of the one part, and T. H. Carter, of the County aforesaid, of the other part. Witnesseth: That the said Ephraim McCalla, as aforesaid, does by these presents bind out his said Daughter Martha McCalla, of said County, as Apprentice to said T. H. Carter in the trade or craft of Farm Laborer or as Laborer upon the plantation of the said Thoˢ H. Carter, to be taught the Said Craft or trade of Farm Laborer or laborer, & to live with, Continue, & serve the said Thomas H. Carter as an Apprentice from the date hereof for and during the term of one year. During all of which time, said Ephraim McCalla, as aforesaid, doth Covenant with the said T. H. Carter that the said Martha McCalla shall well & faithfully demean her self as such faithful Apprentice, observing fully the Command of the said T. H. Carter, and in all things deporting and behaving her Self as a faithful Apprentice to the said T. H. Carter, neither revealing his secrets, nor at any time leaving or neglecting the business of the said T. H. Carter. And for & in Consideration of the service well and faithfully rendered by the said Martha McCalla, of the first part, said T. H. Carter, of the Second part, doth Covenant, promise, & agree to instruct his said Apprentice, or otherwise cause her to be well & faithfully instructed, in the said trade or Craft of Farm Laborer or Laborer, and shall also allow, furnish, & provide his Said Apprentice with meat & drink & clothing during the said term, & all other

necessaries meet & proper, in sickness & in health, & shall also, at the expiration of the said term, allow & pay the said Apprentice Twenty five Dollars.

Witness our hands & seals the day & year first before written.

Executed Before Us
J. J. Burch, Ordinary
George Haslett

Ephraim + McCalla, his mark
T. H. Carter

Georgia }   [388]
Elbert County } This Indenture, made this the 2nd day January 1901, between Sam White and William White for & in behalf of them selves and Sam White for his minor son Sol & George White, being of the age of 59, 35, 18, 15 years, of the one part, & Geº P. Norman, of the County aforesaid, of the other part. Witnesseth: That the said Sam & William White, as aforesaid, does by these presents bind out them selves & Sam White his said sons Sol & George White, of said County, as Apprentices to said Geº P. Norman in the trade or craft of Farm Laborers or as Laborers upon the plantation of the said Geº P. Norman, to be taught the said craft or trade of Farm Laborers or laborers, & to live with, continue, and serve the said Geº P. Norman as Apprentices from the date hereof for & during the term of 15 months.

During all of which time, said Sam & William White, as afore Said, doth covenant with the said Geº P. Norman that the said Sam & William White & Sam for his sons Sol & George White shall well & faithfully demean them selves as such faithful apprentices, observing fully the Command of the said Geº P. Norman, & in all things deporting & behaving them selves as faithful Apprentices to the said Geº P. Norman, neither revealing his secrets, nor at any time leaving or neglecting the business of the said Geº P. Norman. And for & in consideration of the Service well & faithfully rendered by the said Sam & William White & Said Sam for his Sons Sol & George White, of the first part, said Geº P. Norman, of the second part, doth Covenant, promise, & agree to instruct his said Apprentices, or otherwise Cause them to be well & faithfully instructed as said Apprentices, or otherwise Cause them to be well & faithfully instructed, in the said trade or craft of Farm Laborers or Laborers, & also allow, furnish, & provide his Said Apprentices with meat & drink & clothing during the said term, & all other necessaries meet and proper, in sickness & in health, & shall also, at the expiration of the said term, allow & pay the said Apprentices Fifty Six Dollars & Thirty Cents.

Witness our hands & seals the day & year first before written.

Executed Before Us	Sam + White, his mark
T. W. Brown	W. M. White
J. J. Burch, ordinary	G. P. Norman

Georgia　　　} [389]
Elbert County } This Indenture, made this the 2nd day of January 1901, between Henry White, of said County, for & in behalf of him self, Henry White, being of the age of 28 years, of the one part, & G. P. Norman, of the County aforesaid, of the other part. Witnesseth: That the said Henry, as aforesaid, does by these presents bind out him self, Henry White, of said County, as Apprentice to said Ge° P. Norman in the trade or Craft of Farm Laborer or as laborer upon the plantation of the said Ge° P. Norman, to be taught the said craft or trade of Farm Laborer or laborer, & to live with, Continue, & serve the said Ge° P. Norman as an Apprentice from the date hereof for & during the term of 15 months. During all of which time, said Henry White, as aforesaid, doth Covenant with the Said Ge° P. Norman that he, the said Henry White, shall well & faithfully demean his self as such faithful Apprentice, observing fully the Command of the said George P. Norman, & in all things deporting & behaving his self as a faithful Apprentice to the said Ge° P. Norman, neither revealing his secrets, nor at any time leaving or neglecting the business of the said Ge° P. Norman. And for & in Consideration of the Service well & faithfully rendered by the said Henry White, of the first part, said Ge° P. Norman, of the Second part, doth Covenant, promise, & agree to instruct his said Apprentice, or otherwise cause him to be well & faithfully instructed, in the said trade or craft of Farm Laborer or laborer, & shall also allow, furnish, & provide his said Apprentice with meat & drink & Clothing during the said term, & all other necessaries meet & proper, in sickness & in health, & shall also, at the expiration of the said term, allow & pay the said Apprentice Fifty six & $^{30}/_{100}$ Dollars.

Witness our hands & seals the day & year first before written.

Executed Before Us in Duplicate	
T. J. Brown	Henry White
J. J. Burch, ordinary	G. P. Norman

Georgia　　　} [390]
Elbert County } This Indenture, made this the 2nd day of January 1901, between Vina Hill, alias Vina Blackwell, of said County, for & in behalf of her self & her minor children, to wit, Minnie, Lula, Ann, Peter, & Jim Hill, Abner Blackwell,

being of the age of 58, 18, 14, 20, 13, 8 years, of the one part, and J. Y. Swift, of the County aforesaid, of the other part. Witnesseth: That the said Vina Hill, alias Blackwell, as aforesaid, does by these presents bind out her self & said minor children, Minnie, Lula, Ann, Peter, & Jim Hill, Abner Blackwell, of said County, as Apprentices to said J. Y. Swift in the trade or craft of Farm Laborers or as Laborers upon the plantation of the said J. Y. Swift, to be taught the said craft or trade of Farm Laborers or Laborers, and to live with, Continue, & serve the said J. Y. Swift as apprentices from the date hereof for and during the term of one year. During all of which time, said Vina Hill, alias Blackwell, as aforesaid, doth Covenant with the said J. Y. Swift that the said Vina Hill, alias Blackwell, and her said minor children, Minnie, Lula, Ann, peter, & Jim Hill, Abner Blackwell, shall well & faithfully demean them selves as such faithful apprentices, observing fully the Command of the said J. Y. Swift, & in all things deporting & behaving them selves as faithful Apprentices to the said J. Y. Swift, neither revealing his secrets, nor at any time leaving or neglecting the business of the Said J. Y. Swift. And for & in consideration of the service well and faithfully rendered by the said Vina Hill, alias Blackwell, Minnie, Lula, Ann, Peter, & Jim Hill, abner Blackwell, of the first part, said J. Y. Swift, of the second part, doth covenant, promise, & agree to instruct his said Apprentices, or otherwise cause them to be well & faithfully instructed, in the said trade or craft of Farm Laborers or Laborers, & shall also allow, furnish, & provide them, said Apprentices, with meat & drink & clothing during the said term, And shall also, at the expiration of the said term, allow & pay the said Apprentices One Third part of all crop serviced or gathered by them, Said Apprentices. All interlineations made before Signed.

Witness our hands & seals the day & year first before written.

Executed Before Us
E. B. Edward   Vina + Hill, alias Blackwell, her mark
J. J. Burch, ordinary   J. Y. Swift

Georgia   }   [391]
Elbert County } This Indenture, made this the 5 day of Jany 1900, between H. A. Blackwell, of said County, for & in behalf of him self & his minor children, to wit, W^m, Alexander, Minnie, Mary, & Lizzie, being of the age of 50, 18, 16, 14, 12, & 10 years, of the one part, and W. M. Hudgens, of the County aforesaid, of the other part. Witnesseth: That the said H. A. Blackwell, as aforesaid, does by these presents bind out him self & his said children, W^m, Alexander, Lizzie, Mary, Minnie, & Lizzie Blackwell, County, as Apprentices to said W. M. Hudgens in the trade or craft of Farm Laborers or as Laborers upon the plantation of the said W. M. Hudgens, to be taught the said craft or trade of Farm Laborers or laborers,

& to live with, continue, & serve the said W. M. Hudgens as apprentices from the date hereof for & during the term of 2 years. During all of which time, said H. A. Blackwell, as aforesaid, doth Covenant with the said W. M. Hudgens that the said H. A. Blackwell & his minor Children, to wit, W^m, Alexander, Lizzie, Mary, & Minnie Blackwell, Shall well & faithfully demean them selves as such faithful apprentices, observing fully the Command of the said W. M. Hudgens, & in all things deporting & behaving them self as a faithful Apprentice to the said W. M. Hudgens, neither revealing his secrets, nor at any time leaving or neglecting the business of the said W. M. Hudgens. And for & in consideration of the service well and faithfully rendered by the said H. A. Blackwell & his children, W^m, Alexander, Lizzie, Mary, & Minnie Blackwell, of the first part, said W. M. Hudgens, of the second part, doth covenant, promise, & agree to instruct his said Apprentices, or otherwise cause them to be well & faithfully instructed, in said trade of Farm Laborers or Laborers, & shall also allow, furnish, & provide his said Apprentices with meat & drink & clothing during the said term, & shall also, at the expiration of the said term, allow & pay the Said apprentices half of all crops service & gathered by them, said apprentices, they paying time over expenses. Witness our hands & seals the day & year first before written.

Executed Before Us
W. A. Rucker   H. A. Blackwell
J. J. Burch, ordinary   W. M. Hudgens

Georgia   }   [392]
Elbert County } This Indenture, made this the 25th day of January 1901, between Asbury Eberhart, of said County, for & in behalf of him self & his minor boys, to wit, Charley, York, Alexander, & Jess Eberhart, being of the age of 64, 19, 16, 12, & 11 years, of the one part, and G. A. Lunsford, of the County aforesaid, of the other part. Witnesseth: That the said Asbury Eberhart, as aforesaid, does by these presents bind out himself & his boys, Charley, York, Alexander, & Jess Eberhart, of said County, as Apprentices to said G. A. Lunsford in the trade or Craft of Farm Laborers or as Laborers upon the plantation of the said G. A. Lunsford, to be taught the said craft or trade of Farm Laborers or laborers, & to live with, continue, & serve the said G. A. Lunsford as apprentices from the 1st Jany 1902 for and during the term of 2 years. During all of which time, said Asbury Eberhart, as aforesaid, doth Covenant with the said G. A. Lunsford that the said Asbury, Charley, York, Alexander, & Jesse Eberhart shall well & faithfully demean them selves as faithful Apprentices, observing fully the Command of the said G. A. Lunsford, & in all things deporting and behaving them selves as faithful Apprentices to the said G. A. Lunsford, neither revealing his

secrets, nor at any time leaving or neglecting the business of the said G. A. Lunsford. And for & in consideration of the service well & faithfully rendered by the said Asbury, Charley, York, Alexander, & Jesse Eberhart, of the first part, said G. A. Lunsford, of the second part, doth covenant, promise, & agree to instruct his said Apprentices, or otherwise cause them to be well & faithfully instructed, in the said trade or craft of Farm Laborers or Laborers, and Shall also allow, furnish, & provide his said Apprentices with meat & drink & Clothing during the said term, & all other necessaries meet & proper, in sickness & in health, & shall also, at the expiration of the said term, allow & pay the said Apprentices what is now allowed by the statute in such case made & provided.

Witness our hands & seals the day & year first before written.

Executed Before Us In Duplicate
W. A. Rucker   Asbury + Eberhart, his mark
J. J. Burch, ordinary   G. A. Lunsford

Georgia   }   [393]
Elbert County } This Indenture, made this the 25th day of January 1901, between Bud Eberhart, of said County, for & in behalf of him self, he the Bud Eberhart, being of the age of 25 years, of the one part, & W. C. Gunter, of the County aforesaid, of the other part. Witnesseth: That the said Bud Eberhart, as aforesaid, does by these presents bind out himself, of said County, as Apprentice to said W. C. Gunter in the trade or craft of Farm Laborer or as Laborer upon the plantation of the said W. C. Gunter, to be taught the said craft or trade of Farm Laborer or Laborer, & to live with, Continue, & serve the said W. C. Gunter as an apprentice from the date hereof for and during the term of 6 & ½ months (6½ months). During all of which time, said Bud Eberhart, as aforesaid, doth covenant with the said W. C. Gunter that the said Bud Eberhart shall well & faithfully demean his self as such faithful apprentice, observing fully the Command of the said W. C. Gunter, and in all things deporting & behaving him self as a faithful Apprentice to the said W. C. Gunter, neither revealing his secrets, nor at any time leaving or neglecting the business of the said W. C. Gunter. And for & in consideration of the service well & faithfully rendered by the said Bud Eberhart, of the first part, said W. C. Gunter, of the second part, doth Covenant, promise, & agree to instruct his said Apprentice, or otherwise cause him to be well & faithfully instructed, in the said trade or craft of Farm Laborer or Laborer, and shall also allow, furnish, & provide his said Apprentice with meat & drink & clothing during the said term, & all other necessaries meet & proper, in sickness & in health, and shall also, at the expiration of the said term, allow & pay the said Apprentice Thirty Nine

Dollars, Six Dollars per month, and he, the said Bud Eberhart, paying for his clothing out of his wages.

Witness our hands & seals the day & year first before written. Executed Before Us In Duplicate.

W. A. Rucker	Bud + Eberhart, his mark
J. J. Burch, ordinary	W. C. Gunter

Georgia } [394]
Elbert County } This Indenture, made this the 26 day of January 1901, between Marshal Stone, of said County, for & in behalf of him self & his minor son Luther Stone, being of the age of 60, 17 years, of the one part, and W. T. M. Brown, of the County aforesaid, of the other part. Witnesseth: That the said Marshal Stone, as aforesaid, does by these presents bind himself & his son Luther Stone, of said County, as Apprentices to said W. T. M. Brown in the trade or craft of Farm Laborer or as Laborers upon the plantation of the said W. T. M. Brown, ~~as apprentices from the date hereof for and during one year~~ to be taught the said Craft or trade of Farm Laborers or Laborers, and to live with, Continue, & serve the said W. T. Brown as apprentices from the date hereof for & during the term of one year. During all of which time, said Marshal Stone, as aforesaid, doth Covenant with the said W. T. M. Brown that the said Marshal and Luther Stone shall well & faithfully demean them selves as such faithful Apprentices, observing fully the command of the said W. T. M. Brown, & in all things deporting and behaving them selves as faithful Apprentices to the said W. T. M. Brown, neither revealing his secrets, nor at any time leaving or neglecting the business of the said W. T. M. Brown. And for & in Consideration of the service well & faithfully rendered by the said Marshal & Luther Stone, of the first part, said W. T. M. Brown, of the second part, doth covenant, promise, & agree to instruct his said Apprentices, or otherwise cause them to be well & faithfully instructed, in the said trade or craft of Farm Laborers or Laborers, and shall also allow, furnish, & provide his said Apprentices with meat & drink & clothing during the said term, and all other necessaries meet and proper, in sickness & in health, And shall also, at the expiration of the said term, allow & pay the said Apprentices Seven Dollars per month, or Eighty four Dollars.

Witness our hands & seals the day & year first before written.

Executed Before us In Duplicate
C. M. Allen	Marshal + Stone, his mark
J. J. Burch, ordinary	W. T. M. Brown

Georgia } [395]
Elbert County } This Indenture, made this the 30th day of January 1901, between J. P. Harper, of said County, for & in behalf of him self, J. P. Harper, being of the age of 25 years, of the one part, and M. E. Maxwell, of the County aforesaid, of the other part. Witnesseth: That the said J. P. Harper, as aforesaid, does by these presents bind out himself, J. P. Harper, of said County, as Apprentice to said M. E. Maxwell in the trade or craft of Farm Laborer or as Laborer upon the plantation of the said M. E. Maxwell, to be taught the said Craft or trade of Farm Laborer or laborer, & to live with, continue, & serve the said M. E. Maxwell as an apprentice from the first of January 1902 for and during the term of Two years.

During all of which time, said J. P. Harper, as aforesaid, doth Covenant with the said M. E. Maxwell that the said J. P. Harper shall well & faithfully demean his self as a faithful Apprentice ~~to the said M. E. Maxwell~~, observing fully the Command of the said M. E. Maxwell, and in all things deporting and behaving his self as a faithful Apprentice to the said M. E. Maxwell, neither revealing his secrets, nor at any time leaving or neglecting the business of the said M. E. Maxwell.

And for & in consideration of the service well & faithfully rendered by the said J. P. Harper, of the first part, said M. E. Maxwell, of the second part, doth covenant, promise, & agree to instruct his said Apprentice, or otherwise cause him to be well & faithfully instructed, in the said trade or craft of Farm Laborer or laborer, and shall also allow, furnish, and provide his said Apprentice with meat & drink & clothing during the said term, & all other necessaries meet and proper, in sickness & in health, and shall also, at the expiration of the said term, allow & pay the said Apprentice Seventy five Dollars.

Witness our hands & seals the day & year first before written.

Executed Before Us. Executed in Duplicate.

| J. B. Jones, S^r } | J. P. + Harper, his mark |
| J. J. Burch, ordinary } | M. E. Maxwell |

Georgia } [396]
Elbert County } This Indenture, made this the 1st day of February 1901, between Sam White, of said County, for & in behalf of his son George White, being of the age of 15 years, of the one part, & George P. Norman, of the County aforesaid, of the other part. Witnesseth: That the said Sam White, as aforesaid, does by these presents bind out his said son George White, of said County, as Apprentice to said George P. Norman in the trade or Craft of Farm Laborer or as Laborer upon the

plantation of the said Geº P. Norman, to be taught the said craft or trade of Farm Laborer or Laborer, & to live with, continue, & serve the said Geº P. Norman as an apprentice from the date hereof for & during the term of 4 months.

During all of which time, said Sam White, as aforesaid, doth Covenant with the said Geº P. Norman that the said George White shall well & faithfully demean his self as such faithful apprentice, observing fully the command of the said George P. Norman, and in all things deporting & behaving his self as a faithful Apprentice to the said Geº P. Norman, neither revealing his secrets, nor at any time leaving or neglecting the business of the said Geº P. Norman. And for & in Consideration of the service well & faithfully rendered by the said George White, of the first part, said George P. Norman, of the second part, doth Covenant, promise, & agree to instruct his said Apprentice, or otherwise Cause him to be well & faithfully instructed, in the said trade or craft of Farm Laborer or Laborer, and shall also allow, furnish, & provide his Said Apprentice with meat and drink and clothing during the said term, and all other necessaries meet & proper, in sickness and in health, & shall also, at the expiration of the Said term, allow & pay the said Apprentice Twenty Four Dollars, or Six Dollars per month.

Witness our hands & seals the day & year first before written.

Executed Before Us In Duplicate
T. J. Brown   Sam + White, his mark
J. J. Burch, ordinary   G. P. Norman

Georgia   }   [397]
Elbert County } This Indenture, made this the 22nd day of January 1901, between Frank Brown & Wife Georgia Brown, of said County, for & in behalf of him self & his wife Georgia Brown, being of the age of 26, 21 years, of the one part, and John C. Hudgens, of the County aforesaid, of the other part. Witnesseth: that the said Frank Brown & wife Georgia, as aforesaid, does by these presents bind out him self and his said wife Georgia Brown, of said County, as Apprentices to said John C. Hudgens in the trade or Craft of Farm Laborers or as Laborers upon the plantation of the said John C. Hudgens, to be taught the said Craft or trade of Farm Laborers or Laborers, & to live with, Continue, & serve the said John C. Hudgens as apprentices from the date hereof for and during the term of 2 years. During all of which time, said Frank & Georgia Brown, as aforesaid, doth Covenant with the said Jnº C. Hudgens that the Said Frank & wife Georgia Brown shall well & faithfully demean them selves as such faithful Apprentices, observing fully the command of the said Jnº C. Hudgens, and in all things deporting and behaving them selves as faithful Apprentices to the said J. C. Hudgens, neither revealing

his secrets, nor at any time leaving or neglecting the business of the said J. C. Hudgens. And for & in consideration of the service well & faithfully rendered by the said Frank & wife Georgia Brown, of the first part, said J. C. Hudgens, of the second part, doth Covenant, promise, & agree to instruct his Said Apprentices, or otherwise cause them to be well & faithfully instructed, in the said trade or craft of Farm Laborers or Laborers, and shall also allow, furnish, & provide his said apprentices with meat & drink & Clothing during the said term, & all other necessaries meet & proper, in sickness & in health, & shall also, at the expiration of the Said term, allow & pay the said apprentices Sixty five Dollars.

Witness our hands & seals the day & year first before written.

Executed Before Us In Duplicate
George T. McGill
J. J. Burch

Frank + White, his mark
Jn° C. Hudgens

Georgia } [398]
Elbert County } This Indenture, Made this the 14th Feby 1901, between John & Mary Humble, of said County, for & in behalf of them selves, John & Mary Humble, being of the age of 22, 17 years, of the one part, and Ge° W. Caldwell, of the County aforesaid, of the other part. Witnesseth: That the said John & Mary Humble, as aforesaid, does by these presents bind out them selves, of said County, as Apprentices of said Ge° W. Caldwell in trade or Craft of Farm Laborers or as Laborers upon the plantation of the said Ge° W. Caldwell, to be taught the said craft or trade of Farm Laborers or laborers, & to live with, Continue, & serve the said Ge° W. Caldwell as apprentices from the date hereof for and during the term of one year. During all of which time, said John & Mary Humble, as aforesaid, doth Covenant with the said Ge° W. Caldwell that the said John & Mary Humble shall well & faithfully ~~Apprentice the said John & Mary Humble, of the first part~~ demean them selves as such faithful apprentices, observing fully the Command of the said Ge° W. Caldwell, & in all things deporting and behaving them selves as faithful Apprentices to the said Ge° W. Caldwell, neither revealing his secrets, nor at any time leaving or neglecting the business of the said Ge° W. Caldwell.

And for & in consideration of the service well and faithfully rendered by the said John & Mary Humble, of the first part, said Ge° W. Caldwell, of the second part, doth covenant, promise, & agree to instruct his said apprentices, or otherwise Case them to be well & faithfully instructed, in the said trade or craft of Farm Laborers or Laborers, and shall also allow, furnish, & provide his said apprentices with meat & drink & clothing during the said term, & all other necessaries meet and proper, in sickness & in health, & shall also, at the expiration of the said term, allow & pay the said Apprentices Sixty Dollars.

Witness our hands & seals the day & year first before written. Executed Before Us In Duplicate.

G. C. Taylor	John Humble
J. J. Burch, ordinary	Mary Humble
	G. W. Caldwell

Georgia   }   [399]
Elbert County } This Indenture, made this the 14th day February 1901, between Will Bond and Roda Bond, of said County, for & in behalf of them selves, Will & Roberta Bond, being of the age of 21, 18 years, of the one part, & M. J. Brown, of the County aforesaid, of the other part. Witnesseth: That the said Will & Roberta Bond, as aforesaid, does by these presents bind out them selves, of said County, as Apprentices to said M. J. Brown in the trade or craft of Farm Laborers or as laborers upon the plantation of the said M. J. Brown, to be taught the said Craft or trade of Farm Laborers or laborers, & to live with, Continue, & serve the said M. J. Brown as apprentices from the date hereof for and during the term of 2 years. During all of which time, said Will & Roberta Bond, as aforesaid, doth Covenant with the said M. J. Brown that the said Will & Roberta Bond shall well and faithfully demean them selves as such faithful Apprentices, observing fully the Command of the said M. J. Brown, And in all things deporting & behaving them selves as faithful faithful Apprentices to the said M. J. Brown, neither revealing his secrets, nor at any time leaving or neglecting the business of the said M. J. Brown. And for & in Consideration of the service well & faithfully rendered by the said Will & Roberta Bond, of the first part, said M. J. Brown, of the second part, doth Covenant, promise, & agree to instruct his said Apprentices, or otherwise Cause them to be well & faithfully instructed, in the said trade or craft of Farm Laborers or laborers, and shall also allow, furnish, & provide his said Apprentices with meat & drink & clothing during the said term, & all other necessaries meet & proper, in sickness & in health, & shall also, at the expiration of the said term, allow & pay the said Apprentices Fifty Eight $^{45}/_{100}$ Dollars. Witness our hands and seals the day & year first before written.

Executed Before Us In Duplicate	Will + Bond, his mark
J. C. Hudgens	Roberta + Bond, her mark
J. J. Burch, ordinary	M. J. Brown

Georgia   } [400]
Elbert County } This Indenture, Made this the 2nd day of March 1901, between Hugh Hatten, of said County, for & in behalf of him son John Frank Hatten, being of the age of 12 years, of the one part, & S. S. Brown, of the County aforesaid, of the other part. Witnesseth: That the said Hugh Hatten, as aforesaid, does by these presents bind out his said son John Frank Hatten, of said County, as Apprentice to said S. S. Brown in the trade or Craft Farm Laborer or as Laborer upon the plantation of the said S. S. Brown, to be taught the said craft or trade of Farm Laborer or Laborer, & to live with, Continue, & serve the said S. S. Brown as an Apprentice from the 1st Jany 1902 for and during the term of 3 years. During all of which time, said Hugh Hatten, as aforesaid, doth Covenant with the said S. S. Brown that the said John Frank Hatten Shall well & faithfully demean his self as such faithful Apprentice, observing fully the Command of the said S. S. Brown, & in all things deporting & behaving his self as a faithful Apprentice to the said S. S. Brown, neither revealing his secrets, nor at any time leaving or neglecting the business of the Said S. S. Brown. And for & in Consideration of the service well & faithfully rendered by the said John Frank Hatten, of the first part, said S. S. Brown, of the second part, doth Covenant, promise, & agree to instruct his said Apprentice, or otherwise Cause him to be well & faithfully instructed, in the said trade or Craft of Farm Laborer or Laborer, And Shall also allow, furnish, & provide his Said Apprentice with meat & drink & clothing during the said term, and all other necessaries meet & proper, in sickness & in health, & shall also, at the expiration of the said term, allow & pay the said Apprentices Eighty Dollars.

Witness our hands & seals the day & year first before written.

Executed Before Us In Duplicate
R. M. Heard   Hugh + Hatten, his mark
J. J. Burch, Ordinary   S. S. Brown

Georgia   } [401]
Elbert County } This Indenture, made this the 4th day of March 1901, between Alice Starke, of said County, for & in behalf of her son Luther Starke, being of the age of 14 years, of the one part, & S. S. Brown, of the County aforesaid, of the other part. Witnesseth: That the said Alice Starke, as aforesaid, does by these presents bind out her said son Luther Starke, of said County, as Apprentice to said S. S. Brown in the trade or craft Farm Laborer or as Laborer upon the plantation of the said S. S. Brown, to be taught the said craft or trade of Farm Laborer or Laborer, & to live with, Continue, & Serve the said S. S. Brown as an Apprentice from the 1st day January 1902 for and during the term of 3 years. During all of which time, said Alice Starke, as aforesaid, doth Covenant with the said S. S.

Brown that the said Luther Starke shall well & faithfully demean his self as such faithful Apprentice, observing fully the Command of the said S. S. Brown, And in all things deporting & behaving his Self as a faithful Apprentice to the said S. S. Brown, neither revealing his secrets, nor at any time leaving or neglecting the business of the Said S. S. Brown.

And for & in Consideration of the service well & faithfully rendered by the Said Luther Starke, of the first part, Said S. S. Brown, of the second part, doth covenant, promise, & agree to instruct his said Apprentice, or otherwise cause him to be well & faithfully instructed, in the said trade or craft of Farm Laborer or Laborer, And Shall also allow, furnish, & provide his Said Apprentice with meat & drink and clothing during the said term, And all other necessaries meet & proper, in sickness & in health, and shall also, at the expiration of the said term, allow & pay the said Apprentice Sixty five Dollars. Witness our hands & seals the day & year first before written. Executed Before Us In Duplicate.

T. J. Brown	Alice + Starke, her mark
J. J. Burch, Ordinary	S. S. Brown

Georgia   }   [402]
Elbert County } This Indenture, Made this the 7 day of March 1901, between Sue Burton, of Said County, for & in behalf of her son Jim Burton, being of the age of 8 years, of the one part, & J. H. Brown, of the County aforesaid, of the other part. Witnesseth: That the said Sue Burton, as aforesaid, does by these presents bind out her said son Jim Burton, of said County, as Apprentice to said J. H. Brown in the trade or craft House Servant or as Laborer upon the plantation of the said J. H. Brown, to be taught the said craft or trade of House Servant or Laborer, and to live with, continue, & serve the said J. H. Brown as an Apprentice from the date hereof for and during the term of Ten months. During all of which time, said Sue Burton, as aforesaid, doth covenant with the said J. H. Brown that the said Jim Burton shall well & faithfully demean his self as such faithful Apprentice, observing fully the Command of the said J. H. Brown, And in all things deporting and behaving his self as a faithful Apprentice to the said J. H. Brown, neither revealing his secrets, nor at any time leaving or neglecting the business of the said J. H. Brown. And for & in Consideration of the service well & faithfully rendered by the said Jim Burton, of the first part, said J. H. Brown, of the second part, doth Covenant, promise, and agree to instruct his said Apprentice, or otherwise Cause him to be well and faithfully instructed, in the said trade or craft of House Servant or Laborer, And Shall also allow, furnish, and provide his said Apprentice with meat and drink and clothing during the said term, and all other necessaries meet and proper, in sickness and in health, and shall also,

at the expiration of the said term, allow and pay the said apprentice Twelve Dollars.

Witness our hands & seals the day & year first before written.

Executed Before Us In Duplicate
S. S. Brown   Sue + Burton, her mark
J. J. Burch, ordinary   J. H. Brown

Georgia   }   [403]
Elbert County   } This Indenture, made this the 14 day of March 1901, between John Henry Strange, of said County, for & in behalf of him self, John Henry Strange, being of the age of 25 years, of the one part, & J. W. Harper, of the County aforesaid, of the other part. Witnesseth: That the Said John Henry Strange, as aforesaid, does by these presents bind out him self, of Said County, as apprentice to said J. W. Harper, jr in the trade or craft Farm Laborer or as Laborer upon the plantation of the said J. W. Harper, jr,, to be taught the said Craft or trade of Farm Laborer or Laborer, & to live with, continue, & serve the said J. W. Harper as an Apprentice from the date hereof for & during the term of 4 months.

During all of which time, said John Henry Strange, as aforesaid, doth Covenant with the said J. W. Harper, J^r that the said John Henry Strange shall well and faithfully demean his self as such faithful Apprentice, observing fully the Command of the said J. W. Harper, jr, and in all things deporting & behaving his self as a faithful Apprentice to the said J. W. Harper, jr, neither revealing his secrets, nor at any time leaving or neglecting the business of the said J. W. Harper, jr.

And for & in Consideration of the service well & faithfully rendered by the said John Henry Strange, of the first part, said J. W. Harper, jr, of the second part, doth covenant, promise, & agree to instruct his said Apprentice, or otherwise Cause him to be well & faithfully instructed, in the said trade or craft of Farm Laborer or Laborer, & shall also allow, furnish, & provide his Said Apprentice with meat & drink during the said term, & all other necessaries meet & proper, in sickness & in health, & shall also, at the expiration of the said term, allow & pay the said Apprentice Fifteen Dollars.

Witness our hands & seals the day & year first before written.

Executed Before Us In Duplicate
T. J. Brown   John Henry + Strange, his mark
J. J. Burch, Ordinary   J. W. Harper, jr

Georgia } [404]
Elbert County } This Indenture, made this the 23 day of March 1901, between William Smith, of said County, for & in behalf of him self and his boy Willie Smith, being of the age of 38, 15 years, of the one part, & S. S. Brown, of the County aforesaid, of the other part. Witnesseth: That the said William Smith, as aforesaid, does by these presents bind out him self & his son Willie Smith, of said County, as Apprentices to Said S. S. Brown in the trade or Craft Farm Laborers or as Laborers upon the plantation of the said S. S. Brown, to be taught the said Craft or trade of Farm Laborers or Laborers, And to live with, Continue, & serve the said S. S. Brown as Apprentices from the 1st January 1902 for and during the term of one Year. During all of which time, said William Smith, as aforesaid, doth Covenant with the said S. S. Brown that the said William & Willie Smith Shall well & faithfully demean them selves as such faithful Apprentices, observing fully the Command of the said S. S. Brown, and in all things deporting & behaving them selves as faithful Apprentices to the said S. S. Brown, neither revealing his secrets, nor at any time leaving or neglecting the business of the said S. S. Brown. And for & in consideration of the service well and faithfully rendered by the said William & Willie Smith, of the first part, said S. S. Brown, of the second part, doth covenant, promise, & agree to instruct his said Apprentices, or otherwise Cause them to be well & faithfully instructed, in the said trade or craft of Farm Laborers or Laborers, and Shall also allow, furnish, and provide his Apprentices with meat & drink & Clothing during the Said term, & all other necessaries meet & proper, in sickness and in health, & shall also, at the expiration of the said term, allow & pay the said Apprentices Thirty five Dollars.

Witness our hands & seals the day & year first before written. Executed Before Us In Duplicaate.

Abda Oglesby	William + Smith, his mark
J. J. Burch, Ordinary	S. S. Brown

State of Georgia } [405]
Elbert County } This Indenture made this March the 23, 1901, between Fayett Dye, of Elbert County said State, and C. E. Earle, of Elbert County, said State. Witnesseth: that the said Fayett Dye, in Consideration of the promises & undertakings of the said C. E. Earle herewith set forth, does hereby bind him self to the said C. E. Earle for the full term of one year from March the 23^{d} 1901, & he hereby agrees & contracts with said C. E. Earle to work faithfully under his direction at such place & at such labor as said C. E. Earle may desire & direct, & to respect & obey all orders & Commands of the said C. E. Earle, & at all times

to demean himself orderly & soberly. And the said Fayet Dye further agrees to account to the said C. E. Earle for all lost time, except in cases of temporary sickness not exceeding three days, the same to be deducted from the wages hereinafter set forth and at the same rate. And the said C. E. Earle, in Consideration of the promises & undertakings of the said Fayett Dye, agrees & Contracts with said Fayett Dye to furnish him with board, lodging, & six Dollars per month, to be paid at the expiration of said Contract, March 23rd 1902. It is further agreed, that should this Contract be terminated by the death of either party during either of said years, said Fayett Dye shall be paid prorata for the time he served during said year at the price fixed for said year. In Witness Whereof, the said Fayett Dye and C. E. Earle have hereunto set their hands & seals the day & year first above written.

Signed, sealed, delivered,& executed in in duplicate, in presence of

W. B. Adams	Fayett + Dye, his mark
J. J. Burch, ordinary	C. E. Earle

Georgia   }   [406]
Elbert County } This Indenture, made this the 4 day April 1901, between Charlotte Fleming, of said County, for & in behalf of her minor son Will Fleming, being of the age of 19 years, of the one part, & H. T. Hammond, of the County aforesaid, of the other part. Witnesseth: That the said Charlotte Fleming, as aforesaid, does by these presents bind out her said son Will Fleming, of said County, as Apprentice to said H. T. Hammond in the trade or craft of Farm Laborer or laborer upon the plantation of the said H. T. Hammond, to be taught the said craft or trade of Farm Laborer or laborer, & to live with, continue, & serve the said H. T. Hammond as an apprentice from the date hereof for & during the term of 2 years.

During all of which time, said Charlotte Fleming, as aforesaid, doth Covenant with the said H. T. Hammond that the said Will Fleming shall well & faithfully demean his self as such faithful Apprentice, observing fully the Command of the said H. T. Hammond, And in all things deporting & behaving his self as a faithful Apprentice to the said H. T. Hammond.

And for & in consideration of the service well and faithfully rendered by the said Will Fleming, of the first part, said H. T. Hammond, of the second part, doth Covenant, promise, & agree to instruct his said Apprentice, or otherwise Cause him to be well & faithfully instructed, in the said trade or craft of Farm Laborer or Laborer, & shall also allow, furnish, & provide his said Apprentice with meat

& drink and Clothing during the said term, & all other necessaries meet & proper, in sickness & in health, & shall also, at the expiration of the said term, allow & pay the said apprentice what is now allowed by the statute in such case made & provided.

Witness our hands & seals the day & year first before written.

Executed Before Us In Duplicate
R. M. Heard }
J. J. Burch, ordinary }

Charlotte + Fleming, her mark
H. T. Hammond

Georgia } [407]
Elbert County } This Indenture, made this the 4 day of April 1901, between Robert Rembert & Russel Fleming, of said County, for in behalf of them selves, being of the age of 35, 22 years, of the one part, & H. T. Hammond, of the County aforesaid, of the other part. Witnesseth: That the said Robert Rembert & Russel Fleming, as aforesaid, does by these presents bind out them selves, of said County, as Apprentices to said H. T. Hammond in the trade or Craft of Farm Laborers or Laborers upon the plantation of the said H. T. Hammond, to be taught the said craft or trade of Farm Laborers or Laborers, & to live with, continue, & serve the said H. T. Hammond as Apprentices from the date hereof for & during the term of 5 years.

During all of which time, said Robert Rembert & Russel Fleming, as aforesaid, doth covenant with the said H. T. Hammond that they, the said said Robert Rembert & Russel Fleming, shall well and faithfully demean them selves as such faithful Apprentices, observing fully the command of the said H. T. Hammond, & in all things deporting & behaving them selves as such faithful Apprentices to the said H. T. Hammond, neither revealing his secrets, nor at any time neglecting or leaving the business of the said H. T. Hammond.

And for & in consideration of the service well & faithfully rendered by the said Robert Rembert & Russel Fleming, of the first part, said H. T. Hammond, of the second part, doth Covenant, promise, & agree to instruct his Said Apprentices, or otherwise Cause them to be well & faithfully instructed, in the said trade or craft of Farm Laborers or Laborers, & shall also allow, furnish, & provide his said Apprentices with meat & drink & clothing during the said term, & all other necessaries meet & proper, in sickness & in health, & shall also, at the expiration of the said term, allow & pay the said Apprentices what is now allowed by the statute in such case made & provided.

Witness our hands & seals the day & year first before written.

Executed Before Us In Duplicate Robert + Rembert, his mark
R. M. Heard Russel + Fleming, his mark
J. J. Burch, ordinary H. T. Hammond

Georgia } [408]
Elbert County } This Indenture, made this the [blot] of April 1901, between Calvin [blot], of said County, for & in behalf of [blot] sons Mathew Brawner & Thomas Brawner, being of the age of 13, 15 years, of the one part, & McAlpin Arnold, of the County aforesaid, of the other part. Witnesseth: That the said Calvin Brawner, as aforesaid, does by these presents bind out his said sons Mathew & Thomas, of said County, as apprentices to said McAlpin Arnold in the trade or craft of Farm Laborer or Laborers upon the plantation of the said McAlpin Arnold, to be taught the said craft or trade of Farm Laborers or Laborers, & to live with, Continue, & serve the said McAlpin Arnold as apprentices from the first day of January 1902 for & during the term of 2 years.

During all of which time, said Calvin Brawner, as aforesaid, doth covenant with the said McAlpin Arnold that the said Mathew & Thos Brawner shall well & faithfully demean themselves as such faithful Apprentices, observing fully the Command of the said McAlpin Arnold, & in all things deporting & behaving them selves as faithful Apprentices to the said McAlpin Arnold. And for & in Consideration of the service well & faithfully rendered by the said Mathew Brawner & Thos Brawner, of the first part, said McAlpin Arnold, of the second part, doth Covenant, promise, & agree to instruct his said Apprentices, or otherwise Cause them to be well & faithfully instructed, in the said trade or craft of Farm Laborer or Laborers, & shall also allow, furnish, & provide his said Apprentices with meat & drink & clothing during the said term, & all other necessaries meet & proper, in sickness & in health, & shall also, at the expiration of the said term, allow & pay the said Apprentices what is now allowed by the statute in such case made and provided.

Witness our hands & seals the day & year first before written.

Executed Before Us In Duplicate
Abda Oglesby Calvin + Brawner, his mark
J. J. Burch, ordinary McAlpin Arnold

Georgia } [409]
Elbert County } This Indenture, made this the 6 day April 1901, between Eliza Ann Hudson, of said County, for & in behalf of her two minor Children Zanie

Hudson & Hattie Hudson, being of the age of 7, 10 years, of the one part, & Geº H. McLanahan, of the County aforesaid, of the other part. Witnesseth: That the said Eliza Ann Hudson, as aforesaid, does by these presents bind out her two minor children Zanie & Hattie, of said County aforesaid, of said County, as apprentices to said Geº H. McLanahan in the trade or craft of House Servant or as Laborers upon the plantation of the said Geº H. McLanahan as an Apprentices from the first January 1902 for and during the term of 5 years.

During all of which time, said Eliza Ann Hudson, as aforesaid, doth Covenant with the said Geº H. McLanahan that the said Zanie & Hattie Hudson shall well & faithfully demean them selves as such faithful Apprentices, observing fully the Command of the said Geº H. McLanahan, & in all things deporting & behaving them selves as faithful Apprentices to the said Geº H. McLanahan. And for & in consideration of the service well & faithfully rendered by the said Zanie & Hattie Hudson, of the first part, said Geº H. McLanahan, of the second part, doth Covenant, promise, & agree to instruct his said Apprentices, or otherwise cause them to be well & faithfully instructed, in the said trade or craft of House servant or Laborers, and shall also allow, furnish, and provide his said Apprentices with meat and drink and clothing during the said term, and all other necessaries meet and proper, in sickness and in health, and shall also, at the expiration of the said term, allow and pay the said Apprentices Forty Dollars.

Witness our hands & seals the day & year first before written.

Executed Before Us In Duplicate
James McIntosh   Eliza Ann + Hudson, her mark
J. J. Burch, Ordinary   G. H. McLanahan

Georgia   }   [410]
Elbert County } This Indenture, made this the 19 day of April 1901, between Will Blackwell, of said County, for & in behalf of him self, Will Blackwell, being of the age of 17 years, of the one part, & J. C. Brown, of the County aforesaid, of the other part. Witnesseth: That the said Will Blackwell, as aforesaid, does by these presents bind out him self, Will Blackwell, of said County, as Apprentice to said J. C. Brown in the trade or craft of Farm Laborer or Laborer upon the plantation of the said J. C. Brown, to be taught the said craft or trade of Farm Laborer or Laborer, & to live with, Continue, & serve the said J. C. Brown as an Apprentice from the date hereof for & during the term of 15 Months. During all of which time, said Will Blackwell, as aforesaid, doth covenant with the said J. C. Brown that the said Will Blackwell shall well & faithfully demean his self as such faithful Apprentice, observing fully the command of the said J. C. Brown or his

agent, & in all things deporting & behaving his self as a faithful Apprentice to the said J. C. Brown.

And for & in consideration of the service well & faithfully rendered by the said Will Blackwell, of the first part, said J. C. Brown, of the second part, doth Covenant, promise, & agree to instruct his said Apprentice, or otherwise Cause him to be well and faithfully instructed, in the said trade or craft of Farm Laborer, & shall also allow, furnish, & provide his said Apprentice with meat & drink during the said term, & shall also, at the expiration of the said term, allow & pay the said apprentice Five Dollars per month.

Witness our hands & seals the day & year first before written.

Executed Before Us In Duplicate
T. J. Brown   Will + Blackwell, his mark
J. J. Burch, ordinary   J. C. Brown

Georgia   }   [411]
Elbert County } This Indenture, Made this the 15 day of May 1901, between Gilbert Mattox, of said County, for & in behalf of his son Green Mattox, being of the age of 16 years, of the one part, and John T. Heard, of the County aforesaid, of the other part. Witnesseth: That the said Gilbert Mattox, as aforesaid, does by these presents bind out his said son Green Mattox, of said County, as Apprentice to said John T. Heard in the trade or craft of Farm Laborer or as Laborer upon the plantation of the said John T. Heard, to be taught the said Craft or trade of Farm Laborer or Laborer, and to live with, Continue, & serve the said John T. Heard as an apprentice from the date hereof for & during the term of 2 years. During all of which time, said Gilbert Mattox, as aforesaid, doth covenant with the said John T. Heard that the said Green Mattox shall well and faithfully demean his self as such faithful Apprentice, observing fully the Command of the said Jn° T. Heard, And in all things deporting & behaving his self as a faithful Apprentice to the said John T. Heard, neither revealing his secrets, nor at any time neglecting or leaving the business of the said John T. Heard. And for & in consideration of the service well & faithfully rendered by the said Green Mattox, of the first part, said John T. Heard, of the second part, doth Covenant, promise, & agree to instruct his said Apprentice, or otherwise Cause him to be well & faithfully instructed, in the said trade or craft of Farm Laborer or Laborer, & shall also allow, furnish, & provide his said Apprentice with meat & drink during the said term, & all other necessaries meet & proper, in sickness & in health, & shall also, at the expiration of the said term, allow & pay the say apprentice Forty Dollars.

Witness our hands & seals the day & year first before written.

Executed Before us In Duplicate
James McIntosh   Gilbert + Mattox, his mark
J. J. Burch, ordinary   Jn° T. Heard

Georgia   }   [412]
Elbert County } This Indenture, made this the 17 day of June 1901, between Robert McIntosh, of said County, for & in behalf of him self, Robert McIntosh, being of the age of 21 years, of the one part, & M. E. Maxwell, of the County aforesaid, of the other part. Witnesseth: That the said Robert McIntosh, as aforesaid, does by these presents bind out him self, Robert McIntosh, of Said County, as apprentice to said M. E. Maxwell in the trade or craft of Farm Laborer or laborer upon the plantation of the said M. E. Maxwell, to be taught the said craft or trade of Farm Laborer or Laborer, and to live with, Continue, & serve the said M. E. Maxwell as an Apprentice from the date hereof for & during the term of 2 years. During all of which time, said Robert McIntosh, as aforesaid, doth Covenant with the said M. E. Maxwell that the said Robert McIntosh shall well & faithfully demean his self as such faithful Apprentice, observing fully the Command of the said M. E. Maxwell, & in all things deporting & behaving his self as a faithful Apprentice to the said M. E. Maxwell, neither revealing his secrets, nor at any time neglecting or leaving the business of the said M. E. Maxwell. And for & in Consideration of the service well & faithfully rendered by the said Robert McIntosh, of the first part, said M. E. Maxwell, of the second part, doth covenant, promise, & agree to instruct his said apprentice, or otherwise Cause him to be well & faithfully instructed, in the said trade or craft of Farm Laborer or Laborer, and Shall also allow, furnish, & provide his said Apprentice with meat & drink & clothing during the said term, & all other necessaries meet & proper, in sickness & in health, & shall also, at the expiration of the said term, allow & pay the said apprentice One hundred Dollars.

Witness our hands & seals the day & year first before written.

Executed Before Us In Duplicate
Abda Oglesby   }   Robert McIntosh
J. J. Burch, Ordinary }   M. E. Maxwell

Georgia   }   [413]
Elbert County } This Indenture, made this the 17 day of June 1901, between Elijah McIntosh, of said County, for & in behalf of his son Albert McIntosh, being of the age of 15 years, of the one part, & M. E. Maxwell, of the County aforesaid,

of the other part. Witnesseth: That the said Elijah McIntosh, as aforesaid, does by these presents bind out his said son Albert, of Said County, as apprentice to said M. E. Maxwell in the trade or Craft of Farm Laborer or as Laborer upon the plantation of the said M. E. Maxwell, to be taught the said craft or trade of Farm Laborer or Laborer, & to live with, Continue, & serve the said M. E. Maxwell as an Apprentice from the date hereof for & during the term of 2 years. During all of which time, said Elijah McIntosh, as aforesaid, doth Covenant with the said M. E. Maxwell that the said Albert McIntosh shall well & faithfully demean his self as such faithful Apprentice, observing fully the Command of the said M. E. Maxwell, And in all things deporting & behaving his self as a faithful Apprentice to the said M. E. Maxwell, neither revealing his secrets, nor at any time neglecting or leaving the business of the said M. E. Maxwell. And for & in Consideration of the service well & faithfully rendered by the said Albert McIntosh, of the first part, said M. E. Maxwell, of the second part, doth covenant, promise, & agree to instruct his said apprentice, or otherwise Cause him to be well & faithfully instructed, in the said trade or craft of Farm Laborer or Laborer, and Shall allow, furnish, & provide his said Apprentice with meat & drink & clothing during the said term, & all other necessaries meet & proper, in sickness & in health, & shall also, at the expiration of the said term, allow & pay the said Apprentice One hundred dollars.

Witness our hands & Seals the day & year first before written.

Executed Before Us In Duplicate
Abda Oglesby   Elijah + McIntosh, his mark
J. J. Burch, ordinary   M. E. Maxwell

Georgia   }   [414]
Elbert County   } This Indenture, made this the 10th day of July 1901, between Mat Harper, of said County, for and in behalf of him self, being of the age of 25 years, of the one part, & J. A. Cauthen, of the County aforesaid, of the other part. Witnesseth: that the said Mat Harper, as aforesaid, does by these presents bind out him self, of Said County, as apprentice to said J. A. Cauthen in the trade or Craft of Farm Laborer or as Laborer upon the plantation of the said J. A. Cauthen, to be taught the said Craft or trade of Farm Laborer or Laborer, & to live with, Continue, & serve the said J. A. Cauthen as an Apprentice from the date hereof for and during the term of one year. During all of which time, said Mat Harper, as aforesaid, doth Covenant with the said J. A. Cauthen that he, the said Mat Harper, shall well & faithfully demean his self as such faithful Apprentice, observing fully the Command of the said J. A. Cauthen, & in all things deporting & behaving his self as a faithful Apprentice to the said J. A. Cauthen, Neither revealing his secrets,

nor at any time neglecting or leaving the business of the said J. A. Cauthen. And for & in Consideration of the service well & faithfully rendered by the said Mat Harper, of the first part, said J. A. Cauthen, of the second part, doth covenant, promise, & agree to instruct his said Apprentice, or otherwise Cause him to be well & faithfully instructed, in the said trade or craft of Farm Laborer or Laborer, and shall also allow, furnish, & provide his said Apprentice with meat and drink & clothing during the said term, & all other necessaries meet & proper, in sickness & in health, & shall also, at the expiration of the said term, allow & pay the said apprentice Eighty four Dollars. Witness our hands & seals the day & year first before written.

Executed Before Us In Duplicate
Abda Oglesby   Mat Harper
J. J. Burch, ordinary   J. A. Cauthen

Georgia } [415]
Elbert County } This Indenture, Made this 21st day of June 1901, between William Blackwell, of Elbert County, for & in behalf of him self, being of the age of 37 years, of the one part, & E. B. Higginbotham, of the County aforesaid, of the other part. Witnesseth: That the said William Blackwell, as aforesaid, doth by these presents bind out him self, of Elbert County, as Apprentice to said E. B. Higginbotham in the trade or Craft of Farm Laborer or as Laborer upon the plantation of the said E. B. Higginbotham, to be taught the said craft or trade of Farm Laborer or Laborer, & to live with, Continue, & serve the said E. B. Higginbotham as an apprentice from the date hereof for and during the term of two years. During all of which time, said William Blackwell, as aforesaid, doth covenant ~~promise & agree~~ with the said E. B. Higginbotham that the said William Blackwell shall well & faithfully demean his self as such faithful Apprentice, observing fully the Command of the said E. B. Higginbotham, & in all things deporting & behaving his self as a faithful Apprentice to the said E. B. Higginbotham, neither revealing their secrets, nor at any time neglecting or leaving the business of the said E. B. Higginbotham. And for & in consideration of the service well & faithfully rendered by the said William Blackwell, of the first part, said E. B. Higginbotham, of the second part, doth covenant, promise, & agree to instruct his said Apprentice, or otherwise cause him to be well & faithfully instructed, in the said trade or craft of Farm Laborer or Laborer, and shall also allow, furnish, & provide his said Apprentice with meat & drink & clothing during the said term, & all other necessaries meet & proper, in sickness & in health, & shall also, at the expiration of the said term, allow & pay the said Apprentice what is now allowed by the statute in such case made and provided.

Witness our hands & seals the day & year first before written.

Executed Before Us In duplicate
H. C. Wansley   William + Blackwell, his mark
C. T. Bond, J. P.   E. B. Higginbotham

Georgia   }   [416]
Elbert County } This Indenture, made this the 23 day of July 1901, between Burl Faust, of said County, for & in behalf of minor son James Faust, being of the age of 9 years, of the one part, & R. E. Hudgens, of the County aforesaid, of the other part. Witnesseth: That the said Burl Faust, as aforesaid, does by these presents bind out his said son James Faust, of Said County, as apprentice to said R. E. Hudgens in the trade or craft of Farm Laborer or Laborer upon the plantation of the said R. E. Hudgens, to be taught the said craft or trade of Farm Laborer or Laborer, and to live with, continue, & serve the said R. E. Hudgens as an apprentice from the date hereof for & during the term of 5 years. During all of which time, said Burl Faust, as aforesaid, doth Covenant with the said R. E. Hudgens that the said James Faust shall well & faithfully demean his self as such faithful apprentice, observing fully the Command of the said R. E. Hudgens, & in all things deporting & behaving his self as such a faithful Apprentice to the said R. E. Hudgens, neither revealing his secrets, nor at any time neglecting or leaving the business of the Said R. E. Hudgens. And for & in Consideration of the service well & faithfully rendered by the said James Faust, of the first part, said R. E. Hudgens, of the second part, doth covenant, promise, & agree to instruct his said Apprentice, or otherwise cause him to be well & faithfully instructed, in the said trade or craft of Farm Laborer or Laborer, & also to read the english language, & shall also allow, furnish, & provide his said apprentice with meat & drink & clothing during the said term, and all other necessaries meet & proper, in sickness & in health, & shall also, at the expiration of the said term, allow & pay the Said Apprentice what is now allowed by the statute in such case made & provided.

Witness our hands & seals the day & year first before written.

Executed Before us In Duplicate
Abda Oglesby   }   Burl + Faust, his mark
J. J. Burch, ordinary }   R. E. Hudgens

Georgia   }   [417]
Elbert County } This Indenture, made this the 12 day August 1901, between Ben H. Hicks, of said County, for & in behalf of him self & minor son Charley Hicks, being of the age of 14 years, of the one part, & Henry Wilkins, of the County

aforesaid, of the other part. Witnesseth: That the said Ben Hicks, as aforesaid, does by these presents bind out himself & his son Charley Hicks, of said County, as Apprentices to said Henry Wilkins in the trade or craft of farm Laborer or Laborer upon the plantation of the said Henry Wilkins, to be taught the said craft or trade of farm Laborers or Laborers, and to live with, Continue, & serve the said Henry Wilkins as Apprentices from the first of Jany 1902 for and during the term of one year. During all of which time, said Ben Hicks, as aforesaid, doth covenant with the said Henry Wilkins that the said Ben & Charley Hicks shall well & faithfully demean them selves as such faithful Apprentices, observing fully the command of the said Henry Wilkins, & in all things deporting & behaving them selves as faithful Apprentices to the said Henry Wilkins, neither revealing his secrets, nor at any time neglecting or leaving the business of the said Henry Wilkins.

And for & in consideration of the service well & faithfully rendered by the said Ben & Charley Hicks, of the first part, said Henry Wilkins, of the second part, doth covenant, promise, & agree to instruct his said Apprentices, or otherwise cause them to be well & faithfully instructed, in the said trade or Craft of farm Laborers, & shall also allow, furnish, & provide his said Apprentices with meat & drink & clothing during the said term, & all other necessaries meet & proper, in sickness & in health, & shall also, at the expiration of the said term, allow & pay the said Apprentice Charley Hicks forty Dollars.

Witness our hands & Seals the day & year first before written.

Executed Before Us in Duplicate
A. S. J. Stovall   Ben H. + Hicks, his mark
J. J. Burch, ordinary   Henry + Wilkins, his mark

Georgia   }   [418]
Elbert County } This Indenture, made this the 15th day of August 1901, between William Brawner, W. H. Blackwell, John Brawner, & Orn Moss, of said County, for & in behalf of them selves, being of the age of 21, 26, 60, 27 years, of the one part, & J. W. Cleveland, of the County aforesaid, of the other part. Witnesseth: That the said Wm Brawner, W. H. Blackwell, John Brawner, & Orn Moss, as aforesaid, does by these presents bind out them selves, of said County, as apprentices to said J. W. Cleveland in the trade or craft of Husbandry or as Laborers upon the plantation of the said J. W. Cleveland, to be taught the said craft or trade of Husbandry or Laborers, and to live with, Continue, & serve the said J. W. Cleveland as an Apprentice from the date hereof for & during the term of one year.

During all of which time, said Wm Blackwell, Brawner, Jn° Brawner, & Orn Moss, as aforesaid, doth Covenant with the said J. W. Cleveland that they, the said Blackwell & Brawner & John Brawner & Orn Moss, shall well & faithfully demean them selves as such faithful Apprentices, observing fully the Command of the said J. W. Cleveland, & in all things deporting & behaving them selves as faithful Apprentices to the said J. W. Cleveland, neither revealing his secrets, nor at any time neglecting or leaving the business of the said J. W. Cleveland. And for & in Consideration of the service well & faithfully rendered by the said Brawner, Blackwell, Brawner, & Orn Moss, of the first part, said J. W. Cleveland, of the second part, doth covenant, promise, & agree to instruct his said Apprentices, or otherwise Cause them to be well & faithfully instructed, in the said trade or craft of Husbandry or Laborers, and shall also allow, furnish, & provide his said Apprentices with meat & drink & clothing during the said term, & all other necessaries meet & proper, in Sickness & in health, & shall also, at the expiration of the said term, allow & pay the said apprentices $7.00 per month.

Witness our hands & seals the day & year first before written.

Executed Before Us In Duplicate
W. A. Shumate   }   Wm Brawner
J. J. Burch, ordinary }   W. H. Blackwell
                                       J. W. Cleveland
                                       Orn Moss

Georgia   }   [419]
Elbert County } This Indenture, Made this the 16 day of August 1901, between John Ray & Rena Ray & Mary Martin & son, of said County, for & in behalf of them selves, being of the age of 24, 21, & 34 years, of the one part, & S. S. Brown, of the County aforesaid, of the other part. Witnesseth: That the said John & Rena Ray & Mary Martin, as aforesaid, does by these presents bind out them selves, of said County, as Apprentices to said S. S. Brown in the trade or craft of Farm Laborers or as Laborers upon the plantation of the said S. S. Brown, to be taught the said Craft or trade of Farm Laborers or Laborers, & to live with, Continue, & serve the said S. S. Brown as Apprentices from the date hereof for & during the term of one year. During all of which time, said John & Rena Ray & Mary Martin, as aforesaid, doth Covenant with the said S. S. Brown that the said John & Rena Ray & Mary Martin shall well & faithfully demean them selves as such faithful Apprentices, observing fully the Command of the said S. S. Brown, & in all things deporting & behaving them selves as faithful Apprentices to the said S. S. Brown, neither revealing his secrets, nor at any time neglecting or leaving the business of the said S. S. Brown. And for & in Consideration of the service well & faithfully

rendered by the said John & Rena Ray & Mary Martin, of the first part, said S. S. Brown, of the Second part, doth Covenant, promise, & agree to instruct his said Apprentices, or otherwise Cause them to be well & faithfully instructed, in the said trade or Craft of Farm Laborers or Laborers, and shall also allow, furnish, & provide his said Apprentices with meat & drink & clothing during the said term, & all other necessaries meet & proper, in sickness & in health, & shall also, at the expiration of the said term, allow & pay the Said Apprentices Sixty Dollars.

Witness our hands & seals the day & year first before written.

Executed Before Us In Duplicate
L. H. Turner
J. J. Burch, ordinary

John + Ray, his mark
Rena + Ray, her mark
Mary + Martin, her mark
S. S. Brown

Georgia } [420]
Elbert County } This Indenture, Made this the 19 day of August 1901, between Harman Thompson, of said County, for & in behalf of his self and his minor sons William and George Thompson, being of the age of 15 & 12 years, of the one part, & John C. Hudgens, of the County aforesaid, of the other part. Witnesseth: That the said Harman Thompson, as aforesaid, does by these presents bind out him self and his two minor sons William & George Thompson, of said County, as apprentices to said John C. Hudgens in the trade or craft of Farm Laborers or Laborers upon the plantation of the said J. C. Hudgens, to be taught the said craft or trade of Farm Laborers or Laborers, & to live with, Continue, & serve the said J. C. Hudgens as apprentices from the first Jany 1902 for and during the term of one year.

During all of which time, said Harman Thompson, as aforesaid, doth covenant with the said J. C. Hudgens that the said Harman & William & George Thompson shall well & faithfully demean themselves as such faithful Apprentices, observing fully the command of the said J. C. Hudgens, And in all things deporting & behaving them selves as faithful apprentices to the said J. C. Hudgens, neither revealing his secrets, nor at any time neglecting or leaving the business of the said J. C. Hudgens. And for & in Consideration of the services well & faithfully rendered by the Said Harman, William, & George Thompson, of the first part, said J. C. Hudgens, of the second part, doth covenant, promise, & agree to instruct his said Apprentices, or otherwise cause them to be well & faithfully instructed, in the said trade or craft of Farm Laborers or as Laborers, & Shall also allow, furnish, & provide his said Apprentices with meat & drink & clothing during the said term, & all other necessaries meet and proper, in sickness & in health, & shall also, at the expiration of the said term, allow & pay said Apprentices One hundred & twenty five dollars.

Witness our hands & seals the day & year first before written.

Executed Before Us In Duplicate
George Haslett   Harman + Thompson, his mark
J. J. Burch, Ordinary   J. C. Hudgens

Georgia   }   [421]
Elbert County } This Indenture, made this the 19 day of August 1901, between Walter Oglesby, of said County, for & in behalf of him self, of the one part, and W. O. Jones, of the County aforesaid, of the other part. Witnesseth: That the said Oglesby aforesaid, does by these presents bind out himself, of said County, as Apprentice to said W. O. Jones in the trade or craft of Brick Making or as Laborer upon the Brick yard of the said W. O. Jones, to be taught the said craft or trade of Brick Making or Laborer, and to live with, continue, and serve the said W. O. Jones as an Apprentice from the date hereof for & during the term of 16 Months.

During all of which time, said Oglesby aforesaid doth covenant with the said W. O. Jones that the said Oglesby shall well & faithfully demean him self as such faithful Apprentice, observing fully the command of the said W. O. Jones, And in all things deporting & behaving him self as a faithful Apprentice to the said W. O. Jones, neither revealing his secrets, nor at any time neglecting or leaving the business of the said W. O. Jones. And for & in consideration of the service well & faithfully rendered by the said Oglesby, of the first part, said W. O. Jones, of the second part, doth covenant, promise, & agree to instruct his said Apprentice, or otherwise cause him to be well & faithfully instructed, in the said trade or craft of Brick Making or Laborer, And shall also allow, furnish, & provide his said Apprentice with meat & drink & clothing during the said term, & all other necessaries meet & proper, in sickness & in health, & shall also, at the expiration of the said term, allow & pay the said apprentice what is now allowed by the statute in such case made and provided. Erasures & interlineations before signing.

Witness our hands & seals the day & year first before written.

Executed In Duplicate Before Us
Sam L. Oliver   Walter + Oglesby, his mark
J. J. Burch, ordinary   W. O. Jones

Georgia } [422]
Elbert County } This Indenture, Made this the 19 day of August 1901, between Walter Oglesby, of said County, for & in behalf of his son B. J. Oglesby, being of the age of [blank] years, of the one part, and W. O. Jones, of the County aforesaid, of the other part. Witnesseth: That the said Walter Oglesby, as aforesaid, does by these presents bind out B. J. Oglesby, of said County, as Apprentice to said W. O. Jones in the trade or craft of Brick Making or as Laborer upon the Brick yard of the said W. O. Jones, to be taught the said Craft Craft or trade of Brick Making or Laborer, and to live with, Continue, and serve the said W. O. Jones as an apprentice from the date hereof for & during the term of his minority, the said B. J. Oglesby is 21 years old. During all of which time, said Walter Oglesby, as aforesaid, doth Covenant with the said W. O. Jones that the said B. J. Oglesby Shall well & faithfully demean him self as such faithful Apprentice, observing fully the command of the said W. O. Jones, And in all things deporting & behaving him self as a faithful Apprentice to the said W. O. Jones, neither revealing his secrets, nor at any time neglecting or leaving the business of the said W. O. Jones.

And for & in Consideration of the service well & faithfully rendered by the said B. J. Oglesby, of the first part, said W. O. Jones, of the second part, doth Covenant, promise, & agree to instruct him, said Apprentice, or otherwise cause him to be well and faithfully instructed, in the said trade or craft of Brick Making or Laborer, And also to read the English language, & shall also allow, furnish, & provide his said Apprentice with meat & drink & clothing during the said term, & all other necessaries meet & proper, in sickness & in health, & shall also, at the expiration of the said term, allow & pay the said Apprentice what is now allowed by the statute in such case made and provided. Interlineations & erasures before signing.

Witness our hands & seals the day & year first before written.

Executed Before Us In Duplicate
Sam L. Oliver   Walter + Oglesby, his mark
J. J. Burch, ordinary   W. O. Jones

Georgia } [423]
Elbert County } This Indenture, Made this the 19 day of August 1901, between Dan Goss, of said County, for and in behalf of him self, of the one part, and W. E. Wallis, of the County aforesaid, of the other part. Witnesseth: That the Dan Goss aforesaid, does by these presents bind out himself, of said County, as Apprentice to said W. E. Wallis in the trade or Craft of Brick Making or as Laborer upon the Brick yard of the said Wallis & W. O. Jones, to be taught the said craft or trade of Brick making or Laborer, and to live with, continue, and serve the said

W. E. Wallis as an Apprentice from the date hereof for & during the term of 2 years.

During all of which time, said Dan Goss aforesaid doth covenant with the said W. E. Wallis that the said Dan Goss shall well & faithfully demean himself as such faithful Apprentice, observing fully the Command of the said W. E. Wallis, and in all things deporting & behaving him self as a faithful Apprentice to the said W. E. Wallis, neither revealing his secrets, nor at any time neglecting or leaving the business of the said W. E. Wallis. And for & in Consideration of the service well & faithfully rendered by the said Dan Goss, of the first part, said W. E. Wallis, of the second part, doth covenant, promise, and agree to instruct his said Apprentice, or otherwise cause him to be well & faithfully instructed, in the said trade or Craft of Brick Making or Laborer, and shall also allow, furnish, & provide his said Apprentice with meat & drink & clothing during the said term, and all other necessaries meet & proper, in sickness and in health, and shall also, at the expiration of the said term, allow & pay the said apprentice what is now allowed by the statute in such case made & provided.

Interlined & Erased before signing.

Witness our hands & seals the day & year first before written.

Executed In Duplicate Before Us
Sam L. Oliver   }
J. J. Burch, Ordinary }

Dan + Goss, his mark
W. E. Wallis

Georgia   }   [424]
Elbert County } This Indenture, made this the 19 day of August 1901, between Will Morris himself, of said County, for and in behalf of him self, of the one part, & W. E. Wallis, of the County aforesaid, of the other part. Witnesseth: That the Morris aforesaid, does by these presents bind out himself, of said County, as apprentice to said Wallis in the trade or Craft of Brick Making or as Laborer upon the Brick yard of the said Wallis & W. O. Jones, to be taught the said Craft or trade of Brick Making or Laborer, and to live with, Continue, and serve the said Wallis as an Apprentice from the date hereof for & during the term of one year. During all of which time, said Morris aforesaid doth Covenant with the said Wallis that the said Morris shall well & faithfully demean himself as such faithful Apprentice, observing fully the command of the said Wallis, and in all things deporting & behaving him self as a faithful Apprentice to the said Wallis, neither revealing his secrets, nor at any time neglecting or leaving the business of the said Wallis. And for & in Consideration of the service well & faithfully rendered by

the said Morris, of the first part, said Wallis, of the second part, doth Covenant, promise, & agree to instruct him, said Apprentice, or otherwise Cause him to be well & faithfully instructed, in the said trade or craft of Brick Making or Laborer, & also to read the English language, & shall also allow, furnish, & provide him, said Apprentice, with meat & drink & clothing during the said term, & all other necessaries meet & proper, in sickness and in health, & shall also, at the expiration of the said term, allow & pay the said apprentice what is now allowed by the statute in such case made & provided.

Interlined before signing.

Witness our hands & seals the day & year first before written.

Executed Before Us in Duplicate
Sam L. Oliver   Will + Morris, his mark
J. J. Burch, Ord   W. E. Wallis

Georgia   }   [425]
Elbert County }   This Indenture, made this 26 day of August 1901, between Henry Bullard (father), of said County, for and in behalf of Jessie Bullard, his minor son, being of the age of seventeen years, of the one part, and Jnº W. McCalla, of the County aforesaid, of the other part. Witnesseth: That the said Henry Bullard, father as aforesaid, does by these presents bind out his said son Jessie Bullard, of said County, as Apprentice to said Jnº W. McCalla in the trade or craft of farm Laborer or as Laborer upon the plantation of the said Jnº W. McCalla, to be taught the said Craft or trade of farm laborer or Laborer, & to live with, County, and serve the said Jnº W. McCalla as an Apprentice from the date hereof for & during the term of four years.

During all of which time, said Henry Bullard, father as aforesaid, doth covenant with the said Jnº W. McCalla that the said Jessie Bullard shall well & faithfully demean him self as such faithful Apprentice, observing fully the command of the said Jnº W. McCalla, & in all things deporting & behaving him self as a faithful Apprentice to the said Jnº W. McCalla, neither revealing his secrets, nor at any time neglecting or leaving the business of the said Jnº W. McCalla. And for & in consideration of the service well & faithfully rendered by the said Jessie Bullard, of the first part, Said McCalla, of the second part, doth Covenant, promise, & agree to instruct his said Apprentice, or otherwise cause him to be well & faithfully instructed, in the said trade or craft of farm Laborer or laborer, & also to read the English language, and shall also allow, furnish, & provide his said Apprentice with meat & drink & clothing during the said term, & all other necessaries meet & proper, in sickness and in health, & shall also, at the expiration of the said term, allow & pay the said apprentice what is now allowed by the statute in such case made & provided.

Witness our hands & seals the day & year first before written.

Executed Before us in Duplicate
Witness
E. B. Starke   Henry + Bullard, his mark
M. H. Wyche   J. W. McCalla

Georgia   }   [426]
Elbert County } This Indenture, made this the 9th day of September 1901, between Anna Heard, of said County, for and in behalf of her minor children John Goss, Fannie Goss, & Oister Goss, being of the age of 16, 13, 5 years age, of the one part, and J. W. McCalla, of the County aforesaid, of the other part. Witnesseth: That the said Anna Heard, as aforesaid, does by these presents bind out John Goss, Fannie Goss, & Oyster Goss, of said County, as apprentices to said J. W. McCalla in the trade or craft of Farm Laborer or as Laborer upon the plantation of the said McCalla, to be taught the said craft or trade of Farming or Laborers, & to live with, Continue, and serve the McCalla as apprentices from the date hereof for & during the term of their minority.

During all of which time, said Anna Heard, as aforesaid, doth Covenant with the said McCalla that the above mentioned children shall well & faithfully demean them selves as such faithful Apprentices, observing fully the command of the said McCalla, and in all things deporting & behaving them selves as faithful apprentices to the said McCalla, neither revealing his secrets, nor at any time neglecting or leaving the business of the said J. W. McCalla. And for & in consideration of the service well & faithfully rendered by the said Anna Heard & children aforesaid, of first part, said J. W. McCalla, of the second part, doth covenant, promise, and agree to instruct his said Apprentices, or otherwise cause them to be well & faithfully instructed, in the said trade or Craft of Farm Laborers or laborers, and also to read the English language, & shall also allow, furnish, & provide his said Apprentices with meat & drink & clothing during the said term, & all other necessaries meet & proper, in sickness & in health, & shall also, at the expiration of the said term, allow & pay the said apprentices what is now allowed by the statute in such case made & provided.

Witness our hands & seals the day & year first before written.

Executed Before Us in Duplicate
B. F. Goss, J. P.   Anna + Heard, her mark
J. M. Dixon   Jn° W. McCalla

Georgia, Elbert County   [427]
This Indenture, made this 5th day of September 1901. between Yancy Hill, of the first part, for and T. J. Brownlee, of the second part, all of said County. Witness: That the said Hill, of the first part, for & in consideration of the promises & undertakings of the said Brownlee, of the second part, hereinafter set forth, does hereby bind himself to the said Brownlee for the period of Two years, begining Jan 1st 1902 and ending Dec 31st 1903, as an apprentice to learn the trade or craft of husbandry in all its details. He agrees to faithfully observe all the commands of the said Brownlee and render to said Brownlee an account of all absence on his part not occasioned by sickness. And the said Brownlee, of the second part, promises, agrees, and covenants to furnish said Yancy a sufficient supply of wholesome food & clothing such as is customary on a farm & to teach the said Yancy the trade of husbandry in all its details. Said Brownlee further agrees to furnish said Yancy a house to live in and to furnish him medical attention when sick and to pay Said Yancy fifty dollars at the expiration of his Apprenticeship. Witness our hands and seals the day and year first above written.

Signed, sealed, & delivered in presence of
J. D. Du Bose, J. P.   Yancy Hill
                                            T. J. Brownlee

Georgia   }   [428]
Elbert County   }   This Indenture, Made this the 11th day of October 1901, between Vina Hill, alias Blackwell, of said County, being of the age of 12 years of the one part, and W. A. Swift, of the County aforesaid, of the other part. Witnesseth: That the said Vina Hill, alias Blackwell, as aforesaid, does by these presents bind out her said son Allen aforesaid, of said County, as Apprentice to said W. A. Swift in the trade or craft of Farm Laborer or as Laborer upon the plantation of the said W. A. Swift, to be taught the said craft or trade of Farming or Laborer, & to live with, continue, & serve the said W. A. Swift as an Apprentice from the date hereof for & during the term of his minority. During all of which time, said Vina Hill, alias Blackwell, as aforesaid, doth covenant with the said W. A. Swift that the said Allen Hill, alias Blackwell, shall well & faithfully demean his self as such faithful Apprentice, observing fully the command of the said W. A. Swift, and in all things deporting & behaving his self as a faithful Apprentice

to said W. A. Swift, neither revealing his secrets, nor at any time neglecting or leaving the business of the said W. A. Swift.

And for and in consideration of the service well & faithfully rendered by the said Allen Hill, alias Blackwell, of first part, said W. A. Swift, of the second part, doth Covenant, promise, and agree to instruct his said Apprentice, or otherwise cause him to be well & faithfully instructed, in the said trade or craft of Farm Laborer or Laborer, and also to read the English language, & Shall also allow, furnish, & provide his said Apprentice with meat & drink & clothing during the said term, & all other necessaries meet & proper, in sickness & in health, & shall also, at the expiration of the said term, allow & pay the said Apprentice what is now allowed by the statute in such case made and provided.

Witness our hands & seals the day & year first before written.

Executed in Duplicate Before us
Abda Oglesby.   Vina + Hill, alias Blackwell, her mark
J. J. Burch, ordinary   W. A. Swift

Georgia   }   [429]
Elbert County }   This Indenture, Made this the 11th day of October 1901, between Vina Hill, alias Blackwell, of said County, for and in behalf of her minor children, to wit, Annie, Minnie, Lula, Jun, & Jim Hill, alias Blackwell, 20, 18, 16, 10, 5 years, of the one part, and Ja^s Y. Swift, of the County aforesaid, of the other part. Witnesseth: That the said Vina Hill, alias Blackwell, as aforesaid, does by these presents bind out her said children aforesaid, of said County, as Apprentices to said Ja^s Y. Swift in the trade or craft of Farm Laborers or as Laborers upon the plantation of the said Ja^s Y. Swift, to be taught the said craft or trade of Farm Laborers or Laborers, & to live with, continue, & serve the said Ja^s Y. Swift as an Apprentice from the 2nd day Jan 1902 for & during the term of 3 years. During all of which time, said Vina Hill, alias Blackwell, as aforesaid, doth covenant with the said Ja^s Y. Swift that the said Annie, Millie, Lula, Jun, & Jim Hill, alias Blackwell, shall well & faithfully demean them selves as such faithful Apprentices, observing fully the command of the said Ja^s Y. Swift, and in all things deporting & behaving them selves as faithful Apprentices to said Ja^s Y. Swift, neither revealing his secrets, nor at any time neglecting or leaving the business of the said Ja^s Y. Swift. And for and in consideration of the service well & faithfully rendered by the said Ana, Minnie, Lula, Jun, & Jim Hill, alias Blackwell, of first part, said Ja^s Y. Swift, of the second part, doth covenant, promise, & agree to instruct his said Apprentices, or otherwise cause them to be well and faithfully instructed, in the said trade or craft of Farm Laborers or

Laborers, and shall also allow, furnish, and provide his said Apprentices with meat & drink & clothing during the said term, and shall also, at the expiration of the said term, allow & pay the said Apprentices one Third part of all Crop raised & gathered by the said Apprentices. All Interlinations made before Signing.

Witness our hands and seals the day & year first before written.

Executed Before us In duplicate
Abda Oglesby. Vina + Hill, alias Blackwell, her mark
J. J. Burch, Ordinary Ja^s Y. Swift

Georgia } [430]
Elbert County } This Indenture, Made this the 21st day of October 1901, between Jordan Heard and Ada L. Oglesby, of said County. Witness: That the said Jordan Heard, in consideration of the promises & undertakings of the said Ada L. Oglesby hereinafter set forth, does hereby bind himself, family, wife, & their children to the said Ada L. Oglesby for the full term of 12 Months from the 1st day Jany 1902. And they hereby agree & contract with said Ada L. Oglesby to work faithfully under her direction, respect & obey all orders & Commands of the said Ada L. Oglesby with reference to the business hereinafter set forth, at all times demean them selfes orderly & soberly. & the said Heard & family further agree to account to the Said Ada L. Oglesby for all loss of time, except in case of temporary sickness (If such sickness should be of longer duration at any one time than six days) And the said Ada L. Oglesby, in consideration of the promises & undertakings of the said Jordan Heard & family, agree & Contract with said Heard & family to furnish them lodging. And further agree to pay said one half of all they make on my farm in said year. And said Ada L. Oglesby to furnish said Heard with Stock and feed to make said crop.

In Witness, the said Jordan Heard and the said Ada L. Oglesby have hereto respectively set their hands & seals the day & year first above written.

Executed in duplicate in presence of

Thos D. Biggs Jordan + Heard, his mark
J. M. Almond, J. P. Ada L. Oglesby

Georgia } [431]
Elbert County } This Indenture, Made this the 22nd day of October 1901, between Sam Deadwyler & Ada L. Oglesby, of said County. Witness: That the said Sam Deadwyler, in Consideration of the promises & undertakings of the said A. L. Oglesby hereinafter set forth, does hereby bind his son Jesse to the said A.

L. Oglesby for the full term of 12 months from the 1st Jany 1902. & does hereby agree & contract with said A. L. Oglesby for his son to work faithfully under her direction, respect & obey all orders & Commands of the said A. L. Oglesby with reference to the business hereinafter set forth, at all times demean himself orderly & soberly. And the said Sam for his son Jesse further agrees to account to the said A. L. Oglesby for all loss of time, except in case of temporary sickness. And the said Ada L. Oglesby, in consideration of the promises and undertakings of the Said Deadwyler, agrees & contracts with said Sam Deadwyler to furnish Jesse with board lodging. She further agrees to pay said Sam for Jesse on the 25th day of December next Seventy five Dollars. And she further agrees to teach the said Jesse the trade of Agriculture in all its details.

In Witness, the said Sam Deadwyler and the said Ada L. Oglesby have hereto respectively set their hands & seals the day & year first above written.

Executed in duplicate in presence of

Ge° B. Lumpkin	Sam + Deadwyler, his mark
Thos D. Biggs, J. P.	Ada L. Oglesby

Georgia　　　}　　　　　　　　　　　　　　　　　　　　　　　　[432]
Elbert County } This Indenture, Made this the 22nd day of October 1901, between Minerva Deadwyler and Ada L. Oglesby, of said County. Witness: That the said Minerva Deadwyler, in Consideration of the promises & undertakings of the said Minerva Deadwyler hereinafter set forth, does hereby bind herself to the said A. L. Oglesby for the full term of 12 months from the 1st Jan 1902. And she hereby agrees & Contracts with said A. L. Oglesby to work faithfully under her direction, respect and obey all orders and Commands of the said Ada L. Oglesby with reference to the business hereinafter set forth, at all times demean herself orderly and soberly. And the said Minerva further agrees to account to the Said Ada L. Oglesby for all loss of time, except in case of temporary sickness. And the said Ada L. Oglesby, in Consideration of the promises & undertakings of the said Minerva Deadwyler, agrees & contracts with said Minerva Deadwyler to furnish her with board lodging. She further agrees to pay said Minerva Deadwyler on the 25 day of Dec next Thirty five Dollars. And she further agrees to teach the said Minerva Deadwyler the trade in housework in all its details.

In Witness Whereof, the said Minerva Deadwyler and the said Ada L. Oglesby have hereto respectively set their hands & seals the day & year first above written.

Executed in duplicate in presence of

Ge° B. Lumkin
Thos D. Biggs, J. P.

Minerva + Deadwyler, her mark
Ada L. Oglesby

Georgia } [433]
Elbert County } This Indenture, made this the 7 day of October 1901, between George Jones, of said County, for and in behalf of himself, being of the age of 45 years, of the one part, and Ja^s Y. Swift, of the County aforesaid, of the other part. Witnesseth: That the said George Jones, as aforesaid, does by these presents bind out him self, of said County, As Apprentice to said Ja^s Y. Swift in the trade or craft of Farm Laborer or as Laborer upon the plantation of the said Ja^s Y. Swift, to be taught the said Craft or trade of Farm Laborer or Laborer, & to live with, continue, & serve the said Ja^s Y. Swift as an Apprentice from the date hereof for & during the term of 3 years. During all of which time, said George Jones, as aforesaid, doth covenant with the said Ja^s Y. Swift that he, the said George Jones, shall well & faithfully demean his self as such faithful Apprentice, observing fully the command of the said Ja^s Y. Swift, and in all things deporting & behaving him self as a faithful Apprentice to said Ja^s Y. Swift, neither revealing his secrets, nor at any time neglecting or leaving the business of the said Ja^s Y. Swift. And for & in Consideration of the service well & faithfully rendered by the said George Jones, of first part, said Ja^s Y. Swift, of the second part, doth Covenant, promise, & agree to instruct his said Apprentice, or otherwise Cause him to be well and faithfully instructed, in the said trade or craft of Farm Laborer or Laborer, and shall also allow, furnish, and provide his said Apprentice with meat & drink & clothing during the said term, and shall also, at the expiration of the said term, allow & pay the said Apprentice One Hundred dollars.

Witness our hands and seals the day & year first before written.

Executed Before us In duplicate
E. B. Heard.
W. M. Grogan, N. P. & Ex off J. P.

George + Jones, his mark
Ja^s Y. Swift

Georgia } [434]
Elbert County } This Indenture, made this the 17 day of October 1901, between Jane Cade, alias Eberhart, of said County, for and in behalf of her minor children, to wit, Henry, Corine, Ora, and Sallie Cade, alias Eberhart, being of the age of 13, 8, 6, 4 years, of the one part, and Ja^s Y. Swift, of the County aforesaid, of the other part. Witnesseth: That the said Jane Cade, alias Eberhart, as aforesaid, does by these presents bind out her said children aforesaid, of Said County, as Apprentices

to said Jaˢ Y. Swift in the trade or craft of Farm Laborers or as Laborers upon the plantation of the said Jaˢ Y. Swift, to be taught the said craft or trade of farm Laborers or Laborers, & to live with, continue, & serve the Said Jaˢ Y. Swift as apprentices from the date hereof for & during the term of 3 years.

During all of which time, said Jane Cade, alias Eberhart, as aforesaid, doth covenant with the said Jaˢ Y. Swift that the said Henry, Corine, Ora, Sallie Cade, alias Eberhart, shall well & faithfully demean them selves as such faithful Apprentices, observing fully the Command of the said Jaˢ Y. Swift, And in all things deporting & behaving them selves as faithful Apprentices to the said Jaˢ Y. Swift, neither revealing his secrets, nor at any time neglecting or leaving the business of the said Jaˢ Y. Swift. And for & in Consideration of the service well & faithfully rendered by the said Henry, Corine, Ora, & Sallie Cade, alias Eberhart, of first part, said Jaˢ Y. Swift, of the second part, doth Covenant, promise, & agree to instruct his said Apprentices, or otherwise cause them to be well and faithfully instructed, in the said trade or craft of Farm Laborers or Laborers, and shall also allow, furnish, and provide his said Apprentices with meat & drink & clothing during the said term, and shall also, at the expiration of the said term, allow & pay the Said Apprentices One hundred Dollars. all Interlinations made before Signing.

Witness our hands and seals the day & year first before written.

Executed Before Us In duplicate
E. B. Heard, F. H.   Jane + Cade, alias Eberhart, her mark
W. M. Grogan, N. P. & Ex off J. P.   Jaˢ Y. Swift

Georgia   }   [435]
Elbert County } This Indenture, Made this the 14 day of March 1901, between Matilda Nickols, of said County, for and in behalf of her minor son Henry Nickols, being of the age of 9 years, of the one part, and J. Y. Swift, of the County aforesaid, of the other part. Witnesseth: That the said Matilda Nichols, as aforesaid, does by these presents bind out her said son Henry Nickols, of Said County, as Apprentice to said J. Y. Swift in the trade or Craft of Farm Laborer or as Laborer upon the plantation of the said J. Y. Swift, to be taught the said Craft or trade of farm Laborer or Laborer, and to live with, Continue, & serve the said J. Y. Swift as an apprentice from the date hereof for & during the term of 12 years or his minority.

During all of which time, said Matilda Nickols, as aforesaid, doth Covenant with the said J. Y. Swift that the said Henry Nickols, Shall well & faithfully demean his self as such faithful Apprentice, observing fully the command of the said J. Y. Swift, and in all things deporting and behaving his self as a faithful Apprentice to the Said J. Y. Swift, neither revealing his Secrets, nor at any time neglecting or leaving the business of the said J. Y. Swift. And for and in consideration of the service he well & faithfully rendered by the said Henry Nickols, of the first part, said J. Y. Swift, of the second part, doth Covenant, promise, & agree to instruct his said Apprentice, or otherwise cause him to be well & faithfully instructed, in the said trade or craft of Farm Laborer or Laborer, & also to read the English Language, & shall also allow, furnish, and provide his Said Apprentice with meat & drink & clothing during the said term, & shall also, at the Expiration of the said term, allow & pay the said Apprentice what is now allowed by the statute in such case made & provided.

Witness our hands & seals the day & year first before written.

Executed Before Us In duplicate
T. R. White, N. P.   Matilda Nickols
J. G. Harden   Ja^s Y. Swift

Georgia   }   [436]
Elbert County } This Indenture, made this 2nd day of November 1901, between Asbury, Bud, Jim, Judge, & Charley Eberhart, of said County, for and in behalf of them selves, being of the age of 61, 21, 25, 23, 22 years, of the one part, & Ge^o A. Lunsford, of the County aforesaid, of the other part. Witnesseth: That the said Asbury, Bud, Jim, Judge, & Charley Eberhart, as aforesaid, does by these presents bind out them selves, of Said County in the trade or craft of Farm Laborers or as Laborers upon the plantation of the said Ge^o A. Lunsford, to be taught the said craft or trade of farm Laborers or Laborers, & to live with, Continue, & serve the said Ge^o A. Lunsford as apprentices from the 15 day of November 1902 for & during the term of one year. During all of which time, said Asbury, Bud, Jim, Judge, & Charley Eberhart, as aforesaid, doth covenant with the said Ge^o A. Lunsford that the said Asbury, Bud, Jim, Judge, & Charley Eberhart, shall well & faithfully demean them selves as such faithful Apprentices, observing fully the Command of the said Ge^o A. Lunsford, & in all things deporting & behaving them selves as faithful Apprentices to said Ge^o A. Lunsford, neither revealing his secrets, nor at any time neglecting or leaving the business of the said Ge^o A. Lunsford. And for & in consideration of the service well & faithfully rendered by the said Asbury, Bud, Jim, Judge, & Charley Eberhart, of first part, said Ge^o A. Lunsford, of the second part, doth Covenant, promise, & agree to instruct his said Apprentices, or otherwise cause them to be well & faithfully instructed, in the said trade or craft of Farm Laborers or Laborers, and shall also allow, furnish,

and provide his said Apprentices with meat & drink & clothing during the said term, & shall also, at the expiration of the said term, allow & pay the Said Apprentices One hundred & Twenty Five Dollars. Witness our hands and seals the day & year first before written.

Executed Before Us in Duplicate
J. A. + Brady, his mark
J. J. Burch, ordinary

Asbury + Eberhart, his mark
Bud + Eberhart, his mark
Jim + Eberhart, his mark
Judge + Eberhart, his mark
Charley + Eberhart, his mark
Ge° A. Lunsford

Georgia } [437]
Elbert County } This Indenture, made this the 9th day of November 1901, between Charley Eberhart, of said County, for and in behalf of him self, being of the age of 21 years, of the one part, and J. A. Beasley, of the County aforesaid, of the other part. Witnesseth: That the said Charley Eberhart, as aforesaid, does by these presents bind out him self, of Said County, as Apprentice to said J. A. Beasley in the trade or craft of Farm Laborer or as Laborer upon the plantation of the said J. A. Beasley, to be taught the said craft or trade of Farm Laborer or Laborer, & to live with, continue, & serve the said J. A. Beasley as an apprentice from the 15th day of January 1902 for & during the term of Ten & a half Months. During all of which time, said Charley Eberhart, as aforesaid, doth covenant with the said J. A. Beasley that he, the said Charley Eberhart, shall well & faithfully demean his self as Such faithful Apprentice, observing fully the Command of the said J. A. Beasley, & in all things deporting & behaving his self as a faithful Apprentice to the said J. A. Beasley, neither revealing his secrets, nor at any time neglecting or leaving the business of the said J. A. Beasley. And for & in Consideration of the service well & faithfully rendered by the said Charley Eberhart, of first part, said J. A. Beasley, of the second part, doth Covenant, promise, & agree to instruct his said Apprentice, or otherwise cause him to be well and faithfully instructed, in the said trade or craft of Farm Laborer or Laborer, shall also allow, furnish, and provide his Said Apprentice with meat & drink & clothing during the said term, & shall also, at the expiration of the said term, allow & pay the Said Apprentice Seven & $^{00}/_{100}$ per Month. Said J. A. Beasley also agrees to buy Said Charley Eberhart [illegible]

Witness our hands & seals the day & year first before written.

Executed Before us In duplicate
George Haslett   }   Charley + Eberhart, his mark
J. J. Burch, ordinary }   J. A. + Beasley, his mark

Georgia   }   [438]
Elbert County }   This Indenture, made this the 10th day of November 1901, between Jim Eberhart, of Said County, for and in behalf of him self, he being of the age of 23 years, of the one part, & J. A. Beasley, of the County aforesaid, of the other part. Witnesseth: That the Jim Eberhart, as aforesaid, does by these presents bind out him Self, of said County, as Apprentice to said J. A. Beasley in the trade or craft of Farm Laborer or as Laborer upon the plantation of the Said J. A. Beasley, to be taught the said craft or trade of Farm Laborer or Laborer, & to live with, Continue, & serve the said J. A. Beasley as an apprentice from the first day of Jany 1902 during the term of Twelve months. During all of which time, said Jim Eberhart, as aforesaid, doth Covenant with the said J. A. Beasley that he, the said Jim Eberhart, shall well & faithfully demean his self as such faithful Apprentice, observing fully the Command of the said J. A. Beasley, and in all things deporting & behaving him self as a faithful Apprentice to the said J. A. Beasley, neither revealing his secrets, nor at any time neglecting or leaving the business of the said J. A. Beasley.

And for & in Consideration of the service well & faithfully rendered by the said Jim Eberhart, of first part, said J. A. Beasley, of the second part, doth Covenant, promise, & agree to instruct his said Apprentice, or otherwise Cause him to be well & faithfully instructed, in the said trade or craft of Farm Laborer or Laborer, And shall also allow, furnish, and provide his said Apprentice with meat & drink & clothing during the said term, & shall also, at the expiration of the said term, allow & pay the said Apprentice Seventy Dollars.

Witness our hand & seal the day & year first before written.

Executed Before us in duplicate
E. B. Norman   Jim + Eberhart, his mark
J. J. Burch, ordinary   J. A. + Beasley, his mark

Georgia   }   [439]
Elbert County }   This Indenture, made this the 14th day of November 1901, between Judge Eberhart, of Said County, for and in behalf of him self, he being of the age of 23 years, of the one part, & J. A. Beasley, of the County aforesaid, of the other part. Witnesseth: That the Judge Eberhart, as aforesaid, does by these

presents bind out him self as Apprentice to said J. A. Beasley in the trade or craft of Farm Laborer or as Laborer upon the plantation of the Said J. A. Beasley, to be taught the said craft or trade of Farm Laborer or Laborer, & to live with, Continue, & serve the said J. A. Beasley as an apprentice from the first day of Jany 1902 during the term of Six & a half months. (6½) During all of which time, said Judge Eberhart, as aforesaid, doth Covenant with the said J. A. Beasley that he, the said Judge Eberhart, shall well & faithfully demean his self as such faithful Apprentice, observing fully the Command of the said J. A. Beasley, & in all things deporting & behaving his self as a faithful Apprentice to the said J. A. Beasley, neither revealing his secrets, nor at any time neglecting or leaving the business of the said J. A. Beasley. And for & in consideration of the service well & faithfully rendered by the said Judge Eberhart, of first part, Said J. A. Beasley, of the second part, doth Covenant, promise, & agree to instruct his said Apprentice, or otherwise Cause him to be well & faithfully instructed, in the said trade or craft of Farm Laborer or Laborer, & shall also allow, furnish, and provide his said Apprentice with meat & drink & clothing during the said term, & shall also, at the expiration of the said term, allow & pay the said Apprentice Forty Seven Dollars. ($47.00) Witness our hand & seal the day & year first before written.

Executed Before us In duplicate
L. M. Vickery   Jim + Eberhart, his mark
J. J. Burch, ordinary   J. A. + Beasley, his mark

Georgia   }   [440]
Elbert County } This Indenture, made this the 10th day of November 1901, between Will Wilkins, of Elbert County, for and in behalf of Will Wilkins, being of the age of 24 years, of the one part, & L. H. Hunt, of the County aforesaid, of the other part. Witnesseth: That the Will Wilkins does by these presents bind out him self, of Elbert County, as Apprentice to said L. H. Hunt in the trade or Craft of Farm Laborer or as Laborer upon the plantation of the said L. H. Hunt, to be taught the said craft or trade of Farm Laborer or as Laborer, And to live with, Continue, & serve the said L. H. Hunt as an Apprentice from the date hereof during the term of 4 years.

During all of which time, said Will Wilkins, as aforesaid, doth Covenant with the said L. H. Hunt that the said Will Wilkins shall well & faithfully demean him self as such faithful Apprentice, observing fully the Commands of the said L. H. Hunt, and in all things deporting & behaving him self as a faithful Apprentice to the said L. H. Hunt, neither revealing his secrets, nor at any time neglecting or leaving the business of the said L. H. Hunt.

And for & in Consideration of the service well & faithfully rendered by the said Will Wilkins, of first part, said L. H. Hunt, of the second part, doth covenant, promise, & agree to instruct his said Apprentice, or otherwise Cause him to be well & faithfully instructed, in the said trade or craft of Farm Laborer or laborer, and also to read the English language, & shall also allow, furnish, and provide his said Apprentice with meat & drink & clothing during the said term, & shall also, at the expiration of the said term, allow & pay the said apprentice what is now allowed by the statute in such case made & provided.

Witness our hand & seal the day & year first before written.

Executed Before Us in duplicate
J. W. Black   Will + Wilkins, his mark
J. H. Seymore, N. P.   L. H. Hunt

Georgia   }   [441]
Elbert County } This Indenture, made this the 10th day of November 1901, between Bishop Christian & William Christian, of Said County, for and in behalf of them selves, they being of the age of 22, 50 years, of the one part, & J. W. Seymore, of the County aforesaid, of the other part. Witnesseth: That the said Bishop & William Christian, as aforesaid, does by these presents bind out them selves as Apprentices to said J. W. Seymore in the trade or craft of Farm Labor or as Laborers upon the plantation of the Said J. W. Seymore, to be taught the said Craft or trade of Farm Labor or Laborers, & to live with, Continue, & serve the said J. W. Seymore as Apprentices from the date hereof for & during the term of 2 years.

During all of which time, said Bishop & William Christian, as aforesaid, doth covenant with the said J. W. Seymore that they, the said Bishop & William Christian, shall well & faithfully demean them selves as such faithful Apprentices, observing fully the command of the said J. W. Seymore, and in all things deporting & behaving them selves as faithful Apprentices to the said J. W. Seymore, neither revealing his secrets, nor at any time neglecting or leaving the business of the said J. W. Seymore.

And for & in consideration of the service well & faithfully rendered by the said Bishop Christian & William Christian, of first part, said J. W. Seymore, of the second part, doth covenant, promise, & agree to instruct his said Apprentices, or otherwise cause them to be well & faithfully instructed, in the said trade or craft of Farm Labor or Laborers, And Shall also allow, furnish, and provide his said Apprentices with meat & drink & clothing during the said term, & all other necessaries meet & proper, in sickness & in health, & shall also, at the expiration of the said term, allow & pay the said Apprentices one hundred & four Dollars.

Witness our hands & seals the day & year first before written.

Executed Before us in duplicate
W. H. + Thompson, his mark }   Bishop + Christian, his mark
J. J. Burch, ordinary   } W^m + Christian, his mark
                               }   J. W. Seymore

Georgia   }   [442]
Elbert County } This Indenture, Made this the 20th day of November 1901, between James Peyton, of Said County, for & in behalf of his minor daughter Hellen Peyton, being of the age of one year, of the one part, and Sue Jett Smith, of the County aforesaid, of the other. Witnesseth: That the James Peyton, as aforesaid, does by these presents bind out his said daughter Hellen Peyton, of said County, as apprentice to said Sue Jett Smith in the trade or Craft of House Servant or as Laborer upon the plantation of the said Sue Jett Smith, to be taught the said craft or trade of House Servant or Laborer, & to live with, continue, & serve the said Sue Jett Smith as an Apprentice from the date hereof for & during the time of her minority. During all of which time, said James Peyton, as aforesaid, doth Covenant with the said Sue Jett Smith that the said Hellen Peyton shall well & faithfully demean her self as such faithful apprentice, observing fully the command of the said Sue Jett Smith, and in all things deporting & behaving her self as a faithful Apprentice to the said Sue Jett Smith, neither revealing his secrets, nor at any time neglecting or leaving the business of the said Sue Jett Smith. And for & in consideration of the service well & faithfully rendered by the said Hellen Peyton, of first part, said Sue Jett Smith, of the second part, doth Covenant, promise, & agree to instruct her Apprentice, or otherwise cause her to be well & faithfully instructed, in the said trade or craft of House servant or Laborer, and also to read the English language, & shall also allow, furnish, and provide her said apprentice with meat & drink & clothing during the said term, & shall also, at the expiration of the said term, allow & pay the said Apprentice what is now allowed by the statute in such case made & provided.

Witness our hand & seal the day & year first before written.

Executed Before us in duplicate
Abda Oglesby   }   Ja^s Peyton
J. J. Burch, ordinary }   Sue Jett Smith

Georgia   }   [443]
Elbert County }   This Indenture, Made this the 25th day of November 1901, between D. M. McClain, of Said County, for & in behalf of his minor sons Loyed, Dillard, & Jordan McClain, being of the age of 17, 15, 11 years, of the one part, & Jnº C. Brown, of the County aforesaid, of the other part. Witnesseth: That the said D. M. McClain, as aforesaid, does by these presents bind out his said sons Loyed, Dillard, & Jordan McClain, of said County, as apprentices to said Jnº C. Brown in the trade or Craft of Farm Laborers or as Laborers upon the plantation of the said Jnº C. Brown, to be taught the said craft or trade of Farm Labor or Laborers, & to live with, continue, & serve the said Jnº C. Brown as apprentices from the date hereof for & during the term of their minority. During all of which time, said D. M. McClain, as aforesaid, doth covenant with the said Jnº C. Brown that the said Loyed, Dillard, & Jordan McClain shall well & faithfully demean them selves as such faithful Apprentices, observing fully the Command of the said Jnº C. Brown, or his agent, & in all things deporting & behaving them selves as faithful Apprentices to the said Jnº C. Brow, or agent, neither revealing his secrets, nor at any time neglecting or leaving the business of the said Jnº C. Brown. And for & in consideration of the service well & faithfully rendered by the said Loyed, Dillard, & Jordan McClain, of the first part, said Jnº C. Brown, of the second part, doth Covenant, promise, & agree to instruct his said Apprentices, or otherwise cause them to be well & faithfully instructed, in the said trade or Craft of Farm Labor or Laborers, & also to read the English language, & shall also allow, furnish, and provide his said Apprentices with meat & drink & clothing during the said term, & shall also, at the expiration of the said term, allow & pay the said Apprentices what is now allowed by the statute in such case made and provided.

Witness our hands & seals the day & year first before written.

Executed Before Us In duplicate
L. C. Edwards   D. M. McClain
J. J. Burch, Ordinary   Jnº C. Brown

Georgia   }   [444]
Elbert County }   This Indenture, made this the 25 day of November 1901, between Jim Roebuck, of said County, for & in behalf of him self, he being of the age of 21 years, of the one part, & J. A. Beasley, of County aforesaid, of the other part. Witnesseth: That the said Jim Roebuck, as aforesaid, does by these presents bind out him self, of said County, as apprentice to said J. A. Beasley in the trade or craft of Farm Labor or Laborer upon the plantation of the said J. A. Beasley, to be taught the said craft or trade of Farm Labor or Laborer, & to live with, continue, & serve the said J. A. Beasley as an apprentice from the first day January 1902

for and during the term of one year. During all of which time, said Jim Roebuck, as aforesaid, doth covenant with the said J. A. Beasley that he, the said Jim Roebuck, shall well & faithfully demean his self as such faithful Apprentice to the said J. A. Beasley, observing fully the Command of the said J. A. Beasley, and in all things deporting & behaving his self as a faithful Apprentice to the said J. A. Beasley, neither revealing his secrets, nor at any time neglecting or leaving the business of the said J. A. Beasley. And for & in consideration of the service well & faithfully rendered by the said Jim Roebuck, of the first part, said J. A. Beasley, of the second part, doth covenant, promise, and agree to instruct his said apprentice, or otherwise Cause him to be well & faithfully instructed, in the said trade or craft of Farm Labor or Laborer, And shall also allow, furnish, and provide his said Apprentice with meat & drink & clothing during the said term, & shall also, at the expiration of the said term, allow & pay the said Apprentice Eighty Dollars.

Witness our hands & seals the day & year first before written.

Executed Before us In duplicate
Abda Oglesby   }   Jim + Roebuck, his mark
J. J. Burch, ordinary }   J. A. + Beasley, his mark

Georgia   }   [445]
Elbert County } This Indenture, made this the 27 day of November 1901, between John Haley, of said County, for & in behalf of him self & his minor daughters Ada & Vohamie Haley, being of the age of 40, 13, 10 years, of the one part, & J. G. Seymore, of County aforesaid, of the other part. Witnesseth: That the said John Haley, as aforesaid, does by these presents bind out him self & his minor daughters Ada & Vohamie Haley, of County, as apprentices to said J. G. Seymore in the trade or craft of Farm Labor or as Laborers upon the plantation of the said J. G. Seymore, to be taught the said craft or trade of Farm Labor or Laborer, & to live with, continue, & serve the said J. G. Seymore as Apprentices from the first day January 1902 for & during the term of one year. During all of which time, said John Haley, as aforesaid, doth covenant with the said J. G. Seymore that he, the said John Haley & Ada & Vohamie Haley shall well & faithfully demean them selves as such faithful Apprentices, observing fully the Command of the said J. G. Seymore, and in all things deporting & behaving them selves as faithful Apprentices to the said J. G. Seymore, neither revealing his secrets, nor at any time neglecting or leaving the business of the said J. G. Seymore. And for & in consideration of the service well & faithfully rendered by the said John Haley & Ada & Vohamie Haley, of the first part, said J. G. Seymore, of the second part, doth Covenant, promise, & agree to instruct his said

Apprentices, or otherwise cause them to be well & faithfully instructed, in the said trade or craft of Farm Labor or Laborers, & shall also allow, furnish, & provide his said Apprentices with meat & drink & clothing during the said term, & shall also, at the expiration of the said term, allow & pay the said Apprentices One half of all Crops raised and gathered by said John, Ada, & Vohamie Haley afore Said.

All interlination made before signing.

Witness our Hands & seals the day & year first above written.

Executed Before Us In duplicate
T. D. + Shaw, his mark }   John + Haley, his mark
J. J. Burch, ordinary   }   J. G. Seymore

Georgia   }   [446]
Elbert County } This Indenture, made this the 29th day of November 1901, between Anderson Starke, of said County, for & in behalf of him self & his minor son Robert Starke, of said County, for & in behalf of him self, being of the age of 50, 10 years, of the one part, & D. L. McLanahan, of the County aforesaid, of the other part. Witnesseth: that the said Anderson Starke, as aforesaid, does by these presents bind out him self & his son Robert Starke, of said County, as apprentices to said D. L. McLanahan in the trade or craft of Farm Labor or as Laborers upon the plantation of the said D. L. McLanahan, to be taught the said craft or trade of Farm Labor or Laborers, & to live with, continue, & serve the D. L. McLanahan as apprentices from the date hereof for and during the term of 5 years. During all of which time, said Anderson Starke, as aforesaid, doth covenant with the said D. L. McLanahan that he, the said Anderson & Robert Starke, shall well and faithfully demean them selves as such faithful Apprentices, observing fully the command of the said D. L. McLanahan, & in all things deporting & behaving them selves as faithful Apprentices to the said D. L. McLanahan, neither revealing his secrets, nor at any time neglecting or leaving the business of the said D. L. McLanahan. And for & in Consideration of the service well & faithfully rendered by the said Anderson & Robert Starke, of the first part, said D. L. McLanahan, of the second part, doth covenant, promise, and agree to instruct his said Apprentices, or otherwise Cause them to be well and faithfully instructed, in the said trade or craft of Farm Labor or Laborers, and shall also allow, furnish, & provide his said Apprentices with meat and drink & clothing during the said term, & shall also, at the expiration of the said term, allow & pay the said Apprentices

Sixty Dollars per year, Forty Dollars already having been paid. Witness our hand & seal the day & year first before written.

Executed Before Us In duplicate
T. J. Brown   Anderson + Starke, his mark
J. J. Burch, ordinary   D. L. McLanahan

[The Ordinary wrote the following notation vertically in the left margin of the page.]

This Contract is this day Cancelled between the parties and So Ordered marked in the Record Jany 11th 1904.

J. J. Burch, Ord

Georgia   }   [447]
Elbert County } This Indenture, made this the 30th day of November 1901, between Bud Eberhart, of said County, for and in behalf of him self, being of the age of 27 years, of the one part, & W. C. Gunter, of the County aforesaid, of the other part. Witnesseth: That the said Bud Eberhart, as aforesaid, does by these presents bind out him self, of said County, as apprentice to said W. C. Gunter in the trade or craft of Farm Labor or as Laborer upon the plantation of the said W. C. Gunter, to be taught the said Craft or trade of Farm Labor or Laborer, & to live with, Continue, & serve the said W. C. Gunter as an apprentice from the first day of January 1902 for and during the term of two years. During all of which time, said Bud Eberhart, as aforesaid, doth Covenant with the said W. C. Gunter that he, the said Bud Eberhart, shall well & faithfully demean his self as such faithful Apprentice, observing fully the Command of the said W. C. Gunter, and in all things deporting & behaving his self as a faithful Apprentice to the said W. C. Gunter, neither revealing his secrets, nor at any time neglecting or leaving the business of the said W. C. Gunter. And for & in consideration of the service well & faithfully rendered by the said Bud Eberhart, of the first part, said W. C. Gunter, of the second part, doth covenant, promise, & agree to instruct his said Apprentice, or otherwise Cause him to be well & faithfully instructed, in the said trade or craft of Farm Labor or Laborer, and shall also allow, furnish, & provide his said Apprentice with meat & drink & clothing during the said term, & shall also, at the expiration of the said term, allow & pay the said Apprentice Seventy Eight Dollars per year.

Witness our hands & Seals the day & year first before written.

Executed Before Us In duplicate
J. N. Wall
J. J. Burch, ordinary

Bud + Eberhart, his mark
W. C. Gunter

Georgia   }   [448]
Elbert County } This Indenture, made this the 30th day of November 1901, between Eugene Tate & Reuben Clement, of said County, for and in behalf of them selves, being of the age of 21, 44 years, of the one part, & L. G. Fambrough, of County aforesaid, of the other part. Witnesseth: That the said Eugene Tate & Reuben Clement, as aforesaid, does by these presents bind out them selves, of said County, as apprentices to said L. G. Fambrough in the trade or Craft of Farm Labor or Laborers upon the plantation of the said L. G. Fambrough, to be taught the said craft or trade of Farm Labor or Laborers, & to live with, continue, & serve the said L. G. Fambrough as apprentices from the date hereof for and during the term of Thirteen months.

During all of which time, said Eugene Tate & Reuben Clement, as aforesaid, doth covenant with the said L. G. Fambrough that the said Eugene Tate & Reuben Clement, shall well & faithfully demean them selves as such faithful Apprentices, observing fully the Command of the said L. G. Fambrough, & in all things deporting & behaving them selves as faithful Apprentices to the said L. G. Fambrough, neither revealing his secrets, nor at any time neglecting or leaving the business of the said L. G. Fambrough. And for & in Consideration of the service well & faithfully rendered by the said Eugene Tate & Reuben Clement, of first part, said L. G. Fambrough, of the second part, doth covenant, promise, & agree to instruct his said Apprentices, or otherwise cause them to be well & faithfully instructed, in the said trade or craft of Farm Labor or Laborers, and shall also allow, furnish, & provide his said Apprentices with meat & drink & clothing during the said term, & shall also, at the expiration of the said term, allow & pay the said Apprentices One half of all Crop raised & gathered by them, they agreeing to pay for all clothing & rations furnished by said L. G. Fambrough. All interlinations made before signing.

Witness our hands & seals the day & year first before written.

Executed Before Us In duplicate
C. P. Harris
J. J. Burch, ordinary

Eugene + Tate, his mark
Reuben + Clement, his mark
L. G. Fambrough

Georgia   }   [449]
Elbert County } This Indenture, Made this the 6th day of December 1901, between Mary Jones, of said County, for and in behalf of her minor son Willie Jones, being of the age of 13 years, of the one part, & S. S. Brewer, of the County aforesaid, of the other part. Witnesseth: That the said Mary Jones, as aforesaid, does by these presents bind out her said son Willie Jones of as apprentice to said S. S. Brewer in the trade or craft of Farm Labor or as Laborer upon the plantation of the said S. S. Brewer, to be taught the said craft or trade of Farm labor or Laborers, & to live with, continue, & serve the said S. S. Brewer as apprentices from the first day January 1903 for and during the term of 3 years.

During all of which time, said Mary Jones, as aforesaid, doth Covenant with the said S. S. Brewer that the said Willie Jones shall well & faithfully demean his self as such faithful apprentice, observing fully the command of the said S. S. Brewer, & in all things deporting and behaving his self as a faithful Apprentice to the said S. S. Brewer, neither revealing his secrets, nor at any time neglecting or leaving the business of the said S. S. Brewer. And for & in consideration of the service well & faithfully rendered by the said Willie Jones, of first part, said S. S. Brewer, of the second part, doth Covenant, promise, and agree to instruct his said Apprentice, or otherwise Cause him to be well & faithfully instructed, in the said trade or craft of Farm Labor or Laborer, and also allow, furnish, & provide his said Apprentice with meat & drink & clothing during the said term, & shall also, at the expiration of the said term, allow & pay the said Apprentice Ninety Six & $^{65}/_{100}$ Dollars.

Witness our hands & seals the day & year first before written.

Executed Before Us In Duplicate
James McIntosh   Mary + Jones, her mark
J. J. Burch, ordinary   S. S. Brewer

Georgia   }   [450]
Elbert County } This Indenture, made this the 16th day of December 1901, between Ben Joe Heard, of said County, for & in behalf of his minor sons Gete Heard & John Henry Heard, being of the age of 19, 15 years, of the one part, and J. W. Norman, of the County aforesaid, of the other part. Witnesseth: That the said Ben Joe Heard, as aforesaid, does by these presents bind out said sons Gete & John Henry, of said County, as Apprentices to said J. W. Norman in the trade or Craft of Farm Labor or as Laborers upon the plantation of the said J. W. Norman, to be taught the said Craft or trade of Farm Labor or Laborers, and to live with, Continue, & serve the said J. W. Norman as Apprentices from the first

day of January 1902 for & during the term of one year. During all of which time, said Ben Joe Heard, as aforesaid, doth covenant with the said J. W. Norman that the said Gete & John Henry Heard shall well & faithfully demean them selves as such faithful Apprentices, observing fully the command of the said J. W. Norman, & in all things deporting & behaving them selves as faithful Apprentices to the said J. W. Norman, neither revealing his secrets, nor at any time neglecting or leaving the business of the said J. W. Norman. And for & in consideration of the service well & faithfully rendered by the said Gete & John Henry Heard, of the first part, said J. W. Norman, of the second part, doth Covenant, promise, & agree to instruct his said Apprentices, or otherwise Cause them to be well & faithfully instructed, in the said trade or craft of Farm Labor or Laborers, and shall also allow, furnish, & provide his said Apprentices with meat & drink during the said term, and shall also, at the expiration of the said term, allow & pay the said Apprentices Eleven Dollars per month.

Witness our hands & seals the day & year first before written.

Executed Before Us In Duplicate
J. H. Stovall   Ben Joe + Heard, his mark
J. J. Burch, ordinary   J. W. Norman

Georgia   }   [451]
Elbert County } This Indenture, made this the 17th December 1901, between Harve Hawkins & Isabella Hawkins his wife, of said County, for and in behalf of them selves & their minor children George Hawkins & Ann Hawkins, being of the age of 36, 32, 12, 7 years, of the one part, & C. T. Bond, of the County aforesaid, of the other part. Witnesseth: That the said Harve Hawkins & Isabella Hawkins, as aforesaid, does by these presents bind out them selves & their minor children George & Ann Hawkins, of said County, as Apprentices to said C. T. Bond in the trade or Craft of Farm Labor or as Laborers upon the plantation of the said C. T. Bond, to be taught the said craft or trade of Farm Labor or Laborers, & to live with, continue, & serve the said C. T. Bond as apprentices from the first of January 1902 for & during the term of 2 years.

During all of which time, said Harve Hawkins & Isabella Hawkins, as aforesaid, doth Covenant with the said C. T. Bond that they, the said Harve & Isabella, George & Ann Hawkins, shall well & faithfully demean them selves as such faithful Apprentices, observing fully the command of the said C. T. Bond, & in all things deporting & behaving them selves as faithful Apprentices to the said C. T. Bond, neither revealing his secrets, nor at any time neglecting or leaving the business of the said C. T. Bond. And for & in Consideration of the service well

& faithfully rendered by the said Harve, Isabella, George, & Ann Hawkins, of the first part, said C. T. Bond, of the second part, doth Covenant, promise, & agree to instruct his said Apprentices, or otherwise cause them to be well & faithfully instructed, in the said trade or craft of Farm Labor or Laborers, & shall also allow, furnish, & provide his said Apprentices with meat & drink & clothing during the said term, & shall also, at the expiration of the said term, allow & pay the Said Apprentices Sixty five Dollars.

Witness our hands & seals the day & year first before written.

Executed Before Us In duplicate
M. E. Fortson
J. J. Burch, ordinary

Harve + Hawkins, his mark
Isabella + Hawkins, her mark
C. T. Bond

Georgia   }   [452]
Elbert County } This Indenture, made this the 17 Day December 1901, between Eugene Brawner, of said County, for and in behalf of him self, Eugene Brawner, being of the age of 30 years, of the one part, & A. S. J. Stovall, of the County of Madison, of the other part. Witnesseth: That the said Eugene Browner, as afores Said, does by these presents bind out himself, Eugene Browner, of County, as Apprentice to said A. S. J. Stovall in the trade or craft of Teamster or Laborer upon the plantation of the said A. S. J. Stovall, to be taught the said craft or trade of Teamster or Laborer, & to live with, Continue, & serve the said A. S. J. Stovall as an Apprentice from the date hereof for & during the term of one year.

During all of which time, said Eugene Brawner, as aforesaid, doth covenant with the said A. S. J. Stovall that the said Eugene Brawner shall well & faithfully demean him self as such faithful Apprentice, observing fully the Command of the said A. S. J. Stovall, & in all things deporting & behaving him Self as a faithful Apprentice to the said A. S. J. Stovall, neither revealing his secrets, nor at any time neglecting or leaving the business of the said A. S. J. Stovall. And for & in Consideration of the service well & faithfully rendered by the said Eugene Brawner, of first part, said A. S. J. Stovall, of the second part, doth covenant, promise, & agree to instruct his Said Apprentice, or otherwise cause him to be well & faithfully instructed, in the said trade or craft of Teamster or Laborer, & shall also allow, furnish, & provide his said Apprentice with meat & drink & clothing during the said term, & shall also, at the expiration of the said term, allow & pay the said Apprentice One Hundred & twenty Dollars.

Witness our hands & seals the day & year first before written.

Executed Before Us In Duplicate
H. W. Cauthen   Eugene + Brawner, his mark
J. J. Burch, Ordinary   A. S. J. Stovall

Georgia   }   [453]
Elbert County } This Indenture, made this the 23rd day of December 1901, between Fayette Dye, of said County, for & in behalf of him self, he being of the age of 21 years, of the one part, & J. A. Cauthen, of the County aforesaid, of the other part. Witnesseth: That the said Fayette Dye, as aforesaid, does by these presents bind out him self, of said County, as apprentice to said J. A. Cauthen in the trade or Craft of Farm Labor or as Laborer upon the plantation of the said J. A. Cauthen, to be taught the said Craft or trade of Farm Labor or laborer, & to live with, Continue, & serve the said J. A. Cauthen as an apprentice from the date hereof until the first day of August 1902.

During all of which time, said Fayette Dye, as aforesaid, doth Covenant with the said J. A. Cauthen that the said Fayette Dye, shall well & faithfully demean his Self as such faithful Apprentice, observing fully the command of the said J. A. Cauthen, & in all things deporting & behaving his self as a faithful Apprentice to the said J. A. Cauthen, neither revealing his secrets, nor at any time neglecting or leaving the business of the said J. A. Cauthen. And for & in Consideration of the service well & faithfully rendered by the said Fayette Dye, of the first part, said J. A. Cauthen, of the second part, doth Covenant, promise, & agree to instruct his said Apprentice, or otherwise cause him to be well & faithfully instructed, in the said trade or craft of Farm Labor or laborer, and shall also allow, furnish, & provide his said Apprentice with meat & drink during the said term, and shall also, at the expiration of the said term, allow & pay the Said Apprentice Forty Dollars expiration of the said term allow & pay the said.

Witness our hands & seals the day & year first before written. Executed Before Us in Duplicate

W. H. Kerlin   Fayette + Dye, his mark
J. J. Burch, ordinary   J. A. Cauthen

Georgia   }   [454]
Elbert County } This Indenture, Made this the 24 day of December 1901, between Luther Herndon, of said County, for & in behalf of him self, being of the age of 28 years, of the one part, & J. J. McLanahan, of the County aforesaid, of the other part.

Witnesseth: That the said Luther Herndon, as aforesaid, does by these presents bind out him self, of said County, as apprentice to said J. J. McLanahan in the trade or craft of Farm Labor or as Laborer upon the plantation of the said J. J. McLanahan, to be taught the said Craft or trade of Farm Labor or Laborer, & to live with, Continue, & serve the said J. J. McLanahan as an Apprentice from the first day of Jany 1902 for & during the term of seven months.

During all of Which time, said Luther Herndon, as aforesaid, doth covenant with the said J. J. McLanahan that the said Luther Herndon shall well & faithfully demean his self as such faithful Apprentice, observing fully the command of the said J. J. McLanahan, and in all things deporting & behaving his self as a faithful Apprentice to the said J. J. McLanahan, neither revealing his secrets, nor at any time neglecting or leaving the business of the said J. J. McLanahan.

And for & in Consideration of the service well & faithfully rendered by the said Luther Herndon, of the first part, said J. J. McLanahan, of the second part, doth Covenant, promise, & agree to instruct his said Apprentice, or otherwise Cause him to be well & faithfully instructed, in the said trade or craft of Farm Labor or Laborer, & shall also allow, furnish, and provide his said Apprentice with meat & drink during the said term, and shall also, at the expiration of said term, allow & pay the said Apprentice Forty Five Dollars.

Witness our hands & seals the day & year first before written.

Executed Before Us In Duplicate
J. H. Maxwell   Luther + Herndon, his mark
J. J. Burch, ordinary   J. J. McLanahan

Georgia   }   [455]
Elbert County }   This Indenture, Made this the 24 day of December 1901, between Jep Brawner, of said County, for & in behalf of his minor son Henry Brawner, being of the age of 15 years, of the one part, and W. H. Downer, of the County aforesaid, of the other part. Witnesseth: That the said Jep Brawner, as aforesaid, does by these presents bind out his said son Henry Brawner, of said County, as Apprentice to said W. H. Downer in the trade or craft of Farm Labor or as Laborer upon the plantation of the said W. H. Downer, to be taught the said craft or trade of Farm Labor or Laborer, & to live with, Continue, & serve the said W. H. Downer as an Apprentice from the first day of January 1902 for and during the term of his minority.

During all of which time, said Jep Brawner, as aforesaid, doth Covenant with the said W. H. Downer that the said Henry Brawner, shall well & faithfully demean his Self as such faithful Apprentice, observing fully the Command of the said W. H. Downer, & in all things deporting & behaving his self as a faithful Apprentice to the said W. H. Downer, neither revealing his secrets, nor at any time neglecting or leaving the business of the said W. H. Downer.

And for & in consideration of the service well & faithfully rendered by the said Henry Brawner, of the first part, said W. H. Downer, of the second part, doth Covenant, promise, & agree to instruct his Said Apprentice, or otherwise Cause him to be well & faithfully instructed, in the said trade or craft of Farm Labor or Laborer, & also to read the English language, & shall also allow, furnish, & provide his said Apprentice with meat & drink & clothing during the said term, & all other necessaries meet & proper, in sickness & in health, & shall also, at the expiration of the said term, allow & pay the said Apprentice what is now allowed by the statute in such case made & provided.

Witness our hands & Seals the day & year first before written.

Executed Before Us In Duplicate
J. H. Stovall   Jep + Brawner, his mark
J. J. Burch, ordinary   W. H. Downer

Georgia   }   [456]
Elbert County } This Indenture, made this the 2nd day of January 1902, between Ransom Fortson, of said County, for & in behalf of his son Ira Fortson, being of the age of 14 years, of the one part, & Tom Fortson, of the County aforesaid, of the other part. Witnesseth: That the said Ransom Fortson, as aforesaid, does by these presents bind out his said son Ira Fortson, of said County, as Apprentice to said Tom Fortson in the trade or craft of Farm Labor or as Laborer upon the plantation of the said Tom Fortson, to be taught the said craft or trade of Farm Labor or Laborer, & to live with, Continue, & serve the said Tom Fortson as an Apprentice from the date hereof for & during the term of one year. During all of which time, said Ransom Fortson, as aforesaid, doth Covenant with the said Tom Fortson that the said Ira Fortson, shall well & faithfully demean his self as such faithful Apprentice, observing fully the command of the said Tom Fortson, & in all things deporting & behaving his self as a faithful Apprentice to the said Tom Fortson, neither revealing his secrets, nor at any time neglecting or leaving the business of the said Tom Fortson. And for & in consideration of the service well & faithfully rendered by the said Ira Fortson, of the first part, said Tom Fortson, of the second part, doth Covenant, promise, & agree to instruct his said Apprentice, or otherwise Cause him to be well & faithfully instructed, in the said trade or craft of Farm Labor or Laborer, & shall also allow, furnish, & provide his

said Apprentice with meat & drink & clothing during the said term, & all other necessaries meet & proper, in sickness & in health, & shall also, at the expiration of the said term, allow & pay the said Apprentice Twenty Five Dollars.

Witness our hands & seals the day & year first before written.

Executed Before Us In Duplicate
I. D. Glove   Ransom + Fortson, his mark
J. J. Burch, ordinary   T. F. Fortson

Georgia   }   [457]
Elbert County } This Indenture, Made this the 12th day of November 1901, between Lindsey Gray, of said County, for & in behalf of Alexander Gray, being of the age of 15 years, of the one part, And J. W. McCalla, of the County aforesaid, of the other part. Witnesseth: That the said Lindsey Gray, as aforesaid, does by these presents bind out Elexander Gray, of said County, as Apprentice to said J. W. McCalla in the trade or craft of Farmer or as Laborer upon the plantation of the said J. W. McCalla, to be taught the said craft or trade of Farming or Laborer, & to live with, Continue, and Serve the said J. W. McCalla as an Apprentice from the date hereof for & during the term of Six years.

During all of which time, said Linsy Gray, as aforesaid, doth Covenant with the said J. W. McCalla that the said Elexander Gray, shall well and faithfully demean his self as such faithful Apprentice, observing fully the Command of the said J. W. McCalla, and in all things deporting & behaving him self as a faithful Apprentice to the said J. W. McCalla, neither revealing his secrets, nor at any time neglecting or leaving the business of the said J. W. McCalla. And for & in Consideration of the service well & faithfully rendered by the said Elexander Gray, of the first part, said J. W. McCalla, of the second part, doth covenant, promise, & agree to instruct his said apprentice, or otherwise Cause him to be well & faithfully instructed, in the said trade or craft of Farming or Laborer, & also to read the English language, & shall also allow, furnish, & provide his said Apprentice with meat & drink & clothing during the said term, & all other necessaries meet & proper, in sickness & in health, & shall also, at the expiration of the said term, allow & pay the said Apprentice what is now allowed by the statute in such Case made & provided.

Witness our hands & seals the day & year first before written.

Executed Before Us
J. M. Dixon   Lindsy + Gray, his mark
B. F. Goss, J. P.   Jn° W. McCalla

Georgia } [458]
Elbert County } This Indenture, made this the 11th day of January 1902, between Sam White, of said County, for & in behalf of his son Solomon White, being of the age of 13 years, of the one part, & Ge° P. Norman, of the County aforesaid, of the other part. Witnesseth: That the said Sam White, as aforesaid, does by these presents bind out Solomon White, of Said County, as Apprentice to said Ge° P. Norman in the trade or Craft of Husbandry or as Laborer upon the plantation of the said Ge° P. Norman, And to live with, Continue, & serve the said Ge° P. Norman as an apprentice from the date hereof for & during the term of 2¼ years begining Jany 1st 1902 & ending April 1st 1904. During all of which time, Sam White, as aforesaid, doth Covenant with the said Ge° P. Norman that the said Solomon White, shall well & faithfully demean him self as such faithful apprentice, observing fully the command of the said Ge° P. Norman, & in all things deporting & behaving him self as a faithful Apprentice to the said Ge° P. Norman, neither revealing his secrets, nor at any time neglecting or leaving the business of the Said Ge° P. Norman. And for & in Consideration of the service well & faithfully rendered by the said Solomon White, of the first part, said Ge° P. Norman, of the second part, doth Covenant, promise, & agree to instruct his said Apprentice, or otherwise cause him to be well & faithfully instructed, in the said trade or craft of Husbandry or Laborer, & shall also allow, furnish, & provide him, said Apprentice, with meat & drink & clothing house & bed during the said term, & all other necessaries meet & proper, in sickness & in health, said Norman to allow said Solomon to visit Sam White every 1st & 3 Sunday. Witness our hands & seals the day & year first before written.

Executed Before us In duplicate
C. T. Bond   Sam + White, his mark
J. J. Burch, ordinary   G. P. Norman

Georgia } [459]
Elbert County } This Indenture, made this the 11th day of Jany 1902, between Henry White & Mamie White, of said County, for & in behalf of Rosa White 7 years old, Ida White 5 years, & Henry White being of the age of 3 years, of the one part, & C. T. Bond, of the County aforesaid, of the other part. Witnesseth: That the Henry & Mamie, as aforesaid, does by these presents bind out Rosa, Ida, & Henry, of said County, as Apprentices to said C. T. Bond in the trade or craft of Husbandry or as Laborer upon the plantation of the said C. T. Bond, to be taught the said craft or trade of Husbandry or Laborer, & to live with, Continue, & serve the said C. T. Bond as Apprentices from the date hereof for & during the term of their minority. During all of which time, said Henry & Mamie, as aforesaid, doth

covenant with the said C. T. Bond that the said Apprentices shall well & faithfully demean them selves as such faithful apprentices, observing fully the command of the said C. T. Bond, & in all things deporting & behaving them selves as faithful Apprentices to the said C. T. Bond, neither revealing his secrets, nor at any time neglecting or leaving the business of the said C. T. Bond. And for & in consideration of the service well & faithfully rendered by the said Apprentices, of the first part, said C. T. Bond, of the second part, doth Covenant, promise, & agree to instruct them, said Apprentices, or otherwise Cause them to be well & faithfully instructed, in the said trade or craft of Husbandry or Laborers, & also to read the English language, & shall also allow, furnish, & provide them, said Apprentices, with meat & drink & clothing during the said term, & all other necessaries meet & proper, in sickness & in health, & shall also, at the expiration of the said term, allow & pay the said Apprentices what is now allowed by the statute in such case made & provided.

Witness our hands & seals the day & year first before written.

Executed Before us In duplicate
Sam L. Oliver   Mamie + White, her mark
J. J. Burch, ordinary   Henry + White. his mark
                                           C. T. Bond

Georgia   }   [460]
Elbert County } This Indenture, made this the 11th Day Jan 1902, between Henry & Mamie White, of said County, for & in behalf of them selves, of the one part, & C. T. Bond, of the County aforesaid, of the other part. Witnesseth: That the said Henry & Mamie White, as aforesaid, does by these presents bind out them selves, of said County, as Apprentices to said C. T. Bond in the trade or craft of Husbandry or Laborers upon the plantation of the said C. T. Bond, to be taught the said craft or trade of Husbandry or Laborers, & to live with, Continue, & serve the said C. T. Bond as Apprentices from the date hereof for & during the term of 5 years.

During all of which time, said Henry & Mamie, as aforesaid, doth covenant with the said C. T. Bond that the said Henry & Mamie shall well & faithfully demean them selves as such faithful apprentices, observing fully the command of the said C. T. Bond, & in all things deporting and behaving them selves as faithful apprentices to the said C. T. Bond, neither revealing his secrets, nor at any time neglecting or leaving the business of the said C. T. Bond. And for & in consideration of the service well & faithfully rendered by the said Henry & Mamie, of the first part, said C. T. Bond, of the second part, doth Covenant, promise, & agree to instruct them, said Apprentices, or otherwise Cause them to be well & faithfully instructed, in the said trade or craft of Husbandry or Laborer, & Shall also allow, furnish, & provide them, said Apprentices, with meat & drink & clothing during the said term, & And all other necessaries meet & proper, in sickness & in health, & shall also, at the expiration of the said term, allow & pay the said Apprentices what is now allowed by the statute in such case made & provided.

Witness our hands & seals the day & year first before written.

Executed Before Us In duplicate
Sam L. Oliver   }   Mamie + White, her mark
J. J. Burch, ordinary }   Henry + White. his mark
                                          C. T. Bond

Georgia   }   [461]
Elbert County } This Indenture, Made this the 13 day of January 1902, Between Ben Hicks, of said County, for & in behalf of him self & his minor sons Charley, John, & Jim Hicks, being of the age of 13, 12, & 5 years, of the one part, & L. M. Brown, of the County aforesaid, of the other part. Witnesseth: That the said Ben Hicks, as aforesaid, does by these presents bind out him self & his sons, Charley, John, & Jim Hicks, of said County, as Apprentices to said L. M. Brown in the trade or Craft of Husbandry or as Laborers upon the plantation of the said L. M. Brown, to be taught the said Craft or trade of Husbandry or Laborers, & to live with, Continue, & serve the said L. M. Brown as Apprentices from the date hereof for & during the term of 2 years.

During all of which time, said Ben Hicks, as aforesaid, doth covenant with the said L. M. Brown that the said Ben, Charley, John, & Jim Hicks shall well & faithfully demean them selves as such faithful apprentices, observing fully the Command of the said L. M. Brown, & in all things deporting & behaving them selves as faithful Apprentices to the said L. M. Brown, neither revealing his secrets, nor at any time neglecting or leaving the business of the said L. M. Brown. And for & in consideration of the service well & faithfully rendered by the said Ben, Charley, John, & Jim Hicks, of the first part, said L. M. Brown, of the second part, doth Covenant, promise, & agree to instruct them, said Apprentices, or otherwise Cause them to be well & faithfully instructed, in the said trade or craft of Husbandry or Laborers, and shall also allow, furnish, & provide his said Apprentices with meat & drink & clothing during the said term, and shall also, at the expiration of the said term, allow & pay the said Apprentices One half of all

Crops raised & gathered by them. They also paying for all advances for food & clothing out of their part of the crop.

Witness our hands & seals the day & year first before written.

Interlination made before signing.

Executed Before Us In Duplicate
J. B. Jones, Sr Ben + Hicks, his mark
J. J. Burch, ordinary   L. M. Brown

Georgia   }   [462]
Elbert County } This Indenture, made this the 14 day of January 1902, between Jack Deadwyler, of said County, for and in behalf of him self, being of the age of 21 years, of the one part, & A. S. Oliver, of the County aforesaid, of the other part. Witnesseth: That the said Jack Deadwyler, as aforesaid, does by these presents bind out himself, Jack Deadwyler, of said County, as Apprentice to said A. S. Oliver in the trade or Craft of Farm Labor or as Laborer upon the plantation of the said A. S. Oliver, to be taught the said Craft or trade of Farm Labor or Laborer, & to live with, Continue, & serve the said A. S. Oliver as an Apprentice from the date hereof for & during the term of five years. During all of which time, said Jack Deadwyler, as aforesaid, doth covenant with the said A. S. Oliver that the said Jack Deadwyler shall well & faithfully demean him self as such faithful Apprentice, observing fully the Command of the said A. S. Oliver, And in all things deporting & behaving him self as a faithful Apprentice to the said A. S. Oliver, neither revealing his secrets, nor at any time neglecting or leaving the business of the said C. T. Bond. And for & in consideration of the service well & faithfully rendered by the said Jack Deadwyler, of the first part, said A. S. Oliver, of the second part, doth Covenant, promise, & agree to instruct him, said Apprentice, or otherwise Cause him to be well and faithfully instructed, in the said trade or craft of farm Labor or Laborer, And also to read the English language, & shall also allow, furnish, & provide him, said Apprentice, with meat & drink & clothing during the said term, & all other necessaries meet and proper, in sickness & in health, and shall also, at the expiration of the said term, allow & pay the said Apprentice what is now allowed by the Statute in such case made & provided.

Witness our hands & seals the day & year first before Written.

Executed Before Us In duplicate
N. M. Motes   Jack + Deadwyler, his mark
J. J. Burch, ordinary   A. S. Oliver

[The Ordinary wrote the following notation vertically in the left margin of the page.]

This contract Cancelled by order of A. S. Oliver.

           J. J. Burch, ordinary, Jany 3, 1903

Georgia   }   [463]
Elbert County } This Indenture, Made this the 15th day of January 1902, between Sam White, Father of said County, for and in behalf of his son George White, being of the age of 15 years, of the one part, & W. M. Cauthen, of the County aforesaid, of the other part. Witnesseth: That the said Sam White, Father as aforesaid, does by these presents bind out his said son George, of said County, as Apprentice to said W. M. Cauthen in the trade or craft of Husbandry or Laborer upon the plantation of the said W. M. Cauthen, to be taught the said Craft or trade of Husbandry or Laborer, & to live with, Continue, & serve the said W. M. Cauthen as an apprentice from the date hereof for & during the term of 11½ months. During all of which time, said Sam White, father as aforesaid, doth Covenant with the said W. M. Cauthen that the said George White shall well & faithfully demean his self as such faithful Apprentice, observing fully the Command of the said W. M. Cauthen, & in all things deporting and behaving his self as a faithful Apprentice to the said W. M. Cauthen, neither revealing his secrets, nor at any time neglecting or leaving the business of the said W. M. Cauthen. And for & in Consideration of the service well & faithfully rendered by the said George White, of the first part, said W. M. Cauthen, of the second part, doth Covenant, promise, & agree to instruct his said Apprentice, or otherwise Cause him to be well & faithfully instructed, in the said trade or craft of Husbandry or Laborer, And shall also allow, furnish, & provide him, said Apprentice, with meat and drink During the said term, & shall also, at the expire of the said term, allow & pay the said Apprentice Sixty Nine Dollars. Said Sam White Father agrees & promises to make good all lost time by Said George White.

Interlination before Signing.

Witness our hands & seals the day & year first before Written.

Executed Before Us In duplicate
George Haslett   Sam + White, his mark
J. J. Burch, ordinary   W. M. Cauthen

Georgia   }   [464]
Elbert County } This Indenture, made this the 16 Jany 1902, between Sid

Rucker, of said County, for and in behalf of him self, he being of the age of 21 years, of the one part. Witnesseth: That the said Sid Rucker, as aforesaid, does by these presents bind out him self as apprentice to said W. S. Gaines in the trade or craft of Husbandry or as Laborer upon the plantation of the said W. S. Gaines, to be taught the said craft or trade of Husbandry or Laborer, & to live with, Continue, & serve the said W. S. Gaines as an Apprentice from the date hereof for and during the term of one year. During all of which time, Said Sid Rucker, as aforesaid, doth Covenant with the said W. S. Gaines that the said Sid Rucker shall well & faithfully demean his self as such faithful apprentice, observing fully the command of the said W. S. Gaines, & in all things deporting and behaving him self as a faithful apprentice to the said W. S. Gaines, neither revealing his secrets, nor at any time neglecting or leaving the business of the said W. S. Gaines. And for & in consideration of the service well & faithfully rendered by the said Sid Rucker, of the first part, said W. S. Gaines, of the second part, doth covenant, promise, & agree to instruct him, said Apprentice, or otherwise Cause him to be well & faithfully instructed, in the said trade or craft of Husbandry or Laborer, & Shall also allow, furnish, & provide him, said Apprentice, with meat & drink & clothing during the said term, & shall also, at the Expiration of the said term, allow & pay the said Apprentice Seven dollars per month, said Apprentice paying for his said clothing out of said wages.

All Interlinations before Signing.

Witness our hands & seals the day & year first before Written.

Executed Before Us In duplicate
P. M. Hawes   Sid + Rucker, his mark
J. J. Burch, ordinary   W. S. Gaines

Georgia   }   [465]
Elbert County   } This Indenture, made this the 11th day January 1902, between Lige McIntosh, of said County, for and in behalf of Peter McIntosh & Albert McIntosh, being of the age of 18, 16 years, of the one part, and A. S. Oliver, of the County aforesaid, of the other part. Witnesseth: That the said Lige McIntosh, as aforesaid, does by these presents bind out Peter McIntosh & Albert McIntosh, of said County, as Apprentice to said A. S. Oliver in the trade or craft of farm Labor or Laborer upon the plantation of the said A. S. Oliver, to be taught the said craft or trade of farm Labor or Laborer, & to live with, continue, & serve the said A. S. Oliver as an Apprentice from the date hereof for & during the term of five years.

During all of which time, said Lige McIntosh, as aforesaid, doth Covenant with the said A. S. Oliver that the said Peter McIntosh & Albert McIntosh shall well & faithfully demean themselves as such faithful Apprentice, observing fully the command of the said A. S. Oliver, & in all things deporting & behaving them selves as faithful Apprentices to the said A. S. Oliver, neither revealing his secrets, nor at any time neglecting or leaving the business of the said C. T. Bond.

And for & in Consideration of the service well & faithfully rendered by the said Peter & Albert, of the first part, said A. S. Oliver, of the second part, doth covenant, promise, & agree to instruct them, said Apprentices, or otherwise cause them to be well & faithfully instructed, in the said trade or craft of Farm Labor or Laborer, & also to read the English language, & shall also allow, furnish, & provide them, said Apprentices, with meat & drink and clothing during the said term, & all other necessaries meet & proper, in sickness & in health, & shall also, at the expiration of the said term, allow & pay the said Apprentices what is now allowed by the statute in such case made & provided.

Witness our hands & seals the day & year first before Written.

Executed Before Us In duplicate
James McIntosh   Lige + McIntosh, his mark
J. J. Burch, ordinary   A. S. Oliver

[The Ordinary wrote the following notation diagonally across the foregoing indenture.]

This contract is hereby Cancelled by order of A. S. Oliver This Febr^y 21st 1903.

J. J. Burch, Ord

Georgia   } [466]
Elbert County } This Indenture, made this the 18 day of January 1902, between Jep Brawner, of said County, for and in behalf of him self, He being of the age of 43 years, of the one part, & W. T. M. Brown, of the County aforesaid, of the other part. Witnesseth: That the said Jep Brawner, as aforesaid, does by these presents bind out him self, of said County, as apprentice to said W. T. M. Brown in the trade or craft of Husbandry or laborer upon the plantation of the said W. T. M. Brown, to be taught the said Craft of Husbandry or Laborer, and to live with, continue, and serve the said W. T. M. Brown as an apprentice from the first day of January 1903 for and during the term of one year. During all of which time, said Jep Brawner, as aforesaid, doth Covenant with the said W. T. M. Brown that he, the said Jep Brawner, shall well & faithfully demean his self as such faithful

Apprentice, observing fully the command of the said W. T. M. Brown, & in all things deporting & behaving him self as a faithful Apprentice to the said W. T. M. Brown, neither revealing his secrets, nor at any time neglecting or leaving the business of the said W. T. M. Brown And for & in Consideration of the service well & faithfully rendered by the said Jep Brawner, of the first part, said W. T. M. Brown, of the second part, doth Covenant, promise, & agree to instruct him, Said Apprentice, or otherwise Cause him to be well and faithfully instructed, in the said trade or craft of Husbandry or Laborer, and shall also allow, furnish, & provide him, said Apprentice, with meat & drink and clothing during the said term, & shall also, at the expiration of the said term, allow & pay the said Apprentice sixty dollars, bearing even date with this Contract at the time specified in per of said note then this Contract to be null & void, else in full force & effect.

Witness our hands & seals the day & year first before Written.

Executed Before Us in Duplicate
C. M. Heard Jep + Brawner, his mark
J. J. Burch, ordinary W. T. M. Brown

Georgia   }   [467]
Elbert County } This Indenture, made this the 22nd day of January 1902, Between Harrison Banks, of said County, for & in behalf of his minor sons, to wit, Paul Banks & John Banks, being of the age of 15, 14 years, of the one part, & E J. Bell, of the County aforesaid, of the other part. Witnesseth: That the said Harrison Banks, as aforesaid, does by these presents bind out his sons Paul & John Banks, of said County, as apprentices to said E. J. Bell in the trade or craft of Farm Labor or as Laborers upon the plantation of the said E. J. Bell, to be taught the said craft or trade of Farm Labor or Laborers, & to live with, Continue, & serve the said E. J. Bell as apprentices from the 27th of January 1902 for & during the term of Eleven months, or until the 25th day of December 1902. During all of which time, said Harrison Banks, as aforesaid, doth covenant with the said E. J. Bell that the said Paul & John Banks shall well & faithfully demean them selves as such faithful Apprentices, observing fully the Command of the said E. J. Bell, & in all things deporting & behaving them selves as faithful Apprentices to the said E. J. Bell, neither revealing his secrets, nor at any time neglecting or leaving the business of the said E. J. Bell. And for & in Consideration of the service well & faithfully rendered by the said Paul & John Banks, of the first part, said E. J. Bell, of the second part, doth Covenant, promise, & agree to instruct them, said Apprentices, or otherwise Cause them to be well and faithfully instructed, in the said trade or Craft of farm Labor or Laborers, And also to read the English language, & shall also allow, furnish, & provide his said apprentices with meat &

drink & House to live in during the said term, & shall also, at the expiration of the said term, allow & pay the said Apprentices Fifty Dollars.

Witness our hands & seals the day & year first before written.

Executed Before us In duplicate
George Haslett   Harrison + Banks, his mark
J. J. Burch, ordinary   E. J. Bell

Georgia } [468]
Elbert County } This Indenture, made this the 30th day of January 1902, between Frank Pressley & Fannie Pressley, of said County, for and in behalf of their Minor children, Bettie, Warren, George, & Cora Pressley, being of the age of 12, 8, 6, 3 years, of the One part, & Jn° W. McCalla, of the County aforesaid, of the other part. Witnesseth: That the said Frank & Fannie Pressley, as aforesaid, does by these presents bind out their aforesaid children, of said County, as Apprentices to said Jn° W. McCalla in the trade or Craft of Husbandry or as Laborers upon the plantation of the said Jn° W. McCalla, to be taught the said craft or trade of Husbandry or Laborers, & to live with, Continue, & serve the said Jn° W. McCalla as Apprentices from the date hereof for & during the term of their minority.

During all of which time, said Frank & Fannie Pressley, as aforesaid, doth Covenant with the said Jn° W. McCalla that the said Bettie, Warren, George & Cora Pressley shall well & faithfully demean them selves as such faithful Apprentices, observing fully the command of the said Jn° W. McCalla, & in all things deporting & behaving them selves as faithful Apprentices to the said Jn° W. McCalla, neither revealing his secrets, nor at any time neglecting or leaving the business of the said Jn° W. McCalla. And for & in consideration of the service well & faithfully rendered by the Said Bettie, Warren, George, & Cora Pressley, of first part, said Jn° W. McCalla, of the second part, doth Covenant, promise, & agree to instruct his said apprentices, or otherwise them to be well & faithfully instructed, in the said trade or Craft of Husbandry or Laborer, & also to read the English language, & shall also allow, furnish, & provide them, said Apprentices, with meat & drink & clothing during the said term, & all other necessaries meet and proper, in sickness & in health, & shall also, at the expiration of the said term, allow & pay the said Apprentices what is now allowed by the Statute in such case made & provided.

Witness our hands & seals the day & year first before Written.

Executed Before Us In Duplicate
James McIntosh   Frank + Pressley, his mark
J. J. Burch, ordinary   Fannie + Pressley, her mark
                                        J. W. McCalla

Georgia   }   [469]
Elbert County } This Indenture, made this the 30th day of Jany 1902, between Marsh Stone, of said County, for and in behalf of his minor son Luther Stone, being of the age of 15 years, of the one part, & E. J. Bell, of the County aforesaid, of the other part. Witnesseth: That the said Marsh Stone, as aforesaid, does by these presents bind out Luther Stone, of said County, as apprentice to said E. J. Bell in the trade or craft of Husbandry or as Laborer upon the plantation of the said E. J. Bell, to be taught the said craft or trade of Husbandry or Laborer, & to live with, continue, & serve the said E. J. Bell as an apprentice from the date hereof for & during the term of one year. During all of which time, said Marsh Stone, as aforesaid, doth covenant with the said E. J. Bell that the said Luther Stone shall well & faithfully demean him self as such faithful apprentice, observing fully the command of the said E. J. Bell, & in all things deporting & behaving his self as a faithful Apprentice to the said E. J. Bell, neither revealing his secrets, nor at any time neglecting or leaving the business of the said E. J. Bell. And for & in consideration of the service well & faithfully rendered by the said Luther Stone, of the first part, said E. J. Bell, of the second part, doth covenant, promise, & agree to instruct his said apprentice, or otherwise cause him to be well & faithfully instructed, in the said trade or craft of Husbandry or Laborer, & shall also allow, furnish, & provide said Apprentice, with meat & drink & clothing during the said term, & all other necessaries meet and proper, in sickness & in health, & shall also, at the expiration of the said term, allow & pay the said apprentice Thirty Dollars. Now, the said E. J. Bell, of the second part, has this day assumed the payment of a debt of thirty Dollars for said Marsh Stone, of the first part. Now, if the said Marsh Stone fails to Comply with a contract entered into of this date with said E. J. Bell, then the said Luther is to work out said amount of thirty Dollars, at Five Dollars per month.

Witness our hands & seals the day & year first before written.

Executed Before Us In duplicate
C. P. Taylor   Marsh + Stone, his mark
J. J. Burch, ordinary   E. J. Bell

Georgia } [not numbered]
Elbert County } This Indenture, Made this 29 day of December 1902, between Ike Rucker, of said County, for & in behalf of Caroline Rucker, being of the age of 16 years, of the one part, & Jn° C. Brown, of the County aforesaid, of the other part. Witnesseth: That the said Ike Rucker, as aforesaid, does by these presents bind out Caroline Rucker, of said County, as Apprentice to said Jn° C. Brown in the trade or craft of Husbandry or as laborer upon the plantation of the said Jn° C. Brown, to be taught the said craft or trade of Husbandry or laborer, and to live with, Continue, & serve the said Jn° C. Brown as an Apprentice from the date hereof for & during the term of Five years. During all of which time, said Ike Rucker, as aforesaid, doth Covenant with the said Jn° C. Brown that the said Caroline Rucker shall well & faithfully demean her self as such faithful Apprentice, observing fully the Command of the said Jn° C. Brown, & in all things deporting & behaving her self as a faithful Apprentice to the said Jn° C. Brown, neither revealing his secrets, nor at any time neglecting or leaving the business of the said Jn° C. Brown. And for & in Consideration of the service well & faithfully rendered by the said Caroline Rucker, of the first part, said Jn° C. Brown, of the second part, doth covenant, promise, & agree to instruct his said Apprentice, or otherwise Cause her to be well and faithfully instructed, in the said trade or craft of Husbandry or laborer, & also to read the English language, & shall also allow, furnish, & provide his said Apprentice with meat & drink & clothing during the said term, & all other necessaries meet & proper, in sickness & in health, & shall also, at the expiration of the said term, allow & pay the said Apprentice what is now allowed by the statute in such case made & provided.

Witness our hands & seals the day & year first before written.

Executed Before us In Duplicate
A. M. Shumate   Ike + Rucker, his mark
J. J. Burch, ordinary   Jn° C. Brown

[The Ordinary wrote the following notation diagonally across the foregoing indenture.]

This Apprentice Married and was never Delivered [illegible] Apprenticeship This Sep^t 1904.

J. J. Burch, ordinary

Georgia } [not numbered]
Elbert County } This Indenture, Made this 24 day December 1902, between Ike Rucker, of said County, for & in behalf of Tinsey Rucker, being of the age of 13

years, of the one part, & Jnº C. Brown, of the County aforesaid, of the other part. Witnesseth: That the said Ike Rucker, as aforesaid, does by these presents bind out Tinsey Rucker, of said County, as Apprentice to said Jnº C. Brown in the trade or craft of Husbandry or as laborer upon the plantation of the said Jnº C. Brown, to be taught the said craft or trade of Husbandry or laborer, and to live with, Continue, & serve the said Jnº C. Brown as an apprentice from the date hereof for & during the term of seven years. During all of which time, said Ike Rucker, as aforesaid, doth covenant with the said Jnº C. Brown that the said Tinsey Rucker shall well & faithfully demean him self as such faithful apprentice, observing fully the Command of the said Jnº C. Brown, & in all things deporting & behaving himself as a faithful Apprentice to the said Jnº C. Brown, neither revealing his secrets, nor at any time neglecting or leaving the business of the said Jnº C. Brown. And for & in consideration of the service well & faithfully rendered by the said Tinsey Rucker, of the first part, said Jnº C. Brown, of the second part, doth covenant, promise, & agree to instruct his said Apprentice, or otherwise Cause him to be well & faithfully instructed, in the said trade or craft of Husbandry or laborer, & also to read the English language, & shall also allow, furnish, & provide the said Apprentice, with meat & drink & clothing during the said term, & all other necessaries meet & proper, in sickness & in health, & shall also, at the expiration of the said term, allow & pay the said Apprentice what is now allowed by the statute in such case made & provided.

Witness our hands & seals the day & year first before written.

Executed Before Us In Duplicate
A. M. Shumate   Ike + Rucker, his mark
J. J. Burch, ordinary   Jnº C. Brown

[The Ordinary wrote the following notation diagonally across the foregoing indenture.]

Cancelled by Order of Court Sep^t 17, 1904.

            J. J. Burch, ordinary

Georgia }   [470]
Elbert County } This Indenture, made this the 2nd day of Febr^y 1902, between Jack Jones & M. E. Maxwell, of said County. Witness: That the said Jack Jones, in Consideration of the promises & undertakings of the said M. E. Maxwell hereafter set forth, does hereby bind him self & his son Eugene Jones to the M. E. Maxwell for the full term of 2 years from first of January 1903 and he hereby agrees agrees & Contracts with said M. E. Maxwell to work faithfully under his

direction, respecting all orders & commands of the said M. E. Maxwell with reference to the business hereinafter set forth, at all times demeaning them selves orderly & soberly. And the said Jack Jones further agrees to account to the said M. E. Maxwell for all loss of time, except in case of temporary sickness. If such Sickness should be of longer duration at any one time than six days, then said lost time is to be accounted for at the same rate per day as they are then receiving pay under this contract. And should this contract be terminated by the death of either of the parties to this indenture, then the said Compensation of said Jack Jones & Eugene Jones shall be prorata for the time Completed for the year in which the death may occur. And the Said M. E. Maxwell, in Consideration of the promises & undertakings of the said Jack Jones, agrees & contracts with said Jack Jones to provide them with board, lodging every day, wearing apparel and washing, and further agrees to pay said Jack & Eugene Jones annually on the 25 day of Decr each year the following sums of money, to wit, On the 25th day of December next Eighty Dollars, on 25 December 1904 Eighty Dollars. And he further agrees to teach the said Jack Jones And Eugene Jones the trade of Husbandry in all its details.

In Witness whereof, the said Jack Jones and the said M. E. Maxwell have hereto respectively set their hands and Seals the day & year first above written, all interlining before Signing.

Executed in Duplicate in the presence of
W. A. Rucker   }   Jack Jones
J. J. Burch, ordinary }   M. E. Maxwell

Georgia   }   [471]
Elbert County } This Indenture, Made this the 12 day of February 1902, between Sol Bullard & George Brawner, of said County. Witness: That the said Sol Bullard, in Consideration of the promises & undertakings of the said George Brawner hereafter set forth, does hereby bind him self to the said George Brawner for the term of 5 months from the sixth February 1902 & he hereby agrees & Contracts with said George Brawner to work faithfully under his direction, respect & obey all orders & commands of the said George Brawner with reference to the business hereinafter set forth, at all times demean him self orderly & soberly. & the said Sol Bullard further agrees to account to the said George Brawner for all loss of time, except in case of temporary sickness. If such sickness should be of longer duration at any one time than six days, then said lost time is to be accounted for at the same rate per day as he is then receiving pay under this contract. And should this Contract be terminated by the death of either of the parties to this indenture, then the said Compensation of said Sol Bullard shall be prorata for the

time Completed for the year in which the death may occur. And the said George Brawner, in Consideration of the promises & undertakings of the said Sol Bullard, agrees & Contracts with said Sol Bullard to provide him with board lodging. Brawner further agrees to pay Said Sol Bullard annually on the 10 day of July next each year the following sums of money, to wit, on the 10 day of July next 27½ Dollars. And he further agrees to teach the said Sol Bullard the trade of Husbandry in all its details.

In Witness Whereof, the said Sol Bullard and the said George Brawner have hereto respectively set their hands & seal the day & year first above written.

Executed in Duplicate in the presence of
W. T. Smith   Sol + Bullard, his mark
J. J. Burch, ordinary   George + Bullard. his mark

Georgia   }   [472]
Elbert County } This Indenture, Made this the 12 day of Feby 1902, between Seven Heard & J. W. McCalla, of said County. Witness: that the said Seven Heard, in Consideration of the promises & undertakings of the said J. W. McCalla hereafter set forth, does hereby bind him self to said J. W. McCalla for the full term of one year from the 12 February 1902. And he hereby agrees & Contracts with said J. W. McCalla to work faithfully under his direction, respect & obey all orders & Commands of the said J. W. McCalla with reference to the business hereinafter set forth, at all times demean himself orderly & soberly. & the said Seven Heard further agrees to account to the said J. W. McCalla for all loss of time, except in Case of temporary sickness. If such sickness should be of longer duration at any one time than six days, then said lost time is to be accounted for at the same rate per day as he is then receiving pay under this contract. And should this Contract be terminated by the death of either of the parties to this indenture, then the said Compensation of said Seven Heard shall be prorata for the time Completed for the year in which the death may occur. And the Said J. W. McCalla, in Consideration of the promises & undertakings of the said Seven Heard, agrees & contracts with said Seven Heard to furnish him with board, lodging every day, wearing apparel & washing. And further agrees to pay said Seven Heard annually on the 12 day of February each year the following sums of money, to wit, On the 12 day of February next Fifty Seven Dollars.

And he further agrees to teach the said Seven Heard the trade of Husbandry in all its details.

In Witness Whereof, the said Seven Heard and the said J. W. McCalla have hereto respectively set their hands & seals the day & year first above written.

Executed in Duplicate in the presence of
James McIntosh   Seven + Heard, his mark
J. J. Burch, ordinary   J. W. McCalla

Georgia   }   [473]
Elbert County } This Indenture, made this the 22nd day of February 1902, between Henry Adams and T. P. Andrews, of said County. Witness: That the Said Henry Adams, in consideration of the promises & undertakings of the said T. P. Andrews hereafter set forth, does hereby bind him self & his children, to wit, Rosa Adams, Minnie Adams, and William Adams to the said T. P. Andrews for the full term of 4 years from 22nd February 1903 & he hereby agrees & contracts with said T. P. Andrews to work faithfully under his direction, respect & obey all orders & Commands of the said T. P. Andrews with reference to the business hereinafter set forth, at all times demeaning them selves orderly & soberly. And the said Henry Adams further agrees to account to the said T. P. Andrews for all loss of time, except in case of temporary sickness. If such sickness should be of longer duration at any one time than six day, then said lost time is to accounted for at the same rate per day as they are then receiving pay under this Contract. And should this Contract be terminated by the death of either of the parties to this indenture, then the said Compensation of said Henry Adams shall be prorata for the time completed for the year in which the death may occur. And The said T. P. Andrews, in Consideration of the promises & undertakings of the said Henry Adams, agrees & contracts with said Henry Adams to furnish them with board lodging every day, wearing apparel, and washing. He further agrees to pay said Henry, Rosa, Minnie, & William Adams annually on the 22 day of February each year the following sums of money, to wit, on the 22 day of February next Fifty Dollars, on 22 February 1903 Fifty Dollars, on 22 February 1904 Fifty Dollars, on 22 February 1905 Fifty Dollars. & he further agrees to teach the said Henry, Rosa, Minnie, & William Adams the trade of Husbandry in all its details. In Witness Whereof, the said Henry Adams & the said T. P. Andrews have hereto respectively set their hands & seals the day & year first above written.

Executed in Duplicate in the presence of
H. A. Fortson   Henry + Adams, his mark
J. J. Burch, Ordinary   T. P. Andrews

Georgia   }   [474]
Elbert County } This Indenture, Made this the 22 day of February 1902, between

Clark Kennebrew and Tom Fortson, of said County. Witness: That the said Clark Kennebrew, in consideration of the promises and of the said Tom Fortson hereafter set forth, does hereby bind him self to the said Tom Fortson for the full term of 7 months from January 1st 1902, and he hereby agrees and contracts with said Tom Fortson to work faithfully under his direction, respect & obey all orders & commands of the said Tom Fortson with reference to the business hereinafter set forth, at all times demean him self orderly and soberly. & the said Clark Kennebrew further agrees to account to the said Tom Fortson for all loss of time, except in case of temporary sickness. If such Sickness should be of longer duration at any one time than six days, then said lost time is to be accounted for at the same rate per day as he is then receiving pay under this contract. And should this Contract be terminated by the death of either of the parties to this indenture, then the said Compensation of said Clark Kennebrew shall be prorata for the time Completed for the year in which the death may occur. And the said Tom Fortson, in consideration of the promises & undertakings of the said Clark Kennebrew, agrees & contracts with said Clark Kennebrew to furnish him with board lodging. And further agrees to pay said Clark Kennebrew Annually on the 1st day of August each year the following sums of money, to wit, On the 1st day of August next Thirty Seven Dollars.

And he further agrees to teach the said Clark Kennebrew the trade of Husbandry in all its details.

In Witness whereof, the said Clark Kennebrew and the said Tom Fortson have hereto respectively set their hands and seals the day & year first above written.

Executed in Duplicate in the presence of
W. A. Rucker   Clark + Kennebrew, his mark
J. J. Burch, ordinary   T. F. Fortson

Georgia   }   [475]
Elbert County } This Indenture, Made this the 22 day of February 1902, between Washington Fortson and Tom Fortson, of said County. Witness: That the said Washington Fortson, in consideration of the promises and undertakings of the said Tom Fortson hereafter set forth, does hereby bind him self to the said Tom Fortson for the full term of 7 months from January 1st 1902. and he hereby agrees & contracts with said Tom Fortson to work faithfully under his direction, respect & obey all orders & commands of the said Tom Fortson with reference to the business hereinafter set forth, at all times demean his self orderly and soberly. & the said Wash Fortson further agrees to account to the said Tom Fortson for all loss of time, except in case of temporary sickness. If such Sickness should be of

longer duration at any one time than six days, then said lost time is to be accounted for at the same rate per day as he is then receiving pay under this Contract. And should this Contract be terminated by the death of either of the parties to this indenture, then the said Compensation of said Wash Fortson shall be prorata for the time Completed for the year in which the death may occur. And the said Tom Fortson, in consideration of the promises & undertakings of the said Wash Fortson agrees & Contracts with said Wash Fortson to furnish him with board, lodging. And further agrees to pay said Wash Fortson annually on the 1st day of August each year the following sums of money, to wit, On the 1st day of August next Thirty six Dollars. And he further agrees to teach the said Wash Fortson the trade of Husbandry in all its details.

In Witness Whereof, the said Wash Fortson and the said Tom Fortson have hereto respectively set their hands seals the day and year first above written.

Executed in Duplicate in the presence of
Executed in Duplicate in the presence of
W. A. Rucker					Wash + Fortson, his mark
J. J. Burch, ordinary				T. F. Fortson

Georgia   }   [476]
Elbert County } This Indenture, made this the 13th day of March 1902, between Harrison Thompson & Emily Thompson, of said County, for & in behalf of their minor Children, George, Henry, Annie, & Rossie Thompson & William Thompson, being of the age of 12, 8, 10, 6, 14 years, of the one part, & John C. Hudgens, of the County aforesaid, of the other part. Witnesseth: That said Harrison & Emily Thompson, as aforesaid, does by these presents bind out their aforesaid named children, of said county, as Apprentices to said John C. Hudgens in the trade or craft of Husbandry or as Laborers upon the plantation of the said Jnº C. Hudgens, to be taught the said craft or trade of Husbandry or Laborers, & to live with, Continue, & serve the said Jnº C. Hudgens as apprentices from the first day of January 1903 for & during the term of 2 years. During all of which time, said Harrison & Emily Thompson, as aforesaid, doth covenant with the said Jnº C. Hudgens that the said George, Henry, Annie, & Rossie Thompson & William Thompson shall well & faithfully demean them selves as such faithful Apprentices, observing fully the command of the said Jnº C. Hudgens, & in all things deporting & behaving them selves as faithful Apprentices to the said Jnº C. Hudgens, neither revealing his secrets, nor at any time neglecting or leaving the business of the said Jnº C. Hudgens. And for & in consideration of the service well & faithfully rendered by the said George, Henry, Annie, & Rossie Thompson and William Thompson, of the first part, said Jnº C. Hudgens, of the second part,

doth covenant, promise, & agree to instruct his said Apprentices, or otherwise Cause them to be well & faithfully instructed, in the said trade or Craft of Husbandry or laborers, & also to read the English Language, & shall also allow, furnish, & provide his said Apprentices with meat & drink & clothing during the said term, & all other necessaries meet and proper, in sickness & in health, & shall also, at the expiration of the said term, allow & pay the said apprentices what is now allowed by the statute in such case made & provided.

Witness our hands & seals the day & year first before written.

Executed Before Us In Duplicate. All interlinations made before signing.
Ja^s McIntosh   Harrison + Thompson, his mark
J. J. Burch, ordinary   Emily + Thompson, her mark
                                   J. C. Hudgens

Georgia   }   [477]
Elbert County } This Indenture, made this the 11th day of April 1902, Between Ben Joe Heard (Parent), of said County, for & in behalf of Jn° Henry Heard, being of the age of sixteen years, of the one part, and A. S. Oliver, of the County aforesaid, of the other part. Witnesseth: That the said Ben Joe Heard, as aforesaid, does by these presents bind out Jn° Henry Heard, of said County, as Apprentice to said A. S. Oliver in the trade or craft of farm labor or as laborer upon the plantation of the said A. S. Oliver, to be taught the said craft or trade of farm labor or laborer, & to live with, continue, & serve the said A. S. Oliver as an Apprentice from the date hereof for & during the term of five years.

During all of which time, said Ben Joe Heard, as aforesaid, doth covenant with the said A. S. Oliver that the said John Henry Heard shall well & faithfully demean himself as such faithful Apprentice, observing fully the Command of the said A. S. Oliver, and in all things deporting & behaving him self as a faithful Apprentice to the said A. S. Oliver, neither revealing his secrets, nor at any time neglecting or leaving the business of the said A. S. Oliver. And for & in consideration of the service well & faithfully rendered by the said Jn° Henry Heard, of first part, said A. S. Oliver, of the second part, doth Covenant, promise, & agree to instruct him, said Apprentice, or otherwise Cause him to be well & faithfully instructed, in the said trade or craft of farm labor or laborer, & also to read the English language, & shall also allow, furnish, & provide his said Apprentice, with meat & drink & clothing during the said term, & all other necessaries meet and proper, in sickness & in health, & shall also, at the expiration of the said term, allow & pay the said Apprentice what is now allowed by the Statute in such case made and & provided.

Witness our hands & seals the day & year first before written. Executed Before Us In Duplicate

Abda Oglesby   }   Ben Joe + Heard, his mark
J. J. Burch, ordinary   }   A. S. Oliver

Georgia   }   [478]
Elbert County } This Indenture, made this the 11th day of April 1902, between Jn° Wilker, J^r, of said County, for and in behalf of him self, being of the age of 26 years, of the one part, and A. S. Oliver, of the County aforesaid, of the other part. Witnesseth: That the said Jn° Wilker, J^r, as aforesaid, does by these presents bind out him self, of said County, as Apprentice to said A. S. Oliver in the trade or craft of farm Labor or as Laborer upon the plantation of the said A. S. Oliver, to be taught the said Craft or trade of farm labor or laborer, & to live with, Continue, & serve the said A. S. Oliver as an Apprentice from the date hereof for & during the term of five years.

During all of which time, said Jn° Wilker, J^r, as aforesaid, doth covenant with the said A. S. Oliver that the said Jn° Wilker, J^r shall well & faithfully demean himself as such faithful Apprentice, observing fully the Command of the said A. S. Oliver, and in all things deporting & behaving him self as a faithful Apprentice to the said A. S. Oliver, neither revealing his secrets, nor at any time neglecting or leaving the business of the said A. S. Oliver.

And for & in Consideration of the service well & faithfully rendered by the said Jn° Wilker, J^r, of first part, said A. S. Oliver, of the second part, doth Covenant, promise, & agree to instruct his said Apprentice, or otherwise Cause him to be well & faithfully instructed, in the said trade or Craft of farm labor or laborer, & also to read the English language, & shall also allow, furnish, & provide him, said Apprentice, with meat and drink & clothing during the said term, & all other necessaries meet and proper, in sickness & in health, & shall also, at the expiration of the said term, allow & pay the said Apprentice what is now allowed by the statute in such case made and & provided.

Witness our hands & seals the day & year first before written.

Executed Before Us In Duplicate
G. B. Rhodes   Jn° + Wilker, J^r, his mark
J. J. Burch, ordinary   A. S. Oliver

Georgia   }   [479]
Elbert County } This Indenture, Made this the 11th day of April 1902, between

Collins Wilker, of said County, for and in behalf of him self, being of the age of 21 years, of the one part, and A. S. Oliver, of the County aforesaid, of the other part. Witnesseth: That the said Collins Wilker, as aforesaid, does by these presents bind out himself, of said County, as Apprentice to said A. S. Oliver in the trade or craft of farm Labor or as Laborer upon the plantation of the said A. S. Oliver, to be taught the said Craft or trade farm labor or laborer, & to live with, Continue, & serve the said A. S. Oliver as an Apprentice from the date hereof for & during the term of five years. During all of which time, said Collins Wilker, as Aforesaid, doth Covenant with the said A. S. Oliver that the said Collins Wilker shall well & faithfully demean himself as such faithful apprentice, observing fully the Command of the said A. S. Oliver, and in all things deporting & behaving himself as a faithful Apprentice to the said A. S. Oliver, neither revealing his secrets, nor at any time neglecting or leaving the business of the said A. S. Oliver. And for & in Consideration of the service well & faithfully rendered by the said Collins Wilker, of first part, said A. S. Oliver, of the second part, doth Covenant, promise, & agree to instruct him, said Apprentice, or otherwise Cause him to be well and faithfully instructed, in the said trade or Craft of farm Labor or laborer, and also to read the English language, and shall also allow, furnish, & provide him, said Apprentice, with meat & drink & clothing during the said term, and all other necessaries meet & proper, in sickness & in health, & shall also, at the expiration of the said term, allow & pay the said Apprentice what is now allowed by the Statute in such Case made and & provided.

Witness our hands & Seals the day & year first before written. Executed Before Us In Duplicate

| G. B. Rhodes } | Collins + Wilker, his mark |
| J. J. Burch, Ordinary } | A. S. Oliver |

Georgia } [480]
Elbert County } This Indenture, made this the 8 day of May 1902, between Clara Hill, of said County, for & in behalf of Isham Hill, her son, being of the age of 15 years, of the one part, & D. P. Oglesby, of the County aforesaid, of the other part. Witnesseth: That the said Clara Hill, as aforesaid, does by these presents bind out Isham Hill, of said County, as Apprentice to said D. P. Oglesby in the trade or Craft of servant or as Laborer upon the plantation of the said D. P. Oglesby, to be taught the said Craft or trade of servant or Laborer, & to live with, continue, & serve the said D. P. Oglesby as an Apprentice from the date hereof for & during the term of Five years. During all of which time, said Clara Hill, as aforesaid, doth Covenant with the said D. P. Oglesby that the said Isham Hill shall well and faithfully demean him self as such faithful Apprentice, observing fully the

Command of the said D. P. Oglesby, & in all things deporting & behaving his self as a faithful Apprentice to the said D. P. Oglesby, neither revealing his secrets, nor at any time neglecting or leaving the business of the said D. P. Oglesby.

And for & in consideration of the service well & faithfully rendered by the said Isham Hill, of first part, said D. P. Oglesby, of the second part, doth Covenant, promise, & agree to instruct his said Apprentice, or otherwise Cause him to be well & faithfully instructed, in the said trade or craft of servant or Laborer, & shall also allow, furnish, & provide his said Apprentice, with meat & drink & clothing during the said term, & all other necessaries meet and proper, in sickness & in health, & shall also, at the expiration of the said term, allow & pay the said Apprentice what is now allowed by the statute in such case made & provided.

Witness our hands & seals the day & year first before written.

Executed Before us in Duplicate
H. J. Brawner   Clara + Hill, her mark
J. J. Burch, ordinary   D. P. Oglesby

Georgia   }   [481]
Elbert County   } This Indenture, made this the 12 day of May 1902, between Lula Blackwell, of said County, for & in behalf of her minor son Henry Stark, being of the age of 15 years, of the one part, & J. H. Blackwell, of the County aforesaid, of the other part. Witnesseth: That the said Lula Blackwell, as aforesaid, does by these presents bind out Said Henry Stark, of said County, as apprentice to said J. H. Blackwell in the trade or Craft of Husbandry or as Laborer upon the plantation of the said J. H. Blackwell, to be taught the said craft or trade of Husbandry or Laborer, and to live with, Continue, & serve the said J. H. Blackwell as an Apprentice from the date hereof for & during the term of five years. During all of which time, said Lula Blackwell, as aforesaid, doth covenant with the said J, H. Blackwell that the said Henry Stark shall well & faithfully demean him self as such faithful Apprentice, observing fully the Command of the said J. H. Blackwell, and in all things deporting & behaving himself as a faithful Apprentice to the said J. H. Blackwell, neither revealing his secrets, nor at any time neglecting or leaving the business of the said J. H. Blackwell. And for & in consideration of the service well & faithfully rendered by the said Henry Stark, of first part, said J. H. Blackwell, of the second part, doth covenant, promise, & agree to instruct him, said Apprentice, or otherwise Cause him to be well & faithfully instructed, in the said trade or craft of husbandry or Laborer, & shall also allow, furnish, & provide him, said Apprentice, with meat & drink & clothing during the said term, & all other necessaries meet and proper, in sickness & in health, And

at the expiration of said five years to give said apprentice back to the Custody of his mother. Witness our hands & seals the day & year first before written. Interlined before signing.

Executed Before us In Duplicate
Sam L. Oliver   Lula + Blackwell, her mark
J. J. Burch, ordinary   J. H. Blackwell

Georgia   }   [482]
Elbert County } This Indenture, Made this the 12 day of May 1902, between Jim Tate, Sarah Tate, and Fox Tate, of said County, for & in behalf of them selves, being of the age of 48, 38, 22 years, of the one part, & J. W. McCalla, of the County aforesaid, of the other part. Witnesseth: That the said Jim Tate, Sarah Tate, & Fox Tate, as aforesaid, does by these presents bind out them selves, of said County, as Apprentices to said J. W. McCalla in the trade or craft of Husbandry or as Laborers upon the plantation of the said J. W. McCalla, to be taught the said craft or trade of Husbandry or laborers, and to live with, Continue, & serve the said J. W. McCalla as apprentices from the date hereof for & during the term of Twenty months.

During all of which time, said Jim, Sarah, & Fox Tate, as aforesaid, doth covenant with the said J. W. McCalla that the said Jim, Sarah, & Fox Tate shall well & faithfully demean them selves as such faithful Apprentices, observing fully the command of the said J. W. McCalla, & in all things deporting & behaving them selves as faithful Apprentices to the said J. W. McCalla, neither revealing his secrets, nor at any time neglecting or leaving the business of the said J. W. McCalla. And for & in Consideration of the service well & faithfully rendered by the said Jim, Sarah, & Fox Tate, of first part, said J. W. McCalla, of the second part, doth covenant, promise, & agree to instruct his said Apprentices, or otherwise cause them to be well & faithfully instructed, in the said trade or craft of Husbandry or Laborers, And shall also allow, furnish, & provide his said Apprentices with meat & drink during the said term, & all other necessaries meet and proper, in sickness & in health, & shall also, at the expiration of the said term, allow & pay the said Apprentices six Dollars per month.

Witness our hands & Seals the day & year first before written.

Executed Before Us In Duplicate
James McIntosh   Jim + Tate, his mark
J. J. Burch, ordinary   Sarah + Tate, her mark
                                  Fox + Tate, his mark
                                  Jnº W. McCalla

Georgia   }   [483]
Elbert County   } This Indenture, made this the 14 day of May 1902, between Anderson Morrison, of said County, for & in behalf of him self, being of the age of 30 years, of the one part, and G. N. Burden, of the County aforesaid, of the other part. Witnesseth: That the said Anderson Morrison, as aforesaid, does by these presents bind out him self, of said County, as apprentice to said G. N. Burden in the trade or craft of Husbandry or as Laborer upon the plantation of the said G. N. Burden, to be taught the said Craft or trade of Husbandry or Laborer, and to live with, Continue, & serve the said G. N. Burden as an Apprentice from the date hereof for & during the term of Seven months. During all of which time, said Anderson Morrison, as aforesaid, doth Covenant with the Said G. N. Burden that the said Anderson Morrison shall well & faithfully demean him self as such faithful Apprentice, observing fully the command of the said G. N. Burden, and in all things deporting & behaving his self as a faithful Apprentice to the said G. N. Burden, neither revealing his secrets, nor at any time neglecting or leaving the business of the said G. N. Burden. And for & in consideration of the service well & faithfully rendered by the said Anderson Morrison, of first part, said G. N. Burden, of the second part, doth covenant, promise, & agree to instruct his said Apprentice, or otherwise cause him to be well & faithfully instructed, in the said trade or Craft of Husbandry or Laborer, and shall also allow, furnish, & provide his said Apprentice with meat and drink during the said term, and shall also, at the expiration of the said term, allow & pay the said Apprentice Ten Dollars per month, And not require the said Morrison to work in bad weather.

Witness our hands & Seals the day & year first before written.

Executed Before Us In Duplicate
Geº C. Grogan   M. A. Morrison
J. J. Burch, ordinary   G. N. Burden

Georgia   }   [484]
Elbert County   } This Indenture, made this the 17 day of May 1902, between Falcon Hudson, of said County, for & in behalf of his minor sons Isaac Hudson

and Falcon Hudson, J^r, being of the age of 15, 13 years, of the one part, & W. J. Hammond, of the County aforesaid, of the other part. Witnesseth: That the said Falcon Hudson, as aforesaid, does by these presents bind out his said sons Isaac and Falcon Hudson, J^r, of said County, as apprentices to said W. J. Hammond in the trade or Craft of Husbandry or as Laborers upon the plantation of the said JW. J. Hammond, to be taught the said Craft or trade of Husbandry or laborers, & to live with, Continue, & serve the said W. J. Hammond as an Apprentice from the first day of January 1903 for & during the term of one year. During all of which time, said Falcon Hudson, as aforesaid, doth covenant with the said W. J. Hammond that the said Isaac & Falcon Hudson, J^r shall well & faithfully demean them selves as such faithful Apprentices, observing fully the command of the said W. J. Hammond, & in all things deporting & behaving themselves as such faithful Apprentices to the said W. J. Hammond, neither revealing his secrets, nor at any time neglecting or leaving the business of the said W. J. Hammond. And for & in consideration of the service well & faithfully rendered by the said Isaac & Falcon Hudson, of the first part, said W. J. Hammond, of the second part, doth covenant, promise, & agree to instruct his said Apprentices, or otherwise Cause them to be well & faithfully instructed, in the said trade or craft of Husbandry or Laborers, & shall also allow, furnish, & provide his said Apprentices with meat & drink & clothing during the said term, & all other necessaries meet & proper, in sickness & in health, & shall also, at the expiration of the said term, allow & pay the said Apprentices Seventy Five Dollars.

Witness our hands & Seals the day & year first before written.

Executed Before Us In Duplicate
J. Allen Miles, J^r Falcon + Hudson, his mark
J. J. Burch, ordinary   W. J. Hammond

Georgia   }   [485]
Elbert County } This Indenture, Made this the 4 day of August 1902, between Margaret Starke, of said County, for & in behalf of her minor sons Marsh Downer & Luther Du Bose, being of the age of 19, 14 years, of the one part, & E. J. Bell, of the County aforesaid, of the other part. Witnesseth: That the said Margaret Starke, as aforesaid, does by these presents bind out her said sons Marsh & Luther, of said County, as Apprentices to said E. J. Bell in the trade or craft of Farm Labor or as Laborers upon the plantation of the said E. J. Bell, to be taught the said craft or trade of Farm Labor or Laborers, & to live with, Continue, & Serve the said E. J. Bell as Apprentices from the date hereof for & during the term of six months.

During all of which time, said Margaret Starke, as aforesaid, doth covenant with the said E. J. Bell that the said Marsh Downer & Luther Du Bose shall well & faithfully demean them selves as such faithful Apprentices, observing fully the Command of the said E. J. Bell, & in all things deporting & behaving them selves as faithful Apprentices to the said E. J. Bell, neither revealing his secrets, nor at any time neglecting or leaving the business of the said E.. J. Bell. And for & in consideration of the service well & faithfully rendered by the said Marsh Downer & Luther Du Bose, of the first part, said E. J. Bell, of the second part, doth Covenant, promise, & agree to instruct his said apprentices, or otherwise cause them to be well & faithfully instructed, in the said trade or craft of Farm Labor or Laborers, & shall also allow, furnish, & provide his said Apprentices with meat & drink during the said term, & shall also, at the expiration of the said term, allow & pay the said apprentices Ten Dollars per month.

Witness our hands & Seals the day & year first before Written.

Executed Before Us In Duplicate
R. M. Heard   }   Margaret + Starke, her mark
J. J. Burch, ordinary }   E. J. Bell

Georgia   }   [486]
Elbert County } This Indenture, made this the 5 day of August 1902, between Ed Gibbs, of said County, for & in behalf of him self, being of the age of 21 years, of the one part, & E. J. Bell, of the County aforesaid, of the other part. Witnesseth: That the said Ed Gibbs, as aforesaid, does by these presents bind out him self, of said County, as apprentice to said E. J. Bell in the trade or craft of Husbandry or laborer upon the plantation of the said E. J. Bell, to be taught the said craft or trade of Husbandry or laborer, & to live with, Continue, & serve the said E. J. Bell as an Apprentice from the date hereof for and during the term of one year. During all of which time, said Ed Gibbs, as aforesaid, doth covenant with the said E. J. Bell that the said Ed Gibbs shall well & faithfully demean his self as such faithful apprentice, observing fully the Command of the said E. J. Bell, & in all things deporting & behaving his self as a faithful Apprentice to the said E. J. Bell, neither revealing his secrets, nor at any time neglecting or leaving the business of the said E. J. Bell. And for & in consideration of the service well & faithfully rendered by the said Ed Gibbs, of the first part, said E. J. Bell, of the second part, doth covenant, promise, & agree to instruct his said Apprentice, or otherwise Cause him to be well & faithfully instructed, in the said trade or craft of Husbandry or laborer, and Shall also allow, furnish, & provide his said Apprentice with meat & drink & clothing during the said term, & shall also, at the expiration of the said term, allow & pay the Said apprentice Sixty Dollars.

Witness our hands & Seals the day & year first before written.

Executed before Us In duplicate
W. D. Tate   Ed + Gibbs, his mark
J. J. Burch, ordinary   E. J. Bell

Georgia   }   [487]
Elbert County } This Indenture, made this the 6 day of August 1902, between Lint McKinley, of said County, for & in behalf of his self, being of the age of 30 years, of the one part, & D. P. Oglesby, of the County aforesaid, of the other part. Witnesseth: That the said Lint McKinley, as aforesaid, does by these presents bind out him self, of said County, as apprentice to Said D. P. Oglesby in the trade or craft of Husbandry or as Laborer upon the plantation of the said D. P. Oglesby, to be taught the said Craft or trade of Husbandry or Laborer, & to live with, Continue, & serve the said D. P. Oglesby as an apprentice from the first day of September 1902 for & during the term of one year. During all of which time, said Lint McKinley, as aforesaid, doth Covenant with the said D. P. Oglesby that the said Lint McKinley shall well & faithfully demean his self as such faithful apprentice, observing fully the command of the said D. P. Oglesby, & in all things deporting & behaving his Self as a faithful Apprentice to the said D. P. Oglesby, neither revealing his secrets, nor at any time neglecting or leaving the business of the said D. P. Oglesby.

And for & in Consideration of the service well & faithfully rendered by the said Lint McKinley, of first part, said D. P. Oglesby, of the second part, doth covenant, promise, & agree to instruct his said Apprentice, or otherwise Cause him to be well & faithfully instructed, in the said trade or craft of Husbandry or laborer, & shall also allow, furnish, & provide his said apprentice with meat & drink during the said term, and shall also, at the expiration of the said term, allow & pay the said apprentice Eighty four Dollars.

Witness our hands & seals the day & year first before written. Executed Before Us In Duplicate

J. N. Wall   Lint + McKinly, his mark
J. J. Burch, ordinary   D. P. Oglesby

Georgia   }   [488]
Elbert County } This Indenture, made this the 6 day of August 1902, between Emanuel Allen, of said County, for & in behalf of his minor daughters Mattie May Allen and Maria Allen, being of the age of 12, 10 years, of the one part, & E. B. Heard, of the County aforesaid, of the other part. Witnesseth: That the said

Emanuel Allen, as aforesaid, does by these presents bind out his said daughters Mattie May & Maria Allen, of said County, as apprentices to said E. B. Heard in the trade or Craft of House servants or as Laborers upon the plantation of the said E. B. Heard, to be taught the said Craft or trade of House Servants or Laborers, & to live with, Continue, & serve the said E. B. Heard as apprentices from the date hereof for and during the term of their minority. During all of which time, said Emanuel Allen, as aforesaid, doth Covenant with the said E. B. Heard that the said Mattie May & Maria Allen shall well & faithfully demean themselves as such faithful Apprentices, observing fully the Command of the said E. B. Heard, & in all things deporting & behaving them selves as faithful Apprentices to the said E. B. Heard, neither revealing his secrets, nor at any time neglecting or leaving the business of the said E. B. Heard. And for & in Consideration of the service well & faithfully rendered by the Said Mattie May & Maria Allen, of the first part, said E. B. Heard, of the second part, doth Covenant, promise, & agree to instruct his said Apprentices, or otherwise Cause them to be well & faithfully instructed, in the said trade or craft of House Servants or laborers, & also to read the English language, & shall also allow, furnish, & provide his said Apprentices with meat & drink & clothing during the said term, & all other necessaries meet & proper, in sickness & in health, & shall also, at the expiration of the said term, allow & pay the said Apprentices what is now allowed by the statute in such case made & provided.

Witness our hands & seals the day & year first before written.

Executed Before us In Duplicate
Ge^o C. Grogan
J. J. Burch, ordinary

Emanuel + Allen, his mark
E. B. Heard

Georgia   }   [489]
Elbert County } This Indenture, Made this the 13 day of August 1902, between Will Blackwell, of said County, for & in behalf of him self, being of the age of 22 years, of the one part, & M. H. Maxwell, of the County aforesaid, of the other part. Witnesseth: That the said Will Blackwell, as aforesaid, does by these presents bind out him self As Apprentice to said M. H. Maxwell in the trade or craft of Husbandry or as laborer upon the plantation of the said M. H. Maxwell, to be taught the said Craft or trade of Husbandry or Laborer, & to live with, Continue, & serve the said M. H. Maxwell as an apprentice from the first day of Jany 1903 for & during the term of Two years.

During all of which time, said Will Blackwell, as aforesaid, doth Covenant with the said M. H. Maxwell that the said Will Blackwell shall well & faithfully demean his self as such faithful Apprentice, observing fully the Command of the said M. H. Maxwell, & in all things deporting & behaving his self as a faithful Apprentice to the said M. H. Maxwell, neither revealing his secrets, nor at any time neglecting or leaving the business of the said M. H. Maxwell. And for & in Consideration of the service well & faithfully rendered by the said Will Blackwell, of the first part, said M. H. Maxwell, of the second part, doth covenant, promise, & agree to instruct his said Apprentice, or otherwise Cause him to be well & faithfully instructed, in the said trade or Craft of Husbandry or Laborer, and shall also allow, furnish, & provide his said apprentice with meat & drink during the Said Term, And shall also, at the expiration of the said term, allow & pay the said apprentice Five Dollars per month.

Witness our hands & seals the day & year first before Written.

Executed Before Us In Duplicate
E. A. Cason   Will + Blackwell, his mark
J. J. Burch, ordinary   M. H. Maxwell

Georgia   }   [490]
Elbert County } This Indenture, Made this the 13th day of August 1902, between Robert Blackwell & Lizzie Blackwell, of said County, for & in behalf of them Selves, being of the age of 26, 23 years, of the one part, and M. H. Maxwell, of the County aforesaid, of the other part. Witnesseth: That the said Robert & Lizzie Blackwell aforesaid, does by these presents bind out them selves as Apprentices to said M. H. Maxwell in the trade or Craft of Husbandry or as Laborers upon the plantation of the said M. H. Maxwell, to be taught the said Craft or trade of Husbandry or Laborers, & to live with, Continue, & serve the said M. H. Maxwell as an Apprentice from the date hereof for & during during the term of two years. During all of which time, said Robert & Lizzie Blackwell, as aforesaid, doth Covenant with the said M. H. Maxwell that the said Robert & Lizzie Blackwell shall well & faithfully demean them selves as such faithful Apprentices, observing fully the Command of the said M. H. Maxwell, & in all things deporting & behaving themselves as faithful Apprentices to the said M. H. Maxwell, neither revealing his secrets, nor at any time neglecting or leaving the business of the Said M. H. Maxwell. And for & in Consideration of the service well & faithfully rendered by the said Robert & Lizzie Blackwell, of the first part, said M. H. Maxwell, of the second part, doth covenant, promise, & agree to instruct his said Apprentices, or otherwise Cause them to be well & faithfully instructed, in the said trade or Craft of Husbandry or Laborers, & shall also allow, furnish, & provide his said Apprentices with meat & drink during the said said Term, and

shall also, at the expiration of the said term, allow & pay the said Apprentices Five Dollars per month.

Witness our hands & seals the day & year first before written.

Executed Before Us In Duplicate
J. J. Burch, ordinary   Robert + Blackwell, his mark
George Haslett   Lizzie + Blackwell, her mark
                                         M. H. Maxwell

Georgia   }   [491]
Elbert County } This Indenture, made this the 18 day of August 1902, between Whit Downer, Edmond Clark, Adam Downer, and Sam Hunt, of said County, for & in behalf of them selves, being of the age of 22, 21, 45, 24 years, of the one part, & J. A. McLanahan, of the County aforesaid, of the other part. Witnesseth: That the said Whit Downer, Edmond Clark, Adam Downer, & Sam Hunt, as aforesaid, does by these presents bind out them selves, of said County, as Apprentices to said J. A. McLanahan in the trade or craft of Farm Labor or as Laborers upon the plantation of the said J. A. McLanahan, to be taught the said Craft or trade of Farm Labor or laborers, & to live with, Continue, & serve the said J. A. McLanahan as Apprentices from the date hereof for & during the term of 18 months. During all of which time, said Whit Downer, Edmond Clark, Adam Downer, & Sam Hunt, as aforesaid, doth Covenant with the said J. A. McLanahan that the said Whit Downer, Edmond, Clark, Adam Downer, & Sam Hunt shall well & faithfully demean them selfs as such faithful Apprentices, observing fully the Command of the said J. A. McLanahan, & in all things deporting & behaving them selves as faithful Apprentices to the said J. A. McLanahan, neither revealing his secrets, nor at any time neglecting or leaving the business of the said J. A. McLanahan.

And for & in Consideration of the service well & faithfully rendered by the said Whit Downer, Edmond Clark, Adam Downer, & Sam Hunt, of the first part, said J. A. McLanahan, of the second part, doth Covenant, promise, & agree to instruct his said Apprentices, or otherwise Cause them to be well & faithfully instructed, in the said trade or Craft of Farm Labor or Laborers, and Shall also allow, furnish, & provide his said Apprentices with meat & drink during the said Term, and shall also, at the expiration of the said Term, allow & pay the said Apprentices Six and one half Dollars per month. All Interlinations made before Signing.

Witness our hands & seals the day & year first before Written.

Executed Before Us In duplicate
J. T. McLanahan
J. J. Burch, ordinary

Whit + Downer, his mark
Edmond + Clark, his mark
Adam + Downer, his mark
Sam + Hunt, his mark
J. A. McLanahan

Georgia } [492]
Elbert County } This Indenture, executed in duplicate this October 2nd 1902, between Emanuel Allen & George C. Grogan, both of said State & County. Witness: That said Emanuel Allen, for & in consideration of the sum of one hundred Dollars per annum to be paid by the said Ge° C. Grogan at the expiration of Each year from and after the date of this Indenture, the first said part being Due Dec 31, 1902 being $25.00, does hereby bind him self to the said Ge° C. Grogan for the full term of Five years next ensuing.

The said Ge° C. Grogan shall be entitled to his reasonable labor from the said Emanuel Allen under the direction of him, the said Ge° C. Grogan. And the said Emanuel Allen shall be entitled to the necessaries of life, including Food, shelter, & clothing, and protection, & humane treatment at the hands of the said Ge° C. Grogan, or those to whom he may hire the said Emanuel. Which right to hire is hereby agreed to by the said Emanuel, provided the party to whom the said Ge° C. Grogan may hire shall observe the Conditions the same as are imposed upon the said Grogan. And the said Emanuel shall be taught the business of husbandry or House Service or both. In witness whereof, the said Contracting parties have hereto set their hands and affixed their seals the day and year first above written.

Signed, sealed, and delivered }
in presence of us Oct 2, 1902 }
J. C. Van Duzer }
A. F. Smith }

Emanuel + Allen, his mark
Ge° C. Grogan

Georgia }
Elbert County } Personally before me, J. J. Burch, ordinary of Elbert County, Comes J. C. Van Duzer who, being duly sworn, says that he saw Ge° C. Grogan sign by writing his name & Emanuel Allen sign by making his mark the foregoing Indenture of service & that the said Emanuel acknowledged that he understood

the Contract and that he & A. F. Smith signed the same as witnesses on said 2nd day of October 1902.

Sworn to & Subscribed }
before us this Oct 2, 1902 } J. C. Vanduzer
J. J. Burch, ordinary }

Georgia } [493]
Elbert County } This Indenture, made this the 7th day of Febr^y, between J. J. Burch, ordinary, of said County, for & in behalf of Oz Bowman, being of the age of 11 years, of the one part, & W. M. Grogan, of the County aforesaid, of the other part. Witnesseth: That the said J. J. Burch, ordinary as aforesaid, does by these presents bind out Oz Bowman, of said County, as Apprentice to said W. M. Grogan in the trade or craft of Husbandry or as laborer upon the plantation of the said W. M. Grogan, to be taught the said Craft or trade of Husbandry or laborer, and to live with, Continue, & serve the said W. M. Grogan as an Apprentice from the date hereof for & during the term of his minority, that is until December 31st 1912. During all of which time, said J. J. Burch, ordinary as aforesaid, doth covenant with the said W. M. Grogan that the said Oz Bowman shall well and faithfully demean him self as such faithful Apprentice, observing fully the Command of the said W. M. Grogan, and in all things deporting & behaving him self as a faithful Apprentice to the said W. M. Grogan, neither revealing his secrets, nor at any time neglecting or leaving the business of the said W. M. Grogan. And for & in consideration of the service well & faithfully rendered by the said Oz Bowman, of the first part, said W. M. Grogan, of the second part, doth covenant, promise, & agree to instruct him, said Apprentice, or otherwise Cause him to be well & faithfully instructed, in the said trade or craft of Husbandry or laborer, & also to read the English language, & shall also allow, furnish, & provide his said Apprentice with meat & drink & clothing during the said term, & all other necessaries meet & proper, in sickness & in health, & shall also, at the expiration of the said Term, allow & pay the said Apprentice what is now allowed by the statute in such case made and provided. Witness our hands & seals the day & year first before written.

Executed Before us in duplicate
Ge^o C. Grogan J. J. Burch, ordinary
Abda Oglesby W. M. Grogan

Georgia } [494]
Elbert County } This Indenture, Made this the 24th August 1902, between Giles Davis, of said County, for & in behalf of him self, being of the age of 50 years, of

the one part, & H. C. Rousey, of the County aforesaid, of the other part. Witnesseth: That the said Giles Davis, as aforesaid, does by these presents bind out him self as apprentice to said H. C. Rousey in the trade or craft of Husbandry or as Laborer upon the plantation of the said H. C. Rousey, to be taught the said Craft or trade of Husbandry or laborer, & to live with, Continue, & serve the said H. C. Rousey as an apprentice from the first day of January 1903 for & during the term of six months. During all of which time, said Giles Davis, as aforesaid, doth Covenant with the said H. C. Rousey that the said Giles Davis shall well & faithfully demean his self as such faithful apprentice, observing fully the Command of the said H. C. Rousey, and in all things deporting & behaving his self as a faithful Apprentice to said H. C. Rousey, neither revealing his secrets, nor at any time neglecting or leaving the business of the said H. C. Rousey. And for & in Consideration of the service well & faithfully rendered by the said Giles Davis, of the first part, said H. C. Rousey, of the second part, doth Covenant, promise, & agree to instruct his said Apprentice, or otherwise Cause him to be well & faithfully instructed, in the said trade or Craft of Husbandry or laborer, and shall also allow, furnish, & provide his said Apprentice Forty with meat & drink during said term, and also, at the expiration of the said term, allow & pay the said Apprentice Forty Dollars.

Witness our hands & Seals the day & year first before written.

Executed Before Us In duplicate
M. R. Bond   Giles + Davis, his mark
J. J. Burch, ordinary   H. C. Rousey

Georgia   }   [495]
Elbert County } This Indenture, made this the 6 day of September 1902, between Mat Wall, of said County, for & in behalf of him self, being of the age of 21 years, of the one part, & Mrs J. J. Nelms, of the County aforesaid, of the other part. Witnesseth: That the said Mat Wall, as aforesaid, does by these presents bind out him self as apprentice to said Mrs J. J. Nelms in the trade or craft of Husbandry or as Laborer upon the plantation of the said Mrs J. J. Nelms, to be taught the said Craft or trade of Husbandry or Laborer, & to live with, continue, & serve the said Mrs J. J. Nelms as an apprentice from the first of January 1903 for & during the term of one year. During all of which time, said Mat Wall, as aforesaid, doth covenant with the said Mrs J. J. Nelms that the said Mat Wall shall well & faithfully demean his self as such faithful apprentice, observing fully the Command of the said Mrs J. J. Nelms, and in all things deporting & behaving his self as a faithful Apprentice to said Mrs J. J. Nelms, neither revealing her secrets, nor at any time neglecting or leaving the business of the said Mrs J. J. Nelms. And

for & in consideration of the service well & faithfully rendered by the said Mat Wall, of the first part, said Mrs J. J. Nelms, of the second part, doth Covenant, promise, & agree to instruct her said Apprentice, or otherwise cause him to be well & faithfully instructed, in the said trade or Craft of Husbandry or laborer, and shall also allow, furnish, & provide her said apprentice with meat & drink during said term, and shall also, at the expiration of the said term, allow & pay the said apprentice Eight Dollars per month.

Witness our hands & seal the day & year first before written.

Executed Before Us In Duplicate
L. C. Edwards   Mat + Wall, his mark
J. J. Burch, ordinary   Mrs J. J. +Nelms, her mark
                                           per J. J. + Nelms, agt, his mark

I hereby, for value received, release the said Mat Wall from the above and foregoing Contract, This August the 17, 1903.

Witness   Mrs J. J. + Nelms, her mark
J. J. Burch   per J. J. + Nelms, his mark

Georgia   }   [496]
Elbert County } This Indenture, made this the 13 day of September 1902, between John Favors, of said County, for & in behalf of him self, being of the age of 28 years, of the one part, & J. B. Hammond, of the County aforesaid, of the other part.

Witnesseth: That the said John Favors, as aforesaid, Does by these presents bind out him self as Apprentice to said J. B. Hammond in the trade or craft of Husbandry or as Laborer upon the plantation of the said J. B. Hammond, to be taught the said craft or trade of Husbandry or laborer, and to live with, Continue, & serve the said J. B. Hammond as an apprentice from first January 1903 for & during the term of seven months. During all of which time, said John Favors, as aforesaid, doth Covenant with the said J. B. Hammond that the said John Favors shall well and faithfully demean his self as such faithful Apprentice, observing fully the Command of the said J. B. Hammond, & in all things deporting & behaving him self as a faithful Apprentice to said J. B. Hammond, neither revealing his secrets, nor at any time neglecting or leaving the business of the said J. B. Hammond. And for & in consideration of the service well & faithfully rendered by the said John Favors, of the first part, said J. B. Hammond, of the second part, doth Covenant, promise, & agree to instruct his said apprentice, or otherwise Cause him to be well & faithfully instructed, in the said trade or Craft of Husbandry or laborer, and shall also allow, furnish, & provide his said apprentice with meat & drink during said term, and shall also, at the expiration of the said term, allow & pay the said apprentice six & one half Dollars per month. Witness our hands & seals the day & year first before written.

Executed Before Us In Duplicate
Thos M. Swift   John + Favors, his mark
J. J. Burch, ordinary   J. B. Hammond

Georgia   }   [497]
Elbert County } This Indenture, made this the 17 day September 1902, between A. P. Davis, of said County, for & in behalf of his minor son Tom Davis, being of the age of 13 years, of the one part, and W. J. Mathews, of the County aforesaid, of the other part. Witnesseth: That the said A. P. Davis, as aforesaid, does by these presents bind out his said son Tom as apprentice to said W. J. Mathews in the trade or craft of Husbandry or as laborer upon the plantation of the said W. J. Mathews, to be taught the said Craft or trade of Husbandry or Laborer, & to live with, Continue, & serve the said W. J. Mathews as an apprentice from the date hereof for & during the term of seven years. During all of which time, said A. P. Davis, as aforesaid, doth covenant with the Said W. J. Mathews that the said Tom Davis shall well & faithfully demean his self as such faithful Apprentice, observing fully the Command of the said W. J. Mathews, and in all things deporting & behaving his self as a faithful Apprentice to said W. J. Mathews, neither revealing his secrets, nor at any time neglecting or leaving the business of the said W. J. Mathews.

And for & in Consideration of the service well & faithfully rendered by the said Tom Davis, of the first part, said W. J. Mathews, of the second part, doth Covenant, promise, & agree to instruct his said Apprentice, or otherwise Cause him to be well & faithfully instructed, in the said trade or Craft of Husbandry or laborer, & also to read the English language, & shall also allow, furnish, & provide his said apprentice with meat & drink and clothing during the said term, & all other necessaries meet & proper, in sickness & in health, & shall also, at the expiration of the said term, allow & pay the said Apprentice what is now allowed by the statute in such case made & provided.

Witness our hands & seal the day & year first before written.

Executed Before Us In Duplicate
W. H. Irwin, J^r A. P. + Davis, his mark
J. J. Burch, ordinary   W. J. Mathews

Georgia } [498]
Elbert County } This Indenture, made the 27 day of September 1902, between Jim Eberhart, of said County, for & in behalf of him self, being of the age of 23 years, of the one part, & J. A. Beasley, of the County aforesaid, of the other part. Witnesseth: That the said Jim Eberhart, as aforesaid, does by these presents bind out him self as apprentice to said J. A. Beasley in the trade or craft of Husbandry or as laborer upon the plantation of the said J. A. Beasley, to be taught the said Craft or trade of Husbandry or Laborer, and To live with, Continue, and serve the said J. A. Beasley as an Apprentice from the first day January 1903 for and during the term of Twelve months. During all of which time, Said Jim Eberhart, as aforesaid, doth Covenant with the said J. A. Beasley that the said Jim Eberhart shall well & faithfully demean his self as such faithful apprentice, observing fully the Command of the said J. A. Beasley, & in all things deporting & behaving his self as a faithful Apprentice to the said J. A. Beasley, neither revealing his secrets, nor at any time neglecting or leaving the business of the said J. A. Beasley. And for & in Consideration of the service well & faithfully rendered by the said Jim Eberhart, of first part, said J. A. Beasley, of the second part, doth covenant, promise, & agree to instruct his said Apprentice, or otherwise Cause him to be well & faithfully instructed, in the said trade or craft of Husbandry or laborer, & shall also allow, furnish, & provide his said Apprentice with meat and drink during the said term, & shall also, at the expiration of the said term, allow & pay the said apprentice Seventy Two dollars.

Witness our hands & seal the day & year first before written.

Executed Before Us In Duplicate
J. M. + Conwell, his mark   Jim + Eberhart, his mark
J. J. Burch, ordinary   J. A. + Beasley, his mark

Georgia } [499]
Elbert County } This Indenture, made this the 5 day of October 1902, between George Rucker, of Elbert County, for and in behalf of Nathaniel Rucker, being of the age of 17 years, of the one part, and L. P. Eberhardt, of the County aforesaid, of the other part. Witnesseth: That the said George Rucker as aforesaid, does by these presents bind out said Nathiel Rucker as apprentice to said L. P. Eberhardt in the trade or craft of Farm Labor or as Laborer upon the plantation of the said L. P. Eberhardt, to be taught the said Craft or trade of Farm Labor or Laborer, & to live with, continue, and serve the said L. P. Eberhardt as an Apprentice from the date hereof for and during the term of one year. During all of which time, the said George Rucker, as aforesaid, doth Covenant with the said L. P. Eberhardt that the said Nathaniel Rucker shall well and faithfully demean him self as such

faithful Apprentice, observing fully the Commands of the said L. P. Eberhardt, and in all things deporting & behaving himself as a faithful apprentice to the said L. P. Eberhardt, neither revealing their secrets, nor at any time neglecting or leaving the business of the said L. P. Eberhardt.

And for & in Consideration of the service well & faithfully rendered by the said Nathaniel Rucker, of the first part, said L. P. Eberhardt, of the second part, doth covenant, promise, and agree to instruct his said apprentice, or otherwise cause him to be well & faithfully instructed, in the said trade or Craft of Farm Labor or Laborer, and also to read the English language, & shall also allow, furnish, & provide his said apprentice with meat & drink and clothing during the said term, & all other necessaries meet & proper, in sickness & in health, & shall also, at the Expiration of said term, allow & pay the said Apprentice what is now allowed by the statute in such case made & provided.

Witness our hands & seal the day & year first before written.

Executed Before Us In duplicate
D. S. Kerlin   George + Rucker, his mark
J. J. Burch, ordinary   L. P. Eberhardt

Georgia   }   [500]
Elbert County } This Indenture, Made this the 17 day of December 1902, between Charlotte Blackwell, of said County, for & in behalf John Blackwell, being of the age of 13 years, of the one part, and W. A. Swift, of the County aforesaid, of the other part. Witnesseth: That the said Charlotte Blackwell, as aforesaid, does by these presents bind out John Blackwell, of Said County, as Apprentice to said W. A. Swift in the trade or craft of Husbandry or as laborer upon the plantation of the said W. A. Swift, to be taught the said Craft or trade of Husbandry or laborer, & to live with, Continue, & serve the said W. A. Swift as an apprentice from the date hereof for & during the term of Eight years. During all of which time, said Charlotte Blackwell, as aforesaid, doth Covenant with the said W. A. Swift that the said John Blackwell shall well & faithfully demean his self as such faithful Apprentice, observing fully the Command of the said W. A. Swift, & in all things deporting and behaving him self as a faithful Apprentice to the Said W. A. Swift, neither revealing his secrets, nor at any time neglecting or leaving the business of the said W. A. Swift. And for & in Consideration of the service well & faithfully rendered by the said John Blackwell, of the first part, said W. A. Swift, of the second part, doth Covenant, promise, & agree to instruct his Said Apprentice, or otherwise Cause him to be well & faithfully instructed, in the said trade or craft of Husbandry or laborer, & also to read the English

language, & shall also allow, furnish, & provide him, said apprentice, with meat & drink & clothing during the said term, & all other necessaries meet & proper, in sickness & in health, & shall also, at the expiration of the said term, allow & pay the said apprentice what is now allowed by the Statute in such case made & provided.

Witness our hands & seal the day & year first before written.

Executed Before us In Duplicate
G. L. A. Almond   Charlotte + Blackwell, her mark
J. J. Burch, ordinary   W. A. Swift

Georgia   }   [501]
Elbert County }   This Indenture, Made this the 31st day of December 1902, between Lucinda Webb, of said County, for & in behalf of Joe Upshaw, being of the age of 14 years, of the one part, and Peter Fortson, of the County aforesaid, of the other part. Witnesseth: That the said Lucinda Webb, as aforesaid, does by these presents bind out said Joe Upshaw as Apprentice to said Peter Fortson in the trade or Craft of Husbandry or as laborer upon the plantation of the said Peter Fortson, to be taught the said craft or trade of Husbandry or laborer, & to live with, continue, & serve the said Peter Fortson as an apprentice from the date hereof for & during the term of one year.

During all of which time, said Lucinda Webb, as aforesaid, doth covenant with the said Peter Fortson that the said Joe Upshaw shall well & faithfully demean his self as such faithful Apprentice, observing fully the command of the said Peter Fortson, And in all things deporting & behaving his self as a faithful Apprentice to said Peter Fortson, neither revealing his secrets, nor at any time neglecting or leaving the business of the said Peter Fortson.

And for & in consideration of the service well & faithfully rendered by the said Joe Upshaw, of the first part, said Peter Fortson, of the second part, doth covenant, promise, & agree to instruct his said Apprentice, or otherwise Cause him to be well & faithfully instructed, in the said trade or craft of Husbandry or laborer, & also to read the English language, & shall also allow, furnish, & provide his said Apprentice with meat & drink & clothing during the said term, & all other necessaries meet & proper, in sickness & in health, & shall also, at the expiration of the said term, allow & pay the said apprentice Sixteen Dollars.

Witness our hands & seal the day & year first before written.

Executed Before Us In Duplicate
Abda Oglesby, J. P.   Lucinda + Webb, her mark
J. J. Burch, ord   Peter + Fortson, his mark

Georgia   }   [502]
Elbert County } This Indenture, made this the 31st day of January 1902, between G. H. McLanahan and Carter Cade, of said County. Witness: That the said Carter Cade for himself & his son Emil Cade, in consideration of the promises and undertakings of the said G. H. McLanahan hereafter set forth, does hereby bind him self & Emil Cade to the said G. H. McLanahan for the full term of 3 years from the 1st day of Feby 1902. And he hereby agrees & Contracts with said G. H. McLanahan to work faithfully under his direction, respect and obey all orders and Commands of the said G. H. McLanahan with reference to the business hereinafter set forth, at all times demean themselves orderly and soberly. And the Said Carter for him self & his son Emil further agrees to account to the said G. H. McLanahan for all loss of time, except in case of temporary sickness if such sickness should be of less duration at any one time than six days, then said lost time is to be accounted for at the same rate per day as they are then receiving pay under this Contract. And should this Contract be terminated by the death of either of the parties to this indenture, then the said Compensation of the said Apprentices shall be prorata for the time Completed for the year in which the death may occur. And the Said G. H. McLanahan, in consideration of the promises & undertakings of the Said Carter Cade, agrees & Contracts with said Carter Cade to furnish them with board lodging every day, wearing apparel, & washing. And he further agrees to pay Said Apprentices Annually on the 5th day of December each year the following sums of money, to wit, on the 25th day of December next One Hundred & Twenty Dollars, on 25 December 1903 One Hundred & Twenty Dollars, on 25 December 1904 One Hundred & Twenty Dollars.

And he further agrees to teach the said Apprentices the trade of Husbandry in all its details.

In witness Whereof, the Said G. H. McLanahan & the said Carter Cade have hereto respectively set their hands & seals the day & year first before written.

Executed in Duplicate in the presence of
Abda Oglesby   Carter + Cade, his mark
J. J. Burch, ord   G. H. McLanahan

Georgia   }   [503]
Elbert County } This Indenture, Made this the 6 day of January 1903, between Tilda Hill, of said County, for and in behalf of her minor children, to wit, Clifford Hill aged fifteen years old, George Hill aged eighteen years, Walter Hill being of the age of fourteen years, Jim Hill aged Twelve years old, and Sally Hill about thirteen years old, of the one part, and S. H. Fortson, of the County aforesaid, of the other part. Witnesseth: That the said Tilda Hill, mother of said children, as aforesaid, does by these presents bind out said named minors, of said County, as apprentices to said S. H. Fortson in the trade or craft of farm laborers or as laborers upon the plantation of the said S. H. Fortson, to be taught the said craft or trade of farm laborers or laborers, & to live with, Continue, & serve the said S. H. Fortson as apprentices from the date hereof for & during the term of five years. During all of which time, said Tilda Hill, as aforesaid, doth covenant with the said S. H. Fortson that the said minors shall well & faithfully demean them selves as such faithful Apprentices, observing fully the Command of the said S. H. Fortson, & in all things deporting & behaving them selves as faithful Apprentices to said S. H. Fortson, neither revealing his secrets, nor at any time neglecting or leaving the business of the said S. H. Fortson.

And for & in consideration of the service well & faithfully rendered by the said Tilda Hill, of the first part, said S. H. Fortson, of the second part, doth covenant, promise, & agree to instruct them, said Apprentices, or otherwise Cause them to be well & faithfully instructed, in the said trade or craft of farm labor or laborer, & also to read the English language, & shall also allow, furnish, & provide them, said Apprentices, with meat & drink & clothing during the said term, & all other necessaries meet & proper, in sickness & in health, & shall also, at the expiration of the said term, allow & pay the said Apprentices what is now allowed by the statute in such case made & provided.

Witness our hands & seals the day & year first before written.

Executed Before us in duplicate
Z. B. Rogers   Tilda + Hill, her mark
J. J. Burch, ordinary   S. H. + Fortson

Georgia   }   [504]
Elbert County } This Indenture, made this the third day of January 1903, between Jack Deadwyler and Ada L. Oglesby, of said County. Witness: That the said Jack Deadwyler, in consideration of the promises and undertakings of the said Ada L. Oglesby hereafter set forth, does hereby bind himself to the said Ada L. Oglesby for the full term of 12 months from 1st January 1903. And he hereby

agrees & contracts with said A. L. Oglesby to work faithfully under her direction, respect & obey all orders and Commands of the said Ada L. Oglesby with reference to the business hereinafter set forth, at all times demean him self orderly & soberly. And the said Jack Deadwyler further agrees to account to the said Ada L. Oglesby for all loss of time. And the said Ada L. Oglesby, in consideration of the promises & undertakings of the said Jack Deadwyler, agrees and Contracts with said Jack Deadwyler to furnish him with board lodging And further agrees to pay said Jack Deadwyler on the 25 day of December next Eighty Dollars.

And he further agrees to teach the said Jack Deadwyler the trade of Agriculture in all its details.

In Witness Whereof, the said Jack Deadwyler and the said Ada L. Oglesby have hereto respectively set their hands & seals the day & year first above written.

Executed in Duplicate in the presence of
T. D. Biggs   Jack Deadwyler, his mark
J. R. Booth, J^r R. P. N. P. Ex off J. P.   Ada L. Oglesby

Georgia   }   [505]
Elbert County } This Indenture, Made this the 3 day of January 1903, between Georgia Gaines, of said County, for & in behalf of her minor son Herbert Gaines, being of the age of 15 years, of the one part, & J. A. McLanahan, of the County aforesaid, of the other part. Witnesseth: that the said Georgia Gaines, as aforesaid, does by these presents bind out her said son Herbert as Apprentice to said J. A. McLanahan in the trade or Craft of Husbandry or as laborer upon the plantation of the said J. A. McLanahan, to be taught the said Craft or trade of Husbandry or laborer, & to live with, Continue, & serve the said J. A. McLanahan as an apprentice from the date hereof for & during the term of 3 years. During all of which time, said Georgia Gaines, as aforesaid, doth Covenant with the said J. A. McLanahan that the said Herbert Gaines shall well & faithfully demean his self as such faithful Apprentice, observing fully the Command of the said J. A. McLanahan, And in all things deporting & behaving his self as a faithful Apprentice to said J. A. McLanahan, neither revealing his secrets, nor at any time neglecting or leaving the business of the said J. A. McLanahan. And for & in Consideration of the service well & faithfully rendered by the said Herbert Gaines, of the first part, said J. A. McLanahan, of the second part, doth Covenant, promise, and agree to instruct his said Apprentice, or otherwise him to be well & faithfully instructed, in the said trade or craft of Husbandry or laborer, & also to read the English language, & shall also allow, furnish, & provide his Said Apprentice with meat & drink & clothing during the said term, & all other necessaries meet &

proper, in sickness & in health, & shall also, at the expiration of the said term, allow & pay the said Apprentice Fifty Dollars per year Or One Hundred & fifty.

Witness our hands & seals the day & year first before written.

Executed Before us in duplicate
C. Chidd   Georgia + Gaines, her mark
J. J. Burch, ordinary   J. A. McLanahan

Georgia   }   [506]
Elbert County } This Indenture, Made this 5 day of January 1903, between Elbert Brawner, of said County, for & in behalf of his son Jesse Brawner, being of the age of 8 years, of the one part, & R. E. Hudgens, of the County aforesaid, of the other part. Witnesseth: That the said Elbert Brawner, as aforesaid, does by these presents bind out his said son Jesse, of said County, as Apprentice to said R. E. Hudgens in the trade or craft of Husbandry or as laborer upon the plantation of the said R. E. Hudgens, to be taught the said Craft or trade of Husbandry or laborer, & to live with, continue, and serve the said R. E. Hudgens as an Apprentice from the date hereof for & during the term of 13 years.

During all of which time, said Elbert Brawner, as aforesaid, doth Covenant with the said R. E. Hudgens that the said Jesse Brawner shall well and faithfully demean his self as such faithful Apprentice, observing fully the Command of the said R. E. Hudgens, and in all things deporting & behaving his self as a faithful apprentice to the said R. E. Hudgens, neither revealing his secrets, nor at any time neglecting or leaving the business of the said R. E. Hudgens. And for and in Consideration of the service well & faithfully rendered by the said Jesse Brawner, of the first part, said R. E. Hudgens, of the second part, doth Covenant, promise, & agree to instruct his said apprentice, or otherwise Cause him to be well & faithfully instructed, in the said trade or craft of Husbandry or laborer, and also to read the English language, & shall also allow, furnish, & provide his said apprentice with meat & drink & clothing during the said term, & all other necessaries meet & proper, in sickness & in health, & shall also, at the expiration of the said term, allow & pay the said apprentice what is now allowed by the statute in such case made and provided.

Witness our hands & seals the day & year first before written.

Executed Before us In duplicate
T. M. Parks   Elbert + Brawner, his mark
J. J. Burch, ordinary   R. E. Hudgens

Georgia   }   [507]
Elbert County } This Indenture, made and entered in to between Ap Davis & Sallie Davis, father & mother of their minor children hereinafter named, all of said State & County, for & in behalf of said minor children, of the one part, & Jnº W. McCalla, of said State & County, of the other part. Witnesseth: That the said Ap Davis & Sallie Davis, parents as aforesaid, does by these presents bind out their following named children, Jim Davis age 19 years, Seaborn Davis aged 17 years, Tom Davis aged 13 years, Joe Davis aged 12 years, Willie Davis aged Eight years, Elizabeth Davis aged Seven years, Andrew Jackson Davis Six years, & Loualla Davis aged three years, as apprentices to said Jnº W. McCalla in the trade or craft of husbandry or as Laborers upon the plantation of the said Jnº W. McCalla, in said County, be taught the said craft or trade of husbandry or farm laborers, & to live with, Continue, & serve the said McCalla as apprentices from the date hereof until each of said children shall severally arrive at the age of twenty one years of age. During all of which time, said Ap and Sallie Davis, parents aforesaid, do covenant with said McCalla that said minor Children shall well and faithfully demean themselves as such faithful Apprentices, observing fully the Command of the said McCalla, and in all things deporting and behaving themselves as faithful apprentices to said McCalla, neither revealing his secrets, nor at any time neglecting or leaving the business of the said McCalla.

And for and in Consideration of the service well & faithfully rendered by the said minor Children said McCalla doth Covenant, promise, & agree to instruct each of said Children during his term of service as such apprentice, or cause him or her to be well & faithfully instructed, in the said trade or craft of farm laborer, and to furnish each with meat & drink and clothing during said term, & all other necessaries meet & proper, in sickness & in health, And that, at the expiration of said term, allow & pay each of said apprentices such allowance as shall be proper and consistent with the service rendered, and the pay given for each during each year during such service.

Witness our hands & seals this the 16th day of January 1903.

Executed before us in Duplicate
James McIntosh   Ap + Davis, his mark
J. J. Burch, ordinary   Sallie + Davis, her mark
                                        J. W. McCalla

Georgia   }   [508]
Elbert County } This Indenture, Made this the 23 day of January 1903, between Willis Wall, Sallie Wall, & Tom Mattox, of said County, for & in behalf them

selves, they being of the age of 25, 20, 50 years, of the one part, & J. E. Herndon, of the County aforesaid, of the other part. Witnesseth: That the said Willis Wall, Sallie Wall, & Tom Mattox, as aforesaid, does by these presents bind out them selves, of said County, as Apprentices to said J. E. Herndon in the trade or craft of Husbandry or as laborers upon the plantation of the said J. E. Herndon, to be taught the said craft or trade of Husbandry or laborers, & to live with, Continue, & serve the said J. E. Herndon as Apprentices from the 24 January 1903 for & during the term of 2 years. During all of which time, said Willis Wall, Sallie Wall, & Tom Mattox, as aforesaid, doth Covenant with the said J. E. Herndon that the said Willis & Sallie Wall & Tom Mattox shall well & faithfully demean them selves as such faithful Apprentices, observing fully the Command of the said J. E. Herndon, And in all things deporting & behaving them selves as faithful Apprentices to the said J. E. Herndon, Neither revealing his secrets, nor at any time neglecting or leaving the business of the said J. E. Herndon. And for & in consideration of the service well & faithfully rendered by the said Willis & Sallie Wall & Tom Mattox, of the first part, said J. E. Herndon, of the second part, doth covenant, promise, & agree to instruct his said Apprentices, or otherwise Cause them to be well & faithfully instructed, in the said trade or craft of Husbandry or laborer, & also to read the English language, & shall also allow, furnish, & provide his said Apprentices with meat & drink during the said term, and shall also, at the expiration of the said term, allow & pay the said apprentice Eighty Dollars per year.

Witness our hands & seals the day & year first before written.

Executed before Us In Duplicate
T. [blot] Brawner
J. J. Burch, ordinary

Willis + Wall, his mark
Sallie + Wall, her mark
Tom + Mattox, his mark
J. E. Herndon

Georgia } [509]
Elbert County } This Indenture, made this the 21 day of April 1902, between Wm Banks, of said County, for & in behalf of Joe Banks age of 5 years, Cynthia Banks Age 3 years, & Sam Banks 10 months old, his minor children, of the one part, & W. O. Jones, of the County aforesaid, of the other part. Witnesseth: That the said Wm Banks, as aforesaid, does by these presents bind out said Children, of said County, as Apprentices to said W. O. Jones in the trade or craft of Husbandry or as laborer upon the plantation of the said W. O. Jones, to be taught the said Craft or trade of Husbandry or laborer, & to live with, Continue, & serve the said W. O. Jones as apprentices from the date hereof for & during the term of their

minority. During all of which time, said Wm Banks, as aforesaid, doth Covenant with the said W. O. Jones that the said Children shall well & faithfully demean them selves as such faithful Apprentices, observing fully the command of the said W. O. Jones, & in all things deporting and behaving them selves as faithful Apprentices to said W. O. Jones, neither revealing his secrets, nor at any time neglecting or leaving the business of the said W. O. Jones. And for & in consideration of the service well & faithfully rendered by the said Children, of the first part, said W. O. Jones, of the second part, doth Covenant, promise, & agree to instruct them, said Apprentices, or otherwise Cause them to be well & faithfully instructed, in the said trade or craft of Husbandry or laborer, and also to read the English language, & shall also allow, furnish, & provide them, said Apprentices, with meat & drink & clothing during the said term, & all other necessaries meet & proper, in sickness & in health, & shall also, at the expiration of the said term, allow & pay the said Apprentices what is now allowed by the Statute in such Case made & provided. Witness our hands & seals the day & year first before written.

Executed Before Us In Duplicate
W. A. Rucker, Clerk S. C. }   W^m + Banks, his mark
Sam L. Oliver   }   W. O. Jones

Georgia   }   [510]
Elbert County } This Indenture, Made this the 21 day of April 1902, between Missy Banks & Will Banks, of said County, of the one part, & W. O. Jones, of the County aforesaid, of the other part. Witnesseth: That the said Missy Banks Will Banks aforesaid, does by these presents bind out them selves, of said County, as apprentices to said W. O. Jones in the trade or craft of Husbandry or as Laborers upon the plantation of the said W. O. Jones, to be taught the said Craft or trade of Husbandry or laborers, & to live with, Continue, & serve the said W. O. Jones as Apprentices from the date hereof for & during the term of one year.

During all of which time, said Missy Banks & Will Banks, as aforesaid, doth Covenant with the said W. O. Jones that the said Missy Banks & Will Banks shall well & faithfully demean them selves as such faithful Apprentices, observing fully the Command of the said W. O. Jones, & in all things deporting and behaving them selves as faithful Apprentices to the said W. O. Jones, neither revealing his secrets, nor at any time neglecting or leaving the business of the said W. O. Jones. And for & in Consideration of the service well & faithfully rendered by the said Missy Banks & Will Banks, of the first part, said W. O. Jones, of the second part, doth Covenant, promise, & agree to instruct them, said Apprentices, or otherwise cause them to be well & faithfully instructed, in the said trade or craft of Husbandry or laborers, & shall also allow, furnish, & provide the said Apprentices with meat & drink and Clothing during the said term, and all other necessaries meet & proper, in sickness & in health, & shall also, at the expiration of the said term, allow & pay the said Apprentices what is now allowed by the statute in such case made and provided.

Witness our hands & Seals the day & year first before written.

Executed Before us in Duplicate
W. A. Ruck, Clerk S. C.   Will + Banks, his mark
Sam L. Oliver   Missy Lizzie + Banks, her mark
                                           W. O. Jones

Georgia   }   [511]
Elbert County } This Indenture, made this the 26 day of January 1903, between John Harper and Mattie Harper, of said County, for & in behalf of them selves, being of the age of 34, 30 years, of the one part, and Felix Mattox, of the County aforesaid, of the other part. Witnesseth: That the said John Harper & Mattie Harper, as aforesaid, does by these presents bind out them selves, of said County, as apprentices to said Felix Mattox in the trade or craft of Husbandry or as laborers upon the plantation of the said Felix Mattox, to be taught the said Craft or trade of Husbandry or laborers, & to live with, Continue, & serve the said Felix Mattox as apprentices from the date hereof for & during the term of 2 years.

During all of which time, said John & Mattie Harper, as aforesaid, doth Covenant with the said Felix Mattox that the said John & Mattie Harper shall well and faithfully demean them selves as such faithful Apprentices, observing fully the command of the said Felix Mattox, & in all things deporting & behaving them selves as faithful Apprentices to said Felix Mattox, neither revealing his secrets, nor at any time neglecting or leaving the business of the said Felix Mattox.

And for & in Consideration of the service well & faithfully rendered by the said John & Mattie Harper, of the first part, said Felix Mattox, of the second part, doth Covenant, promise, & agree to instruct them, said Apprentices, or otherwise Cause them to be well & faithfully instructed, in the said trade or craft of Husbandry or laborers, and shall also allow, furnish, & provide them, said Apprentices, with meat & drink during the said term, and shall also, at the expiration of the said term, allow & pay the said Apprentices Eighty Dollars. Witness our hands & seals the day and year first before written.

A. E. Hammond   John Harper
J. J. Burch, ordinary   Missy + Harper, her mark
                                           Felix + Mattox, his mark

Georgia   } [512]
Elbert County } This Indenture, made this the 3rd day of February 1903, between Will Daniel, of Said County, for & in behalf of him self, being of the age of 27 years, of the one part. Witnesseth: That the said Will Daniel, as aforesaid, does by these presents bind out him self, of said County, As Apprentice to said C. M. Mattox in the trade or craft of Husbandry or as laborer upon the plantation of the said C. M. Mattox, to be taught the said Craft or trade of Husbandry or laborer, and to live with, Continue, & serve the said C. M. Mattox as an apprentice from the date hereof for & during the term of Eleven months. During all of which time, said Will Daniel, as aforesaid, doth covenant with the said C. M. Mattox that the said Will Daniel shall well & faithfully demean himself as a faithful Apprentice to the said C. M. Mattox, neither revealing his secrets, nor at any time neglecting or leaving the business of the said C. M. Mattox.

And for & in Consideration of the service well and faithfully rendered by the said Will Daniel, of the first part, said C. M. Mattox, of the second part, doth covenant, promise, & agree to instruct his said Apprentice, or otherwise cause him to be well & faithfully instructed, in the said trade or craft of Husbandry or laborer, and shall also allow, furnish, & provide his said apprentice, with meat & drink during the said term, & shall also, at the expiration of the said term, allow & pay the said apprentice sixty six Dollars.

Wit our hands & Seals the day and year first before written. Executed Before Us In Duplicate.

J. N. Wall	Will + Daniel, his mark
J. J. Burch, ordinary	C. M. Mattox

Georgia   } [513]
Elbert County } This Indenture, made this the 6 day of February 1903, between George Smith, of said County, for & in behalf of him self, being of the age of 25 years, of the one part, and R. E. Hudgens, of the County aforesaid, of the other part. Witnesseth: That the said George Smith, as aforesaid, does by these presents bind out him self, of said County, as apprentice to said R. E. Hudgens in the trade or Craft of Husbandry or as laborer upon the plantation of the said R. E. Hudgens, to be taught the said craft or trade of Husbandry or laborer, and to live with, continue, & serve the said R. E. Hudgens as an apprentice from the date hereof for & during the term of Eleven months, or until 25 December 1903. During all of which time, said George Smith, as aforesaid, doth covenant with the said R. E. Hudgens that the said George Smith Shall well and faithfully demean his self as such faithful Apprentice, observing fully the Command of the said R. E. Hudgens,

And in all things deporting & behaving his self as a faithful Apprentice to said R. E. Hudgens, neither revealing his secrets, nor at any time neglecting or leaving the business of the said R. E. Hudgens. And for & in Consideration of the service well & faithfully rendered by the said George Smith, of the first part, said R. E. Hudgens, of the second part, doth Covenant, promise, & agree to instruct his said Apprentice, or otherwise Cause him to be well & faithfully instructed, in the said trade or craft of Husbandry or laborer, and Shall also, at the expiration of the said term, allow & pay the said apprentice Eleven Dollars per month.

Witness our hands & seals the day & year first before written.

Executed Before us In Duplicate
A. J. Cleveland   George + Smith, his mark
J. J. Burch, ordinary   R. E. Hudgens

Georgia   }   [514]
Elbert County } This Indenture, made this the 7 day of February 1903, between Charlie Brawner, of said County, for & in behalf of him Self, being of the age of 26 years, of the one part, and Zimri Tate, of the County aforesaid, of the other part. Witnesseth: That the said Charlie Brawner, as aforesaid, does by these presents bind out him self, of Said County, as Apprentice to said Zimri Tate in the trade or craft of Husbandry or as laborer upon the plantation of the said Zimri Tate, to be taught the said craft or trade of Husbandry or laborer, & to live with, Continue, & serve the said Zimri Tate as an Apprentice from the date hereof for & during the term of 2 years. During all of which time, said Charlie Brawner, as aforesaid, doth Covenant with the said Zimri Tate that the said Charlie Brawner shall well & faithfully demean him self as such faithful Apprentice, observing fully the Command of the said Zimri Tate, and in all things deporting & behaving his self as a faithful Apprentice to said Zimri Tate. And for & in Consideration of the service well & faithfully rendered by the said Charlie Brawner, of the first part, said Zimri Tate, of the second part, doth Covenant, promise, & agree to instruct him, said Apprentice, or otherwise Cause him to be well & faithfully instructed, in the said trade or craft of Husbandry or laborer, And shall also allow, furnish, & provide him, said Apprentice, with meat & drink & clothing during the said term, & all other necessaries meet & proper, in sickness & in health, & shall also, at the expiration of the said term, allow & pay the said Apprentice Sixty four & $^{55}/_{100}$ Dollars.

Witness our hands & seals the day and year first before written. Executed Before us In duplicate.

T. J. Brown   Charlie + Brawner, his mark
J. J. Burch, ordinary   Z. A. Tate, J^r

Georgia   }   [515]
Elbert County } This Indenture, made this the 10th February between Richard Fortson & Francis Fortson, of said County, for & in behalf of them selves, of the one part, & J. J. McLanahan, of the County aforesaid, of the other part. Witnesseth: That the said Richard & Francis Fortson, as aforesaid, does by these presents bind out them selves, of said County, as Apprentices to said J. J. McLanahan in the trade or craft of Husbandry or as laborers upon the plantation of the said J. J. McLanahan, to be taught the said craft or trade of Husbandry or laborers, & to live with, Continue, & serve the said J. J. McLanahan as Apprentices from the date hereof for & during the term of 2 years. During all of which time, said Richard and Francis Fortson, as aforesaid, doth covenant with the said J. J. McLanahan that the said Richard & Francis Fortson shall well & faithfully demean them selves as such faithful Apprentices, observing fully the Command of the said J. J. McLanahan, and in all things deporting & behaving them selves as faithful Apprentices to said J. J. McLanahan, neither revealing his secrets, nor at any time neglecting or leaving the business of the said J. J. McLanahan.

And for & in Consideration of the service well & faithfully rendered by the said Richard & Francis Fortson, of the first part, said J. J. McLanahan, of the second part, doth Covenant, promise, & agree to instruct them, said Apprentices, or otherwise Cause them to be well & faithfully instructed, in the said trade or craft of Husbandry or laborers, & shall also allow, furnish, & provide his said apprentices, with meat & drink & clothing during the said term, & all other necessaries meet & proper, in sickness & in health, & shall also, at the expiration of the said term, allow & pay the Apprentices Six Dollars per month.

Witness our hands & seals the day and year first before written.

Executed Before us In Duplicate
J. R. E. Bond   Richard + Fortson, his mark
J. J. Burch, ordinary   Francis + Fortson, his mark
                                                  J. J. McLanahan

Georgia   }   [516]
Elbert County } This Indenture, made this the 10 day of February 1903, between

William Heard, of said County, for & in behalf of his son Eugene Heard, being of the age of 14 years, of the one part, & E. J. Bell, of the County aforesaid, of the other part. Witnesseth: That the said William Heard, as aforesaid, does by these presents bind out his said son Eugene, of said County, as apprentice to said E. J. Bell in the trade or craft of Husbandry or as laborer upon the plantation of the said E. J. Bell, to be taught the said Craft or trade of Husbandry or laborer, & to live with, Continue, & serve the said E. J. Bell as an Apprentice from the date hereof for & during the term of 2 Years. During all of which time, said William Heard, as aforesaid, doth Covenant with the said E. J. Bell that the said Eugene Heard shall well & faithfully demean his self as such faithful Apprentice, observing fully the Command of the said E. J. Bell, & in all things deporting & behaving his self as a faithful Apprentice to the said E. J. Bell, neither revealing his secrets, nor at any time neglecting or leaving the business of the said E. J. Bell. And for & in Consideration of the service well & faithfully rendered by the said Eugene Heard, of the first part, said E. J. Bell, of the second part, doth Covenant, promise, & agree to instruct his said apprentice, or otherwise Cause him to be well & faithfully instructed, in the said trade or Craft of Husbandry or Laborer, & Shall also allow, furnish, & provide him, said Apprentice, with meat & drink & clothing during the said term, & all other necessaries meet and proper, in sickness & in health, & shall also, at the expiration of the said term, allow & pay the said Apprentice Forty Dollars per year.

Witness our hands & seals the day and year first before written.

Executed Before us in duplicate
George Haslett   William + Heard, his mark
J. J. Burch, ordinary   E. J. Bell

Georgia   }   [517]
Elbert County } This Indenture, made this the 11 day February 1903, between Peter Brown, of said County, for & in behalf of him self, of the one part, & J. C. Hudgens, of the County aforesaid, of the other part. Witnesseth: That the said Peter Brown, as aforesaid, does by these presents bind out him self, of said County, as apprentice to said J. C. Hudgens in the trade or craft of Husbandry or as laborer upon the plantation of the said J. C. Hudgens, to be taught the said Craft or trade of Husbandry or laborer, & to live with, Continue, & serve the Said J. C. Hudgens as an apprentice from the date hereof for & during the term of 2 years. During all of which time, said Peter Brown, as aforesaid, doth Covenant with the said J. C. Hudgens that the said Peter Brown shall well & faithfully demean his self as such faithful Apprentice, observing fully the Command of the said J. C. Hudgens, And in all things deporting & behaving his self as a faithful Apprentice

to the said J. C. Hudgens, neither revealing his secrets, nor at any time neglecting or leaving the business of the said J. C. Hudgens. And for & in Consideration of the Service well & faithfully rendered by the said Peter Brown, of the first part, said J. C. Hudgens, of the second part, doth Covenant, promise, & agree to instruct his said Apprentice, or otherwise Cause him to be well & faithfully instructed, in the said trade or Craft of Husbandry or laborer, & shall also allow, furnish, & provide him, said Apprentice, with meat & drink & Clothing during the said term, & all other necessaries meet & proper, in sickness & in health, and shall also, at the expiration of the said term, allow & pay the said Apprentice Eighty Dollars per year.

Witness our hands & seals the day and year first before written.

Executed Before Us /in Duplicate
E. B. Starke, sr   Peter + Brown, his mark
J. J. Burch, ordinary   J. C. Hudgens

Georgia   }   [518]
Elbert County } This Indenture, Made this the 5th day of February 1903, between Capus Ector & Georgia Ector, of said County, for & in behalf of them selves, being of the age of 35, 30 years, of the one part, & C. J. Dickson, of the County aforesaid, of the other part. Witnesseth: That the said Capus & Georgia Ector, as aforesaid, does by these presents bind out them selves, of said County, as apprentices to said C. J. Dickson in the trade or craft of Husbandry or as Laborers upon the plantation of the said C. J. Dickson, to be taught the said Craft or trade of Husbandry or laborers, & to live with, Continue, & serve the said C. J. Dickson as apprentices from the date hereof for & during the term of 2 years. During all of which time, said Capus & Georgia Ector, as aforesaid, doth covenant with the said C. J. Dickson that the Said Capus & Georgia Ector shall well & faithfully demean them selves as such faithful apprentices, observing fully the command of the said C. J. Dickson, & in all things deporting & behaving them selves as faithful Apprentices to the said C. J. Dickson, neither revealing his secrets, nor at any time neglecting or leaving the business of the said C. J. Dickson. And for & in Consideration of the service well & faithfully rendered by the said Capus & Georgia Ector, of the first part, said C. J. Dickson, of the second part, doth covenant, promise, & agree to instruct his said Apprentices, or otherwise Cause them to be well & faithfully instructed, in the said trade or craft of Husbandry or laborers, and shall also allow, furnish, & provide his said Apprentices, with meat & drink & clothing during the said term, & shall also, at the expiration of the said term, allow & pay the said Apprentices Nine Dollars per month.

Witness our hands & seals the day and year first before written.

Executed Before Us In Duplicate
J. J. Burch, ordinary   C. G. Ector
T. J. Brown   G. A. Ector
J. C. Gant   C. J. Dickson
W. N. Dye, N. P.

Georgia   }   [519]
Elbert County } This Indenture, Made this the 24 day February 1903, between Joe Gaines, of Hart County, for & in behalf of him self & their children Henry Gaines, Alice Gaines, & Lois Gaines, being of the age of 18, 13, 7 years, of the one part, and J. A. Cauthen, of the County aforesaid, of the other part. Witnesseth: That the said Joe Gaines, as aforesaid, does by these presents bind out himself, Henry Gaines, Alice Gaines, & Lois Gaines, of said Hart County, as apprentices to said J. A. Cauthen in the trade or craft of Farm Work or as Laborers upon the plantation of the said J. A. Cauthen, to be taught the said craft or trade of Farm Work or laborers, & to live with, Continue, & serve the said J. A. Cauthen as apprentices from the 15 Oct 1903 for & during the term of two years from above date for the Amount of Seventy Two & $^{50}/_{100}$ Dollars money delivered. During all of which time, said Joe Gaines, as aforesaid, doth Covenant with the said J. A. Cauthen that the said children & self shall well & faithfully demean them selves as such faithful Apprentices, observing fully the Command of the said J. A. Cauthen, & in all things deporting & behaving them selves as faithful Apprentices to said J. A. Cauthen, neither revealing his secrets, nor at any time neglecting or leaving the business of the said J. A. Cauthen.

And for & in Consideration of the service well & faithfully rendered by the said Joe, Henry, Alice, & Lois Gaines, of the first part, said J. A. Cauthen, of the second part, doth Covenant, promise, & agree to instruct them, said Apprentices, or otherwise Cause them to be well & faithfully instructed, in the said trade or craft of Farm Work or laborers, and at the expiration of the said term, allow what has been paid by said J. A. Cauthen seventy two & $^{50}/_{100}$ Dollars to said Joe Gaines

Witness our hands & seals the day and year first before written.

Executed before us in Duplicate
R. P. Carter   Joe + Gaines, his mark
W. H. Kerlin, N. P.   J. A. Cauthen
                                              per W. H. Kerlin

Georgia } [520]
Elbert County } This Indenture, Made this the 26 day of February 1903, between Andrew Edwards, of said County, for & in behalf of his minor son Marcus Edwards, being of the age of 15 years, of the one part, and J. T. Heard, of the County aforesaid, of the other part. Witnesseth: That the said Andrew Edwards, as aforesaid, does by these presents bind out his said son Marcus, of said County, as apprentice to said J. T. Heard in the trade or craft of Husbandry or as laborer upon the plantation of the said J. T. Heard, to be taught the said craft or trade of Husbandry or laborer, & to live with, continue, & serve the said J. T. Heard as an Apprentice from the date hereof for & during the term of his minority. During all of which time, said Andrew Edwards, as aforesaid, doth covenant with the said J. T. Heard that the said Marcus Edwards shall well & faithfully demean his self as such faithful Apprentice, observing fully the Command of the said J. T. Heard, & in all things deporting & behaving his self as a faithful Apprentice to said J. T. Heard, neither revealing his secrets, nor at any time neglecting or leaving the business of the said J. T. Heard. And for & in Consideration of the Service well & faithfully rendered by the said Marcus Edwards, of the first part, said J. T. Heard, of the second part, doth Covenant, promise, & agree to instruct his said Apprentice, or otherwise cause him to be well & faithfully instructed, in the said trade or craft of Husbandry or laborer, and shall also allow, furnish, & provide his said Apprentice with meat & drink & clothing during the said term, & all other necessaries meet & proper, in sickness & in health, & shall also, at the expiration of the said term, allow & pay the said Apprentices what is now allowed by the statute in such Case made and provided.

Witness our hands & seals the day & year first before written.

Executed Before us In duplicate
H. A. Roebuck   Andrew + Edwards, his mark
J. J. Burch, ordinary   J. T. Heard

Georgia } [521]
Elbert County } This Indenture, made this the 20th day of October 1902, between Carey Allen, of said County, for & in behalf of his sons Alen, Beverly, & McIntosh Allen, being of the age of 9, 7, 5 years, of the one part, and J. W. McCalla, of the County aforesaid, of the other part.

Witnesseth: That the said Carey Allen, as aforesaid, does by these presents bind out his sons Alen, Beverly, & McIntosh, of said County, as Apprentices to said J. W. McCalla in the trade or craft of Farming or as laborers upon the plantation of the said J. W. McCalla, to be taught the said craft or trade of Farming or Laborers, and to live with, Continue, & serve the said J. W. McCalla as an Apprentices from the date hereof for & during their minority. During all of which time, said Carey Allen, as aforesaid, doth covenant with the said J. W. McCalla that the said Alen, Beverly, & McIntosh Allen shall well & faithfully demean themselves as such faithful Apprentices, observing fully the command of the said J. W. McCalla, & in all things deporting & behaving themselves as faithful Apprentices to said J. W. McCalla, neither revealing his secrets, nor at any time neglecting or leaving the business of the said J. W. McCalla. And for & in consideration of the service well & faithfully rendered by the said Alen, Beverly, & McIntosh Allen, of the first part, said J. W. McCalla, of the second part, doth covenant, promise, & agree to instruct them, said Apprentices, or otherwise Cause them to be well & faithfully instructed, in the said trade or Craft of Farming or Laborers, and also to read the English language, & shall also allow, furnish, & provide them, said Apprentices, with meat & drink & clothing during the said term, & all other necessaries meet and proper, in sickness & in health, and shall also, at the expiration of the said term, allow & pay the said Apprentices what is now allowed by the statute in such case made & provided.

Witness our hands and seals the day & year first before written.

Executed Before us In duplicate
B. F. Goss, J. P.   Carey + Allen, her mark
J. M. Dixon   J. W. McCalla

Georgia   }   [522]
Elbert County } This Indenture, Made this the 20th day of October 1902, between Stephen Calhoun, of said County, for & in behalf of his daughter Winnie and son Sam Calhoun, being of the age of 14, 12 years, of the one part, and J. W. McCalla, of the County aforesaid, of the other part. Witnesseth: That the said Stephen Calhoun, as aforesaid, does by these presents bind out Winnie and Sam Calhoun, of said County, as Apprentices to said J. W. McCalla in the trade or craft of farming or as Laborers upon the plantation of the said J. W. McCalla, to be taught the said Craft or trade of Farming or laborers, & to live with, Continue, & serve the said J. W. McCalla as apprentices from the date hereof for & during the term of their minority. During all of which time, said Stephen Calhoun, as aforesaid, doth covenant with the said J. W. McCalla that the said Winnie & Sam Calhoun shall well & faithfully demean them selves as such faithful Apprentices, observing fully the command of the said J. W. McCalla, and in all things deporting & behaving them selves as faithful Apprentices to said J. W. McCalla, neither revealing his secrets, nor at any time neglecting or leaving the business of the said J. W. McCalla. And for & in Consideration of the service well & faithfully

rendered by the said Winnie & Sam Calhoun, of the first part, said J. W. McCalla, of the second part, doth covenant, promise, & agree to instruct them, said Apprentices, or otherwise Cause them to be well & faithfully instructed, in the said trade or craft of Farming or Laborers, & also to read the English language, & shall also allow, furnish, & provide them, said Apprentices, with meat & drink & clothing during the said term, and all other necessaries meet & proper, in sickness & in health, & shall also, at the expiration of the said term, allow & pay the said Apprentices what is now allowed by the statute in such case made and provided.

Witness our hands & seals the day & year first before written.

Executed Before Us In duplicate
B. F. Goss, J. P.   Stephen + Calhoun, his mark
J. M. Dixon   J. W. McCalla

Georgia   }   [523]
Elbert County } This Indenture, made this the 23rd day of December 1902, between Ann Parks, of said County, for & in behalf of herself and Dennis Parks, Eddie, John, Richard, Lizzie, and Willis Parks, being of the age of 15, 13, 12, 11, 10, 9 years, of the one part, and William Burdett, of the County aforesaid, of the other part. Witnesseth: That the said Ann Parks, as aforesaid, does by these presents bind out herself and children, of said County, as Apprentices to said William Burdett in the trade or Craft of Husbandry or laborers, and to live with, Continue, & serve the said William Burdett as apprentices from the date hereof for & during the term of 12 months from above date. During all of which time, said Ann Parks, as aforesaid, doth covenant with the said William Burdett that the said Children and herself shall well & faithfully demean them selves as such faithful Apprentices, observing fully the command of the said William Burdett, & in all things deporting & behaving them selves as faithful Apprentices to said William Burdett, neither revealing his secrets, nor at any time neglecting or leaving the business of the said William Burdett. And for & in consideration of the service well & faithfully rendered by the said Ann Parks & her children, of the first part, said William Burdett, of the second part, doth covenant, promise, & agree to instruct his said Apprentices, or otherwise cause them to be well & faithfully instructed, in the said trade or craft of Husbandry or Laborers, & also to read the English language, & shall also allow, furnish, & provide his said Apprentices, with meat & drink & clothing during the said term, & all other necessaries meet & proper, in sickness & in health, & shall also, at the expiration of the said term, allow & pay the said Apprentices what is now allowed by the statute in such case made and provided.

Witness our hands and seals the day & year first before written.

Executed Before Us In duplicate
George C. Bond   Ann + Parks, her mark
W. A. Rucker, Clerk S. C.   Wm Burdett

[The Ordinary wrote the following notation vertically along the left margin of the foregoing indenture.]

This Contract between Ann Parks and William Burdett is this day Annuled By Consent of Parties This Sep^t 5, 1903. J. J. Burch, ordinary

Georgia   }   [524]
Elbert County } This Indenture, made this the 10 day of March 1903, between Henry Stowers, of said County, for & in behalf of himself & his minor son Paul Stowers, being of the age of (Paul) 14 years, of the one part, and E. J. Bell, of the County aforesaid, of the other part. Witnesseth: That the said Henry Stowers, as aforesaid, does by these presents bind out him self & his son Paul Stowers, of said County, as apprentices to said E. J. Bell in the trade or craft of Husbandry or as laborers upon the plantation of the said E. J. Bell, to be taught the said trade or craft of Husbandry or Laborers, & to live with, Continue, & serve the said E. J. Bell as Apprentices from the date hereof for & during the term of 2 years. During all of which time, said Henry Stowers, as aforesaid, doth covenant with the said E. J. Bell that the said Henry & Paul Stowers shall well & faithfully demean them selves as such faithful Apprentices, observing fully the command of the said E. J. Bell, and in all things deporting & behaving them selves as faithful Apprentices to said E. J. Bell, neither revealing his secrets, nor at any time neglecting or leaving the business of the said E. J. Bell. And for & in Consideration of the service well & faithfully rendered by the said Henry & Paul Stowers, of the first part, said E. J. Bell, of the second part, doth Covenant, promise, & agree to instruct his said Apprentices, or otherwise Cause them to be well & faithfully instructed, in the said trade or craft of Husbandry or Laborers, and shall also allow, furnish, & provide said apprentices, with meat & drink & clothing during the said term, & all other necessaries meet & proper, in sickness & in health, & shall also, at the expiration of the said term, allow & pay the said Apprentices Nine Dollars per month.

Witness our hands and seals the day & year first before written.

Executed Before Us In Duplicate. The above Contract made to secure the payment for Twenty six dollars.

Executed Before Us In Duplicate
McAlpin Arnold Henry + Stowers, his mark
J. J. Burch, ordinary E. J. Bell

Georgia } [525]
Elbert County } This Indenture, made this the 25 day of March 1903, between Mattie Worton, of said County, for & in behalf her self, being of the age of 25 years, of the one part, & E. J. Bell, of the County aforesaid, of the other part. Witnesseth: That the said Mattie Worton, as aforesaid, does by these presents bind out her self, of said County, as Apprentice to said E. J. Bell in the trade or craft of Husbandry or as Laborer upon the plantation of the said E. J. Bell, to be taught the said trade or craft of Husbandry or laborer, and to live with, Continue, & serve the said E. J. Bell as an apprentice from the date hereof for & during the term of nine months. During all of which time, said Mattie Worton, as aforesaid, doth covenant with the said E. J. Bell that the said Mattie Worton shall well & faithfully demean her self as a faithful Apprentice, observing fully the Command of the said E. J. Bell, And in all things deporting & behaving her self as a faithful Apprentice to said E. J. Bell, neither revealing his secrets, nor at any time neglecting or leaving the business of the said E. J. Bell. And for & in Consideration of the service well & faithfully rendered by the said Mattie Worton, of the first part, said E. J. Bell, of the second part, doth Covenant, promise, & agree to instruct his said Apprentice, or otherwise Cause her to be well & faithfully instructed, in the said trade or craft of Husbandry or Laborer, and Shall also allow, furnish, & provide his said Apprentice with meat & drink during the said term, and shall also, at the expiration of the said term, allow & pay the said apprentice Twenty five Dollars, including lodging & food. Witness our hands and seals the day & year first before written.

Executed Before Us In duplicate
George Haslett Mattie + Worton, her mark
J. J. Burch, ordinary E. J. Bell

Georgia } [526]
Elbert County } This Indenture, made this the 15 day of April 1903, between Laura Mattox, of said County, for & in behalf of her self, being of the age of 23 years, of the one part, & A. J. Mathews, of the County aforesaid, of the other part. Witnesseth: That the said Laura Mattox, as aforesaid, does by these presents bind out her self, of said County, as apprentice to said A. J. Mathews in the trade or

craft of Servant or as laborer upon the plantation of the said A. J. Mathews, to be taught the said trade or craft of servant or as laborer, And to live with, Continue, & serve the said A. J. Mathews as an Apprentice from the date hereof for & during the term of Twelve months. During all of which time, said Laura Mattox, as aforesaid, doth Covenant with the said A. J. Mathews that the said Laura Mattox shall well & faithfully demean her self as such faithful Apprentice, observing fully the Command of the said A. J. Mathews, & in all things deporting & behaving her self as a faithful Apprentice to said A. J. Mathews, neither revealing his secrets, nor at any time neglecting or leaving the business of the said A. J. Mathews, neither revealing his secrets, nor at any time neglecting or leaving the business of the said A. J. Mathews. And for & in Consideration of the service well & faithfully rendered by the said Laura Mattox, of the first part, said A. J. Mathews, of the second part, doth Covenant, promise, & agree to instruct his said apprentice, or otherwise Cause her to be well & faithfully instructed, in the said trade or craft of Servant or Laborer, & shall also allow, furnish, & provide his said Apprentice with meat & drink & clothing during the said term, & all other necessaries meet & proper, in sickness & in health, & shall also, at the expiration of the said term, allow & pay the Said Apprentice Three Dollars per month.

Witness our hands & seals the day & year first before written.

Executed Before us In Duplicate
T. J. Brown   Laura + Mattox, her mark
J. J. Burch, ordinary   A. J. Mathews

Georgia   }   [527]
Elbert County } This Indenture, made this the 15 day of April 1903, between Eli Davenport, of said County, for & in behalf of his minor son Jackson Davenport, being of the age of 13 years, of the one part, and Dr A. S. J. Stovall, of the County aforesaid, of the other part. Witnesseth: That the said Ely Davenport, as aforesaid, does by these presents bind out his said son Jackson, of said County, as Apprentice to said A. S. J. Stovall in the trade or craft of Husbandry or as Laborer upon the plantation of the said A. S. J. Stovall, to be taught the said trade or craft of Husbandry or Laborer, & to live with, Continue, & serve the said A. S. J. Stovall as an Apprentice from the first day of January 1904 for & during the term of One year. During all of which time, said Eli Davenport, as aforesaid, doth covenant with the said A. S. J. Stovall that the said Jackson Davenport shall well & faithfully demean his self as such faithful Apprentice, observing fully the Command of the said A. S. J. Stovall, and in all things deporting & behaving his self as a faithful Apprentice to said A. S. J. Stovall, neither revealing his secrets, nor at any time neglecting or leaving the business of the said A. S. J. Stovall. And

for & in consideration of the service well & faithfully rendered by the said Jackson Davenport, of the first part, said A. S. J. Stovall, of the second part, doth covenant, promise, & agree to instruct his said Apprentice, or otherwise cause him to be well & faithfully instructed, in the said trade or Craft of Husbandry or Laborer, and shall also allow, furnish, & provide his said apprentice with meat & Drink & clothing during the said term, & all other necessaries meet & proper, in sickness & in health, and shall also, at the expiration of the said term, allow & pay the said apprentice Twenty Five Dollars.

Witness our hands and Seals the day & year first before written.

Executed Before us In Duplicate
W. A. Rucker   Eli + Davenport, his mark
J. J. Burch, ordinary   A. S. J. Stovall

Georgia   }   [528]
Elbert County } This Indenture, made this 21st day of April 1903, between Jim Fortson, of said County, for & in behalf of him self, being of the age of 21 years, of the one part, & Jn° T. Heard, of the County aforesaid, of the other part. Witnesseth: That the said Jim Fortson, as aforesaid, does by these presents bind out him self, of said County, As Apprentice to said Jn° T. Heard in the trade or craft of Husbandry or as Laborer upon the plantation of the said Jn° T. Heard, to be taught the said Craft or trade of Husbandry or Laborer, & to live with, Continue, & serve the said Jn° T. Heard as an Apprentice from the date hereof for & during the term of 5 years. During all of which time, said Jim Fortson, as aforesaid, doth Covenant with the said Jn° T. Heard that the said Jim Fortson Shall well & faithfully demean him self as such faithful Apprentice, observing fully the command of the said Jn° T. Heard, & in all things deporting & behaving him self as a faithful Apprentice to said Jn° T. Heard, neither revealing his secrets, nor at any time neglecting or leaving the business of the said Jn° T. Heard. And for & in Consideration of the Service well & faithfully rendered by the said Jim Fortson, of the first part, said Jn° T. Heard, of the second part, doth Covenant, promise, & agree to instruct his said apprentice, or otherwise Cause him to be well & faithfully instructed, in the said trade or Craft of Husbandry or laborer, & shall also allow, furnish, & provide his said apprentice with meat & drink & clothing during the said term, & all other necessaries meet & proper, in sickness & in health, & shall also, at the expiration of the Said term, allow & pay the said Apprentices Seventy five & $^{00}/_{100}$ Dollars.

Witness our hands and seals the day & year first before written.

Executed Before Us In Duplicate
Owen J. Seymore   Jim + Fortson, his mark
J. Alan Miles, N. P. E. C.   Jn° T. Heard

Georgia   }   [529]
Elbert County } This Indenture, made this the 9 day of May 1903, between Bob Brown, of said County, for & in behalf of him self, being of the age of 25 years, of the one part, & M. E. Maxwell, of the County aforesaid, of the other part. Witnesseth: That the said Bob Brown, as aforesaid, does by these presents bind out him self, of said County, as apprentice to said M. E. Maxwell in the trade or craft of Husbandry or as laborer upon the plantation of the said M. E. Maxwell, to be taught the said trade or craft of Husbandry or Laborer, & to live with, Continue, & serve the said M. E. Maxwell as an Apprentice from the 20th day of December 1903 for and during the term of Three years. During all of which time, said Bob Brown, as aforesaid, Doth Covenant with the said M. E. Maxwell that the said Bob Brown shall well & faithfully demean him self as such faithful Apprentice, observing fully the command of the said M. E. Maxwell, And in all things deporting & behaving him self as a faithful Apprentice to said M. E. Maxwell, neither revealing his secrets, nor at any time neglecting or leaving the business of the said M. E. Maxwell.

And for & in Consideration of the service well & faithfully rendered by the said Bob Brown, of the first part, said M. E. Maxwell, of the second part, doth Covenant, promise, & agree to instruct his said Apprentice, or otherwise cause him to be well & faithfully instructed, in the said trade or craft of Husbandry or laborer, & shall also allow, furnish, & provide his said apprentice with meat & drink & clothing during the said term, & all other necessaries meet & proper, in sickness & in health, & shall also, at the expiration of the said term, allow & pay the said Apprentice what is now allowed by the statute in such case made & provided.

Witness our hands & seals the day & year first before written. Executed Before Us In Duplicate

W. A. Rucker   Bob + Brown, his mark
J. J. Burch, ordinary   M. E. Maxwell

Georgia   }   [530]
Elbert County } This Indenture, made this the 13 day of May 1903, between Jep Brawner, of said County, for & in behalf of him self, being of the age of 25 years,

of the one part, & W. O. Jones, of the County aforesaid, of the other part. Witnesseth: That the said Jep Brawner, as aforesaid, does by these presents bind out him self, of said County, as apprentice to said W. O. Jones in the trade or craft of Brickmaker or as laborer upon the Brickyard of the said W. O. Jones, to be taught the said trade or craft of Brick maker or Laborer, & to live with, Continue, & serve the said W. O. Jones as an Apprentice from the date hereof for and during the term of Six months.

During all of which time, said Jep Brawner, as aforesaid, doth Covenant with the said W. O. Jones, or his agent, that the said Jep Brawner shall well & faithfully demean him self as such faithful Apprentice, observing fully the command of the said W. O. Jones, or his agent, & in all things deporting & behaving him self as a faithful Apprentice to said W. O. Jones, neither revealing his secrets, nor at any time neglecting or leaving the business of the said W. O. Jones And for & in Consideration of the service well & faithfully rendered by the said Jep Brawner, of the first part, said W. O. Jones, of the second part, doth Covenant, promise, & agree to instruct his said apprentice, or otherwise Cause him to be well & faithfully instructed, in the said trade or Craft of Brick maker or laborer, & shall also allow, furnish, & provide him, said Apprentice, with meat & drink during the said term, and shall also, at the expiration of the said term, allow & pay the said Apprentice Ten Dollars per month.

Witness our hands & seals the day & year first before written.

Executed Before Us In Duplicate
W. F. Anderson   Jep Brawner
H. D. Hamlin, N. P. E. C.   W. O. Jones
                                             for Elberton Brick C°

Georgia   }   [531]
Elbert County   } This Indenture, made this the 5 day of June 1903, between Hattie Jones of said County, for & in behalf of her daughter Norma Tate (alias Bell), being of the age of 14 years, of the one part, & B. B. Bell, of the County aforesaid, of the other part. Witnesseth: That the said Hattie Jones, as aforesaid, does by these presents bind out her said daughter Norma, of said County, as Apprentice to said B. B. Bell in the trade or craft of House servant or as laborer upon the plantation of the said B. B. Bell, to be taught the said trade or craft of House servant or Laborer, & to live with, Continue, & serve the said B. B. Bell as an apprentice from the date hereof for and during the term of her minority.

During all of which time, said Hattie Jones, as aforesaid, doth covenant with the said B. B. Bell that the Said Norma Tate, alias Bell, shall well & faithfully demean her Self as such faithful apprentice, observing fully the Command of the said B. B. Bell, And in all things deporting & behaving her self as a faithful Apprentice to the said B. B. Bell, neither revealing his secrets, nor at any time neglecting or leaving the business of the said B. B. Bell. And for & in consideration of the service well & faithfully rendered by the said Norma Tate, alias Bell,, of the first part, said B. B. Bell, of the second part, doth covenant, promise, & agree to instruct his said apprentice, or otherwise Cause her to be well and faithfully instructed, in the said trade or craft of House servant or Laborer, & also to read the English language, & shall also allow, furnish, and provide his said Apprentice with meat & drink & clothing during the said term, & all other necessaries meet & proper, in sickness & in health, & shall also, at the expiration of the said term, allow & pay the said apprentice what is now allowed by the Statute in such case made & provided.

Witness our hands & seals the day & year first before written.

Executed Before us In Duplicate
Abda Oglesby, J. P. Hattie + Jones, her mark
W. A. Rucker, clerk S. C. B. B. Bell

Georgia   }   [532]
Elbert County } This Indenture, Made this the 12th day of June 1903, between Charlie Collins, of said County, for & in behalf of him self, being of the age of 25 years, of the one part, & W. O. Jones, of the County aforesaid, of the other part. Witnesseth: That the said Charlie Collins, as aforesaid, does by these presents bind out himself, of said County, as apprentice to said W. O. Jones in the trade or craft of Brick maker or as Laborer upon the Brick Yard of the said W. O. Jones, to be taught the said trade or craft of Brick Maker or Laborer, & to live with, continue, & serve the said W. O. Jones as an apprentice from the date hereof for and during the term of Six months.

During all of which time, said Charlie Collins shall well & faithfully demean him self as such faithful Apprentice, observing fully the Command of the said W. O. Jones, or his agent, and in all things deporting & behaving him self as a faithful Apprentice to said W. O. Jones, neither revealing his secrets, nor at any time neglecting or leaving the business of the said W. O. Jones, or his agent And for & in Consideration of the service well & faithfully rendered by the said Charlie Collins, of the first part, said W. O. Jones, of the second part, doth Covenant, promise, & agree to instruct him, said apprentice, or otherwise Cause him to be well & faithfully instructed, in the said trade or craft of Brick Maker or Laborer, & shall also allow, furnish, & provide him, said apprentice, with meat & drink during the said term, and shall also, at the expiration of the said term, allow & pay the said Apprentice the Sum of Ten Dollars per month during above mentioned period after deducting such amounts as the said Charlie Collins may receive over or may hereafter become indebted to the said W. O. Jones. All Interlinations made before Signing.

Witness our hands & seals the day & year first before written.

Executed Before Us In Duplicate
A. F. Smith   Charlie + Collins, his mark
J. J. Burch, ordinary   W. O. Jones

Georgia   }   [533]
Elbert County } This Indenture, made this the 12 day of June 1903, between Delroe Burdell, of said County, for & in behalf of himself, being of the age of 21 years, of the one part, & W. O. Jones, of the County aforesaid, of the other part. Witnesseth: That the said Delroe Burdell, as aforesaid, does by these presents bind out himself, of said County, as apprentice to said W. O. Jones in the trade or craft of Brick maker or as laborer upon the brick yard of the said W. O. Jones, to be taught the said trade or craft of brick maker or Laborer, & to live with, continue, & serve the said W. O. Jones or his agents as an apprentice from the date hereof for and during the term of six months.

During all of which time, said Delroe Burdell, as aforesaid, doth covenant with the said W. O. Jones, that the said Delroe Burdell shall well & faithfully demean him self as such faithful Apprentice, observing fully the Command of the said W. O. Jones, or his agents, and in all things deporting & behaving him self as a faithful Apprentice to the said W. O. Jones, neither revealing his secrets, nor at any time neglecting or leaving the business of the said W. O. Jones, or his agent And for & in consideration of the service well & faithfully rendered by the said Delroe Burdell, of the first part, said W. O. Jones, of the second part, doth Covenant, promise, & agree to instruct him, said Apprentice, or otherwise Cause him to be well & faithfully instructed, in the said trade or craft of brick maker or laborer, and shall also allow, furnish, & provide him, said apprentice, with meat and drink during the said term, & shall also, at the expiration of the said term, allow & pay the said Apprentice The sum of Ten Dollars per month during above mentioned period after deducting such amounts as the said Delroe Burdell may receive over or may hereafter become indebted to the said W. O. Jones. All Interlinations made before signing.

Witness our hands & seals the day & year first before written.

Executed Before Us In Duplicate
A. F. Smith   Delroe Burdell
J. J. Burch, ordinary   W. O. Jones

Georgia   }   [534]
Elbert County } This Indenture, Made this the 11 day of July 1903, between Jut Brown, of said County, for & in behalf of him self, being of the age of 30 years, of the one part, and W. J. Hammond, of the County aforesaid, of the other part. Witnesseth: That the said Jut Brown, as aforesaid, does by these presents bind out himself, of said County, as Apprentice to said W. J. Hammond in the trade or craft of Husbandry or as Laborer upon the plantation of the said W. J. Hammond, to be taught the said trade or craft of Husbandry or Laborer, & to live with, continue, & Serve the said W. J. Hammond as an apprentice from the 1st day August 1903 for and during one year. During all of which time, said Jut Brown, as aforesaid, does covenant with the said W. J. Hammond that the said Jut Brown shall well & faithfully demean him self as such faithful apprentice, observing fully the Command of the said W. J. Hammond, & in all things deporting & behaving him self as a faithful Apprentice to said W. J. Hammond, neither revealing his secrets, nor at any time neglecting or leaving the business of the said W. J. Hammond. And for & in consideration of the service well & faithfully rendered by the said Jut Brown, of the first part, said W. J. Hammond, of the second part, doth covenant, promise, and agree to instruct him, said Apprentice, or otherwise cause him to be well & faithfully instructed, in the said trade or craft of Husbandry or laborer, And shall also allow, furnish, and provide him, said Apprentice, with meat & drink & clothing during the said term, and all other necessaries meet & proper, in sickness & in health, & shall also, at the expiration of the said term, allow & pay the said Apprentice Seventy Eight Dollars.

Witness our hands & Seals the day & year first before written. Executed Before us In Duplicate.

T. J. Brown   Jut + Brown, his mark
W. A. Rucker, Clerk S. C.   W. J. Hammond

Georgia   }   [535]
Elbert County } This Indenture, made this the 1st day August 1903, between Llewellyn Heard, of said County, for & in behalf of his minor son Jefferson, being of the age of 4 years, of the one part, & Willis Curry, of the County aforesaid, of the other part. Witnesseth: That the said Llewyllyn Heard, as aforesaid, does by

these presents bind out his said son Jefferson, of said County, as Apprentice to said Willis Curry in the trade or Craft of Husbandry or as laborer upon the plantation of the said Willis Curry, to be taught the said trade or Craft of Husbandry or Laborer, & to live with, Continue, & serve the said Willis Curry as an Apprentice from the date hereof for and during the term of 14 years, or until he is eighteen years old. During all of which time, said Llewellyn Heard, as aforesaid, doth Covenant with the said Willis Curry that the said Jefferson Heard shall well & faithfully demean his self as such faithful Apprentice, observing fully the Command of the said Willis Curry, & in all things deporting & behaving his self as a faithful Apprentice to the said Willis Curry, neither revealing his secrets, nor at any time neglecting or leaving the business of the said Willis Curry. And for and in Consideration of the service well & faithfully rendered by the said Jefferson Heard, of the first part, said Willis Curry, of the second part, doth Covenant, promise, and agree to instruct his said Apprentice, or otherwise Cause him to be well & faithfully instructed, in the said trade or Craft of Husbandry or Laborer, & also to read the English language, & shall also allow, furnish, & provide his said Apprentice, with meat & drink & clothing during the said term, and all other necessaries meet & proper, in Sickness & in health, & Shall also, at the expiration of the said term, allow & pay the said Apprentice what is no allowed by the Statute in Such Case made & provided.

Witness our hands & Seals the day & year first before written.

Executed Before Us In Duplicate
J. W. Vanpin   Llewyling Heard
J. J. Burch, ordinary   Willis + Curry, his mark

Georgia   }   [536]
Elbert County } This Indenture, Made this the 10 day of August 1903, between Wes Mattox, of said County, for & in behalf of him self & his sons Tom Mattox, John Mattox, & Early Mattox, being of the age of 21, 15, 10 years, of the one part, & J. C. Hudgens, of the County aforesaid, of the other part. Witnesseth: That the said Wes Mattox, as aforesaid, does by these presents bind out him self & his sons Tom, John, & Early Mattox, of said County, as apprentices to said J. C. Hudgens in the trade or Craft of Husbandry or as laborers upon the plantation of the said J. C. Hudgens, to be taught the said trade or craft of Husbandry or laborers, and to live with, continue, & serve the said J. C. Hudgens as an Apprentice from the first day Jany 1904 for and during the term of one year. During all of which time, said Wes Mattox, as aforesaid, doth covenant with the said J. C. Hudgens that the said Wes, Tom, John, & Early Mattox shall well & faithfully demean them selves as such faithful Apprentices, observing fully the Command of the said J. C. Hudgens,

& in all things deporting & behaving them selves as faithful Apprentices to the said J. C. Hudgens, neither revealing his secrets, nor at any time neglecting or leaving the business of the said J. C. Hudgens. And for & in Consideration of the service well & faithfully rendered by the said Wes, Tom, John, & Early Mattox, of the first part, said J. C. Hudgens, of the second part, doth Covenant, promise, & agree to instruct his said Apprentices, or otherwise Cause them to be well & faithfully instructed, in the said trade or craft of Husbandry or laborers, & Shall also allow, furnish, & provide his said Apprentices with meat & drink during said term, & shall also, at the expiration of the said term, allow & pay the said Apprentice One Hundred Dollars.

Witness our hands & Seals the day & year first before written.

Executed Before us In duplicate
James McIntosh   Wes + Mattox, his mark
J. J. Burch, ordinary   J. C. Hudgens

Georgia   }   [537]
Elbert County } This Indenture, made this the 10th day of August 1903, between Tom Heard & Bill Heard, of said County, for & in behalf of them selves, being of the age of 30, 33 years, of the one part, & J. G. Seymore, of the County aforesaid, of the other part. Witnesseth: That the said Tom & Bill Heard, as aforesaid, does by these presents bind out them selves, of said County, as Apprentices to said J. G. Seymore in the trade or craft of Husbandry (J. G. Seymore) in the trade or Craft of Husbandry or as laborers upon the plantation of the said J. G. Seymore, to be taught the said trade or craft of Husbandry or laborers, & to live with, Continue, & serve the said J. G. Seymore as apprentices from the first Jany 1904 for and during the Term of 2 years.

During all of which time, said Tom & Bill Heard, as aforesaid, doth Covenant with the said J. G. Seymore that the said Tom & Bill Heard shall well & faithfully demean them selves as such faithful Apprentices, observing fully the Command of the said J. G. Seymore, & in all things deporting & behaving them selves as faithful Apprentices to the said J. G. Seymore, Neither revealing his secrets, nor at any time neglecting or leaving the business of the said J. G. Seymore.

And for & in Consideration of the service well & faithfully rendered by the said Tom & Bill Heard, of the first part, said J. G. Seymore, of the second part, doth covenant, promise, & agree to instruct his said Apprentices, or otherwise Cause them to be well & faithfully instructed, in the said trade or craft of Husbandry or laborers, (& shall said term) & Shall also, at the expiration of the said term, allow

& pay the said Apprentices six Dollars per month each or One Hundred & forty Two Dollars.

Witness our hands & Seals the day year first before written.

Executed Before us In Duplicate
O. J. Seymore   Tom + Heard, his mark
J. J. Burch, ordinary   Bill + Heard, his mark
   J. G. Seymore

Georgia } [538]
Elbert County } This Indenture, Made this the 12 day of August 1903, between Margaret Starke, of said County, for & in behalf of her self & her sons Marsh Downer and Luther Du Bose, being of the age of 50, 13, 15 years, of the one part, and G. H. McLanahan, of the County aforesaid, of the other part. Witnesseth: That the said Margaret Starke, as aforesaid, does by these presents bind out her Self & her sons Marsh & Luther, of said County, as apprentices to Said G. H. McLanahan in the trade or Craft of Husbandry or as laborers upon the plantation of the said G. H. McLanahan, to be taught the said trade or Craft of Husbandry or Laborers, & to live with, Continue, & serve the said G. H. McLanahan as apprentices from the date hereof for and during the term of 17 months, or until 25 day December 1904. During all of which time, Said Margaret Starke, as aforesaid, doth Covenant with the said G. H. McLanahan that the said Margaret, Marsh, & Luther shall well & faithfully demean them selves as such faithful Apprentices, observing fully the Command of the said G. H. McLanahan, and in all things deporting & behaving them selves as faithful Apprentices to the said G. H. McLanahan, neither revealing his secrets, nor at any time neglecting or leaving the business of the said G. H. McLanahan. And for and in Consideration of the Services well & faithfully rendered by the said Margaret Starke, Marsh Downer, & Luther Du Bose, of the first part, said G. H. McLanahan, of the second part, doth Covenant, promise, and agree to instruct his said Apprentices, or otherwise Cause them to be well & faithfully instructed, in the said trade or Craft of Husbandry or laborers, & shall also allow, furnish, & provide his said Apprentices with meat & drink during the said term, & shall also, at the expiration of the said term, allow & pay the said Apprentices Eleven Dollars per month.

Witness our hands & Seals the day & year first before written.

Executed Before us In Duplicate
George C. Grogan   Margaret + Starke, her mark
J. J. Burch, ordinary   G. H. McLanahan

Georgia } [539]
Elbert County } This Indenture, made this the 18 day of August 1903, between Anna Parks, of said County, for & in behalf of her son William Dennis Parks, being of the age of 16 years, of the one part, & A. Thurman, of the County aforesaid, of the other part. Witnesseth: That the said Anna Parks, as aforesaid, does by these presents bind out her said son William Dennis, of said County, as Apprentice to said A. Thurman in the trade or craft of Husbandry or as laborer upon the plantation of the said A. Thurman, to be taught the said trade or Craft of Husbandry or laborer, & to live with, Continue, & serve the said A. Thurman as an Apprentice from the first day Jany 1904 for and during the term of one year.

During all of which time, said Anna Parks, as aforesaid, doth Covenant with the said A. Thurman that the said William Dennis Parks shall well & faithfully demean his self as such faithful Apprentice, observing fully the Command of the said A. Thurman, & in all things deporting & behaving his self as a faithful Apprentice to the said A. Thurman, neither revealing his secrets, nor at any time neglecting or leaving the business of the said A. Thurman. And for & in Consideration of the service well & faithfully rendered by the Said William Dennis Parks, of the first part, said A. Thurman, of the second part, doth Covenant, promise, and agree to instruct his said Apprentice, or otherwise Cause him to be well & faithfully instructed, in the said trade or Craft of Husbandry or laborer, & shall also allow, furnish, & provide his said Apprentice with meat & drink & clothing during the said term, & all other necessaries meet & proper, in sickness & in health, & Shall also, at the expiration of the said term, allow & pay the said Apprentice Ten Dollars.

Witness our hands seals the day & year first before written.

Executed Before us In duplicate
D. B. Alexander   Anna + Parks, her mark
J. J. Burch, ordinary   Arthur Thurman

Georgia } [540]
Elbert County } This Indenture, made this the 5 day of Sep^t 1903, between Henry Banks, of said County, for & in behalf of him self, being of the age of 30 years, of the one part, and B. F. Smith, of the County aforesaid, of the other part. Witnesseth: That the said Henry Banks, as aforesaid, does by these presents bind out him self, of said County, as apprentice to said B. F. Smith in the trade or craft of Husbandry or as laborer upon the plantation of the said B. F. Smith, to be taught the said trade or craft of Husbandry or laborer, & to live with, Continue, & Serve the said B. F. Smith as an Apprentice from the date hereof for and during the term

of 17 months, or until 25 December 1904. During all of which time, said Henry Banks, as aforesaid, doth covenant with the said B. F. Smith that the said Henry Banks shall well & faithfully demean his self as such faithful apprentice, observing fully the Command of the said B. F. Smith, & in all things deporting & behaving his self as a faithful Apprentice to the said B. F. Smith, neither revealing his secrets, nor at any time neglecting or leaving the business of the said B. F. Smith. And for & in Consideration of the service well & faithfully rendered by the said Henry Banks, of the first part, said B. F. Smith, of the second part, doth Covenant, promise, and agree to instruct his said Apprentice, or otherwise Cause him to be well & faithfully instructed, in the said trade or craft of Husbandry or laborer, & shall also allow, furnish, & provide his said Apprentice, with meat & drink during the said term & shall also, at the expiration of the said term, allow & pay the said Apprentice Eight & one forth Dollars per month.

Witness our hands & seals the day & year first before written.

Executed Before Us In Duplicate
James McIntosh   Henry Banks
J. J. Burch, ordinary   Barnard F. Smith

Georgia   }   [541]
Elbert County } This Indenture, made this the 5 day of September 1903, between Ann Parks, of said County, for & in behalf of her minor son Eddie Parks, being of the age of 15 years, of the one part, & J. Y. Swift, of the County aforesaid, of the other part. Witnesseth: That the said Ann Parks, as aforesaid, does by these presents bind out her said son Eddie, of said County, as Apprentice to said J. Y. Swift in the trade or craft of Husbandry or as laborer upon the plantation of the said J. Y. Swift, to be taught the said trade or Craft of Husbandry or laborer, & to live with, Continue, & serve the said J. Y. Swift as an apprentice from the date hereof for and during the term of 17 months, or until 25 day of December 1904. During all of which time, said Ann Parks, as aforesaid, doth Covenant with the said J. Y. Swift that the said Eddie Parks shall well & faithfully demean his self as such faithful apprentice, observing fully the Command of the said J. Y. Swift, & in all things deporting and behaving his self as a faithful apprentice to the said J. Y. Swift, neither revealing his secrets, nor at any time neglecting or leaving the business of the said J. Y. Swift. And for & in consideration of the service well & faithfully rendered by the said Eddie Parks, of the first part, said J. Y. Swift, of the second part, doth covenant, promise, and agree to instruct his said Apprentice, or otherwise Cause him to be well & faithfully instructed, in the said trade or craft of Husbandry or laborer, & shall also allow, furnish, & provide his said Apprentice with meat & drink & clothing during the said term, & all other

necessaries meet & proper, in sickness & in health, & Shall also, at the expiration of the said term, allow & pay the said Apprentice Four Dollars per month.

Witness our hands & seals the day & year first before written.

Executed Before Us In duplicate
James McIntosh   Ann + Parks, her mark
J. J. Burch, ordinary   J. Y. Swift

Georgia   }   [542]
Elbert County } This Indenture, made this the 5 day of September 1903, between Ann Parks, of said County, for & in behalf of her minor son John Parks, being of the age of 14 years, of the one part, & E. J. Bell, of the County aforesaid, of the other part. Witnesseth: That the said Ann Parks, as aforesaid, does by these presents bind out her said son John Parks, of said County, as apprentice to said E. J. Bell in the trade or craft of Husbandry or as laborer upon the plantation of the said E. J. Bell, to be taught the said trade or craft of Husbandry or laborer, & to live with, Continue, & serve the said E. J. Bell as an apprentice from the date hereof for and during the term of 17 months, or until 25 day of December 1904. During all of which time, said Ann Parks, as aforesaid, doth Covenant with the said E. J. Bell that the said John Parks shall well & faithfully demean his self as such faithful Apprentice, observing fully the Command of the said E. J. Bell, & in all things deporting and behaving his self as a faithful Apprentice to the said E. J. Bell, neither revealing his secrets, nor at any time neglecting or leaving the business of the said E. J. Bell. And for & in consideration of the service well & faithfully rendered by the said John Parks, of the first part, said E. J. Bell, of the second part, doth Covenant, promise, and agree to instruct his said Apprentice, or otherwise cause him to be well & faithfully instructed, in the said trade or craft of Husbandry or Laborer, & Shall also allow, furnish, & provide his said Apprentice with meat & drink & clothing during the said term, & all other necessaries meet & proper, in Sickness & in health, & shall also, at the expiration of the said term, allow & pay the said Apprentice Four Dollars per month.

Witness our hands & seals the day & year first before written.

Executed Before Us In duplicate
James McIntosh   Ann + Parks, her mark
J. J. Burch, ordinary   E. J. Bell

Georgia   }   [543]
Elbert County } This Indenture, made this the 15th day of Sep^t 1903, between Edmond Blackwell, of said County, for & in behalf of him self, being of the age

of 52 years, of the one part, & A. S. J. Stovall the County aforesaid, of the other part. Witnesseth: That the said Edmond Blackwell, as aforesaid, does by these presents bind out him self, of said County, as Apprentice to said A. S. J. Stovall in the trade or Craft of Husbandry or Laborer upon the plantation of the said A. S. J. Stovall, to be taught the said trade or Craft of Husbandry or laborer, and to live with, Continue, & serve the said A. S. J. Stovall as an apprentice from the first January 1904 for and during the term of one year. During all of which time, said Edmond Blackwell, as aforesaid, doth Covenant with the said A. S. J. Stovall that the said Edmond Blackwell shall well & faithfully demean his self as such faithful Apprentice, observing fully the Command of the said A. S. J. Stovall, and in all things deporting & behaving him self as a faithful Apprentice to the said A. S. J. Stovall, neither revealing his secrets, nor at any time neglecting or leaving the business of the said A. S. J. Stovall.

And for & in Consideration of the service well and faithfully rendered by the said Edmond Blackwell, of the first part, said A. S. J. Stovall, of the second part, doth covenant, promise, and agree to instruct his Said Apprentice, or otherwise Cause him to be well & faithfully instructed, in the said trade or craft of Husbandry or laborer, & shall also allow, furnish, & provide his said Apprentice with meat & drink & clothing during the said term, & all other necessaries meet & proper, in sickness & in health, & shall also, at the expiration of the said term, allow & pay the said Apprentice Seventy five Dollars.

Witness our hands & seals the day & year first before written. Executed Before Us in Duplicate.

J. H. Gaines   }   Edmond Blackwell, his mark
J. J. Burch, ordinary }   A. S. J. Stovall

Georgia   }   [544]
Elbert County } This Indenture, Made this the 23 day of October 1903, between George Maxwell, of said County, for & in behalf of him self, being of the age of 26 years, of the one part, J. B. Stovall the County aforesaid, of the other part. Witnesseth: That the Said George Maxwell, as aforesaid, does by these presents bind out himself, of said County, as Apprentice to said J. B. Stovall in the trade or craft of Husbandry or as laborer upon the plantation of the said J. B. Stovall, to be taught the said trade or Craft of husbandry or laborer, and to live with, Continue, & serve the said J. B. Stovall as an Apprentice from the first January 1904 for & during the term of 2 years.

During all of which time, said George Maxwell, as aforesaid, doth Covenant with the said J. B. Stovall that the said George Maxwell shall well & faithfully demean his self as such faithful Apprentice, observing fully the Command of the said J. B. Stovall, and in all things deporting & behaving his self as a faithful Apprentice to the said J. B. Stovall, neither revealing his secrets, nor at any time neglecting or leaving the business of the said J. B. Stovall. And for & in consideration of the service well and faithfully rendered by the said George Maxwell, of the first part, said J. B. Stovall, of the second part, doth Covenant, promise, and agree to instruct his said Apprentice, or otherwise Cause him to be well & faithfully instructed, in the said trade or Craft of Husbandry or laborer, & shall also allow, furnish, & provide his said Apprentice with meat & drink during the said term, and shall also, at the expiration of the said term, allow & pay the said Apprentice six & ⅔ Dollars per month or one hundred & sixty Dollars.

Witness our hands & Seals the day & year first before written.

Executed Before Us In duplicate.

All interlinations made before signing.

| J. N. Wall } | George Maxwell, his mark |
| J. J. Burch, ordinary } | J. B. Stovall |

Georgia } [545]
Elbert County } This Indenture, Made this the 24 day of October 1903, between Janie Maxwell, of said County, for and in behalf of her self, being of the age of 24 years, of the one part, & Mrs J. L. Heard the County aforesaid, of the other part. Witnesseth: That the said Janie Maxwell, as aforesaid, does by these presents bind out her self, of said County, as Apprentice to said Mrs J. L. Heard in the trade or Craft of Husbandry or as laborer upon the plantation of the said Mrs J. L. Heard, to be taught the said trade or Craft of Husbandry or Laborer, and to live with, Continue, & serve the said Mrs J. L. Heard as an Apprentice from the date hereof for and during the term of 2 years. During all of which time, said Janie Maxwell, as aforesaid, doth Covenant with the said Mrs J. L. Heard that the said Janie Maxwell shall well & faithfully demean her self as such faithful Apprentice, observing fully the command of the said Mrs J. L. Heard, & in all things deporting & behaving her self as a faithful Apprentice to the said Mrs J. L. Heard, neither revealing her secrets, nor at any time neglecting or leaving the business of the said Mrs J. L. Heard. And for & in Consideration of the service well and faithfully rendered by the said Janie Maxwell, of the first part, Mrs J. L. Heard, of the second part, doth covenant, promise, & agree to instruct her said apprentice, or otherwise

Cause her to be well & faithfully instructed, in the said trade or craft of Husbandry or Laborer, & shall also allow, furnish, & provide her said Apprentice with meat & drink during the said term, and shall also, at the expiration of the said term, allow & pay the said apprentice Fifty Dollars.

Witness our hands & seals the day & year first before written.

Executed Before Us In duplicate.
T. J. Brown
J. J. Burch, Ordinary

Jannie Maxwell
Mrs Jannie L. Heard

Georgia } [546]
Elbert County } This Indenture, Made this the 24 day of October 1903, between Luke Green, of said County, for & in behalf of him self, being of the age of 28 years, of the one part, & W. O. Jones, of the County aforesaid, of the other part. Witnesseth: That the said Luke Green, as aforesaid, does by these presents bind out himself, of said County, as Apprentice to said W. O. Jones in the trade or craft of Brick Making, to be taught the said trade or craft of Brick Making, & to live with, Continue, & serve the said W. O. Jones as an Apprentice from the date hereof for & during the term of Two years. During all of which time, said Luke Green, as aforesaid, doth Covenant with the said W. O. Jones that he will well and faithfully demean himself as such faithful Apprentice, observing fully the command of the said W. O. Jones, and in all things deporting & behaving his self as a faithful Apprentice to the said W. O. Jones, neither revealing his secrets, nor at any time neglecting or leaving the business of the said W. O. Jones. And for & in consideration of the service well and faithfully rendered by the said Luke Green, of the first part, said W. O. Jones, of the second part, doth Covenant, promise, and agree to instruct his said Apprentice, or otherwise Cause him to be well & faithfully instructed, in the said trade or Craft of Brick Making, and Shall also allow, furnish, & provide his said Apprentice with meat & drink during the said term, and all other necessaries meet & proper, in sickness & in health, & shall also, at the expiration of the said term, allow & pay the said Apprentice what is now allowed by the statute in such case made and provided.

Witness our hands & seals the day & year first before written.

Executed Before us In duplicate.
James McIntosh
J. J. Burch, ordinary

L. G. Green
W. O. Jones, by
his Att^y Ge^o C. Grogan

Georgia } [547]
Elbert County } This Indenture, made this 9 day of November 1903, between Jane Latimer, of said County, for & in behalf of her minor children Henry Eberhart, Corine Eberhart, Sallie, & Georgia Jones, being of the age of 15, 12, 7, 3 years, of the one part, & J. Y. Swift the County aforesaid, of the other part. Witnesseth: That the said Jane Latimer, as aforesaid, does by these presents bind out her minor children above named, of said County, as Apprentices to said J. Y. Swift in the trade or craft of Husbandry or as laborers upon the plantation of the said J. Y. Swift, to be taught the said trade or Craft of Husbandry or laborers, & to live with, continue, & serve the said J. Y. Swift as apprentices from the date hereof for and during the term of their minority. During all of which time, said Jane Latimer, as aforesaid, doth covenant with the said J. Y. Swift that the said Henry Eberhart, Corine Eberhart, Sallie Eberhart, & Georgia Jones shall well & faithfully demean them selves as such faithful Apprentices, observing fully the command of the said J. Y. Swift, and in all things deporting & behaving them selves as faithful Apprentices to the said J. Y. Swift, Neither revealing his secrets, nor at any time neglecting or leaving the business of the said J. Y. Swift. And for & in Consideration of the service well and faithfully rendered by the said Henry, Corine, & Sallie Eberhart, Georgia Jones, of the first part, said J. Y. Swift, of the second part, doth Covenant, promise, and agree to instruct his said Apprentices, or otherwise Cause them to be well & faithfully instructed, in the said trade or craft of Husbandry or laborers, & also to read the English language, & shall also allow, furnish, & provide them, said Apprentices, with meat & drink & clothing during the said term, & all other necessaries meet & proper, in sickness & in health, & shall also, at the expiration of the said term, allow & pay the said Apprentices what is now allowed by the statute in such case made & provided, and the said Henry Eberhart five Dollars per Month.

Witness our hands & seals the day & year first before written.

Executed Before Us In duplicate.
W. B. Henry   Jane + Latimer, her mark
J. J. Burch, ordinary   J. Y. Swift

Georgia } [548]
Elbert County } This Indenture, made this the 14 day of November 1903, between Alice Clark, of said County, for & in behalf of her minor son Larry Clark, being of the age of 17 years, of the one part, & L. B. Dye the County aforesaid, of the other part. Witnesseth: That the said Alice Clark, as aforesaid, does by these presents bind out her said son Larry Clark, of said County, as Apprentice to said L. B. Dye in the trade or craft of Husbandry or as laborer upon the plantation

of the said L. B. Dye, to be taught the said trade or craft of Husbandry or laborer, and to live with, Continue, & serve the said L. B. Dye as an apprentice from the date hereof for & During the term of One year. During all of which time, Said Alice Clark, as aforesaid, doth covenant with the said L. B. Dye that the said Larry Clark shall well & faithfully demean his self as such faithful Apprentice, observing fully the command of the said L. B. Dye, And in all things deporting and behaving his self as a faithful Apprentice to the Said L. B. Dye, neither revealing his secrets, nor at any time neglecting or leaving the business of the said L. B. Dye. And for & in consideration of the service well and faithfully rendered by the said Larry Clark, of the first part, said L. B. Dye, of the second part, doth Covenant, promise, and agree to instruct his said Apprentice, or otherwise Cause him to be well & faithfully instructed, in the said trade or craft of Husbandry or laborer, And shall also allow, furnish, & provide his said Apprentice with meat & drink & clothing during the said term, & all other necessaries meet and proper, in sickness & in health, & shall also, at the expiration of the said term, allow & pay the Said Apprentice Twenty Five Dollars.

Witness our hands & seals the day & year first before written.

Executed Before us In duplicate.
J. N. Wall   Alice + Clark, her mark
J. J. Burch, ordinary   L. B. Dye

Georgia   }   [549]
Elbert County   } This Indenture, Made this the 14th day of November 1903, between Hodge Blackwell and Mamie Blackwell, of said County, for & in behalf of them selves, being of the age of 30, 25 years, of the one part, & A. S. J. Stovall the County aforesaid, of the other part. Witnesseth: That the said Hodge & Mamie Blackwell, as aforesaid, does by these presents bind out them selves, of said County, as Apprentices to said A. S. J. Stovall in the trade or Craft of Husbandry or as laborers upon the plantation of the said A. S. J. Stovall, to be taught the said trade or Craft of Husbandry or laborers, & to live with, Continue, & serve the said A. S. J. Stovall as apprentices from the date hereof for and during the term of 2 years.

During all of which time, said Hodge & Mamie Blackwell, as aforesaid, doth Covenant with the said A. S. J. Stovall that the said Hodge & Mamie Blackwell shall well & faithfully demean them selves as such faithful Apprentices, observing fully the Command of the said A. S. J. Stovall, and in all things deporting & behaving them Selves as a faithful Apprentices to the said A. S. J. Stovall, neither revealing his secrets, nor at any time neglecting or leaving the business of the said

A. S. J. Stovall. And for & in Consideration of the service well and faithfully rendered by the Said Hodge & Mamie Blackwell, of the first part, said A. S. J. Stovall, of the second part, doth covenant, promise, and agree to instruct his Said Apprentices, or otherwise Cause them to be well & faithfully instructed, in the said trade or craft of Husbandry or laborers, and Shall also allow, furnish, & provide his said Apprentices with meat & drink & clothing during the said term, & all other necessaries meet & proper, in sickness & in health, & shall also, at the expiration of the said term, allow & pay the said Apprentices One Hundred & fifty Dollars.

Witness our hands & seals the day & year first before written. Executed Before Us In duplicate.

D. B. Alexander
J. J. Burch, ordinary

Hodge + Blackwell, his mark
Mamie + Blackwell, her mark
A. S. J. Stovall

Georgia }   [550]
Elbert County } This Indenture, Made this the 16th day of November 1903, between Richard Calloway, of said County, for & in behalf of him Self, being of the age of 22 years, of the one part, and B. F. Smith of the County aforesaid, of the other part. Witnesseth: That the said Richard Calloway, as aforesaid, does by these presents bind out him self, of said County, as Apprentice to said B. F. Smith in the trade or craft of Husbandry or as Laborer upon the plantation of the said B. F. Smith, to be taught the said trade or Craft of Husbandry or laborer, and to live with, Continue, & serve the said B. F. Smith as an apprentice from January 1st 1904 for & during the term of Six months. During all of which time, said Richard Calloway, as aforesaid, doth covenant with the said B. F. Smith that the said Richard Calloway shall well & faithfully demean his self as such faithful Apprentice, observing fully the Command of the said B. F. Smith, and in all things deporting & behaving his self as a faithful Apprentice to the said B. F. Smith, neither revealing his secrets, nor at any time neglecting or leaving the business of the said B. F. Smith. And for & in consideration of the service well and faithfully rendered by the said Richard Calloway, of the first part, said B. F. Smith, of the second part, doth Covenant, promise, and agree to instruct his said Apprentice, or otherwise Cause him to be well & faithfully instructed, in the said trade or craft of Husbandry or laborer, & shall allow, furnish, and provide his said Apprentice with meat and drink during the said term, and shall also, at the expiration of the said term, allow & pay the Said Apprentice Ten Dollars per month.

Witness our hands & Seals the day & year first before written.

J. M. Hilly
J. J. Burch, ordinary

Richard + Calloway, his mark
B. F. Smith

Georgia   } [551]
Elbert County } This Indenture, made this the 19 day of November 1903, between Sophia Oglesby, of said County, for & in behalf of her minor children Martha, Sarah, & Willie Oglesby, being of the age of 19, 17, 14 years, of the one part, & E. W. Bell the County aforesaid, of the other part. Witnesseth: That the said Sophia Oglesby, as aforesaid, does by these presents bind out her said children, of said County, as Apprentices to said E. W. Bell in the trade or craft of Husbandry or as laborers upon the plantation of the said E. W. Bell, to be taught the said trade or craft of Husbandry or laborers, & to live with, Continue, & serve the said E. W. Bell as apprentices from the first day January 1904 for and during the term of twelve months.

During all of which time, said Sophia Oglesby, as aforesaid, doth Covenant with the said E. W. Bell that the said Martha, Sarah, & Willie Oglesby shall well & faithfully demean them selves as such faithful Apprentices, observing fully the Command of the said E. W. Bell, & in all things deporting & behaving them selves as faithful Apprentices to the said E. W. Bell, neither revealing his secrets, nor at any time neglecting or leaving the business of the said E. W. Bell. And for & in consideration of the service well and faithfully rendered by the said Martha, Sarah, & Willie Oglesby, of the first part, said E. W. Bell, of the second part, doth Covenant, promise, & agree to instruct his said Apprentices, or otherwise Cause them to be well & faithfully instructed, in the Said trade or Craft of Husbandry or laborers, And shall also allow & provide his said Apprentices with meat & drink & clothing during the said term, and at the expiration of the said term, allow & pay the said Apprentices Seventy five Dollars.

Witness our hands & seals the day & year first before written.

Executed Before Us in Duplicate.
D. B. Alexander
J. J. Burch, ordinary

Sophia Oglesby
E. W. Bell

Georgia   } [552]
Elbert County } This Indenture, made this the 20th day of November 1903, between Judge Wilker, of Said County, for & in behalf of him Self, being of the age of 35 years, of the one part, & A. S. Oliver, of the County aforesaid, of the other part. Witnesseth: That the said Judge Wilker, as aforesaid, does by these

presents bind out him self, of said County, as Apprentice to said A. S. Oliver in the trade or craft of Husbandry or as Laborer upon the plantation of the said A. S. Oliver, to be taught the said trade or Craft of Husbandry or laborer, and to live with, Continue, and serve the said A. S. Oliver as an Apprentice from the date hereof for and during the term of 5 years.

During all of which time, said Judge Wilker, as aforesaid, doth Covenant with the said A. S. Oliver that the said Judge Wilker shall well & faithfully demean his self as such faithful Apprentice, observing fully the Command of the said A. S. Oliver, & in all things deporting & behaving his self as a faithful Apprentice to the said A. S. Oliver, neither revealing his secrets, nor at any time neglecting or leaving the business of the said A. S. Oliver. And for & in Consideration of the service well and faithfully rendered by the said Judge Wilker, of the first part, said A. S. Oliver, of the second part, doth covenant, promise, and agree to instruct his said Apprentice, or otherwise Cause him to be well & faithfully instructed, in the said trade or craft of Husbandry or laborer, and shall also allow, furnish, & provide his said Apprentice with meat & drink & clothing during the said term, and shall also, at the expiration of the said term, allow & pay the said Apprentice Fifty Dollars Annually.

Witness our hands & seals the day & year first before written.

Executed Before Us in duplicate.
Abda Oglesby
J. J. Burch, ordinary

Judge + Wilker, his mark
A. S. Oliver

Georgia   }   [553]
Elbert County } This Indenture, Made this the 21st day of November 1903, between Alice Starke, of said County, for & in behalf of her minor son Robert Starke, being of the age of 14 years, of the one part, & S. S. Brewer, of the County aforesaid, of the other part. Witnesseth: That the said Alice Starke, as aforesaid, does by these presents bind out her said son Robert, of said County, as Apprentice to said S. S. Brewer in the trade or Craft of Husbandry or as laborer upon the plantation of the said S. S. Brewer, to be taught the said trade or craft of Husbandry or laborer, & to live with, continue, & serve the said S. S. Brewer as an apprentice from the date hereof for & during the term of one year.

During all of which time, said Alice Starke, as aforesaid, doth covenant with the said S. S. Brewer that the said Robert Starke shall well & faithfully demean his self as such faithful Apprentice, observing fully the Command of the said S. S. Brewer, and in all things deporting & behaving his self as a faithful Apprentice to the said S. S. Brewer, neither revealing his secrets, nor at any time neglecting or leaving the business of the said S. S. Brewer. And for & in Consideration of the Service well and faithfully rendered by the said Robert Starke, of the first part, said S. S. Brewer, of the Second part, doth covenant, promise, & agree to instruct his said Apprentice, or otherwise cause him to be well & faithfully instructed, in the said trade or craft of Husbandry or Laborer, And Shall also allow, furnish, & provide his said Apprentice with meat & drink & clothing during the said term, and all other necessaries meet and proper, in sickness and in health, & shall also, at the expiration of the said term, allow & pay the said Apprentice Four Dollars per month.

Witness our hands & seals the day & year first before written.

Executed Before Us In Duplicate.
George Haslett   Alice + Starke, her mark
J. J. Burch, ordinary   S. S. Brewer

Georgia   }   [554]
Elbert County   } This Indenture, Made this the 10th day of October 1903, between Parker Thornton, of Oglethorpe County, for & in behalf of him self, he being of the age of 28 years, of the one part, & Ben Thornton, of the County of Oglethorpe, of the other part. Witnesseth: That the said Parker Thornton, as aforesaid, does by these presents bind out him self, of said Oglethorpe County, as Apprentice to said Ben Thornton in the trade or craft of Husbandry or as laborer upon the plantation of the said Ben Thornton, to be taught the said trade or craft of Husbandry or laborer, & to live with, continue, & serve the said Ben Thornton as an Apprentice from the 1st day January 1904 for and during the term of one year. During all of which time, said Parker Thornton, as aforesaid, doth Covenant with the said Ben Thornton that the said Parker Thornton shall well & faithfully demean his self as such faithful Apprentice, observing fully the command of the said Ben Thornton, & in all things deporting & behaving his self as a faithful Apprentice, observing fully the command of the said Ben Thornton, & in all things deporting & behaving his his self as a faithful Apprentice to said Ben Thornton, neither revealing his secrets, nor at any time neglecting or leaving the business of the said Ben Thornton. And for & in Consideration of the service well and faithfully rendered by the said Parker Thornton, of the first part, said Ben Thornton, of the second part, doth covenant, promise, and agree to instruct his said Apprentice, or otherwise Cause him to be well & faithfully instructed, in the said trade or craft of Husbandry or laborer, & shall also allow, furnish, & provide his said Apprentice with meat & drink & clothing during the said term, & all other

necessaries meet & proper, in sickness & in health, & shall also, at the expiration of the said term, allow & pay the said Apprentice Seventy five Dollars.

Witness our hands & seals the day & year first before written.

Executed Before us in duplicate.
D. B. Alexander   }   Parker Thornton
J. J. Burch, ordinary }   Ben Thornton

Georgia   }   [555]
Elbert County } This Indenture, made this the 27 day of November 1903, between Mary Allen, of said County, for & in behalf of her minor son Clove Allen, being of the age of 13 years, of the one part, and W. B. J. Norman, of the County aforesaid, of the other part. Witnesseth: That the said Mary Allen, as aforesaid, does by these presents bind out her said son Clove Allen, of said County, as Apprentice to said W. B. J. Norman in the trade or craft of Husbandry or as laborer upon the plantation of the said W. B. J. Norman, to be taught the said trade or craft of Husbandry or laborer, & to live with, continue, & serve the said W. B. J. Norman as an Apprentice from the first of January 1904 for and during the term of one year. During all of which time, said Mary Allen, as aforesaid, doth covenant with the said W. B. J. Norman that the said Clove Allen shall well & faithfully demean his self as such faithful apprentice, observing fully the Command of the said W. B. J. Norman, and in all things deporting & behaving his self as a faithful Apprentice to the said W. B. J. Norman, neither revealing his secrets, nor at any time neglecting or leaving the business of the said W. B. J. Norman. And for & in consideration of the service well and faithfully rendered by the said Clove Allen, of the first part, said W. B. J. Norman, of the second part, doth Covenant, promise, and agree to instruct his said Apprentice, or otherwise Cause him to be well & faithfully instructed, in the said trade or craft of Husbandry or laborer, and shall also allow, furnish, & provide his said Apprentice with meat & drink & clothing during the said term, & all other necessaries meet & proper, in sickness & in health, & shall also, at the expiration of the said term, allow & pay the said Apprentice Thirty Dollars.

Witness our hands & seals the day & year first before written.

Executed Before Us In Duplicate.
W. A. Rucker   Mary + Allen, her mark
J. J. Burch, ordinary   W. B. J. Norman

Georgia   }   [556]
Elbert County } This Indenture, Made this the 3rd day December 1903, between

George Rucker, of said County, for & in behalf of his son Ned Rucker, being of the age of 15 years, of the one part, and D. O. Partain, of the County aforesaid, of the other part. Witnesseth: That the said George Rucker, as aforesaid, does by these presents bind out his son Ned Rucker, of Said County, as Apprentice to said D. O. Partain in the trade or craft of Farm Work or as laborer upon the plantation of the said D. O. Partain, to be taught the said trade or Craft of Farm Work or laborer, & to live with, Continue, and serve the said D. O. Partain as an apprentice from the 1st day of January 1904 for and during the term of the year of 1904 at Six Dollars per month. During all of which time, said George Rucker, as aforesaid, doth Covenant with the said D. O. Partain that the said Ned Rucker shall well & faithfully demean him self as such faithful Apprentice, observing fully the Command of the said D. O. Partain, and in all things deporting & behaving him self as a faithful Apprentice to the said D. O. Partain, neither revealing his secrets, nor at any time neglecting or leaving the business of the said D. O. Partain.

And for & in Consideration of the service well and faithfully rendered by the said Ned Rucker, of the first part, said D. O. Partain, of the second part, doth Covenant, promise, and agree to instruct his said Apprentice, or otherwise Cause him to be well & faithfully instructed, in the said trade or craft of farm Work or laborer, & shall also allow, furnish, & provide his said Apprentice with meat & drink during the said term, & shall also, at the expiration of the said term, allow & pay said apprentice what is now allowed by the statute in such Case made & provided. In the event the said Ned Rucker fails to give said D. C. Partain good service or shall leave him, I, George Rucker, agree to put my son Nathaniel Rucker in his place

Witness our hands & seals the day & year first before written. Executed Before us In Duplicate.

W. A. Rucker	George + Rucker, his mark
J. J. Burch, ordinary	D. O. + Partain, his mark

Georgia   }   [557]
Elbert County } This Indenture, made this the 5 day of December 1903, between Frank Mortton, of said County, for & in behalf of him self, being of the age of 22 years, of the one part, and C. H. Allen, of the County aforesaid, of the other part. Witnesseth: That the said Frank Mortton, as aforesaid, does by these presents bind out him self, of said County, as apprentice to said C. H. Allen in the trade or craft of Husbandry or as laborer upon the plantation of the said C. H. Allen, to be taught the said trade or craft of Husbandry or laborer, & to live with, Continue, & serve the said C. H. Allen as an Apprentice from the date hereof for and during the term of 13 months, or until 25 day December 1904. During all of which time, said

Frank Mortton, as aforesaid, doth covenant with the said C. H. Allen that the said Frank Mortton shall well & faithfully demean his self as such faithful apprentice, observing fully the Command of the said C. H. Allen, And in all things deporting and behaving him self as a faithful Apprentice to the said C. H. Allen, neither revealing his secrets, nor at any time neglecting or leaving the business of the said C. H. Allen. And for & in Consideration of the service well & faithfully rendered by the said Frank Mortton, of the first part, said C. H. Allen, of the second part, doth covenant, promise, and agree to instruct his Said Apprentice, or otherwise Cause him to be well & faithfully instructed, in the said trade or craft of Husbandry or laborer, & shall also allow, furnish, and provide his said Apprentice with meat & drink & clothing during the said term, & all other necessaries meet & proper, in sickness & in health, & shall also, at the expiration of the said term, allow and pay the said Apprentice Eight Dollars per month. Witness our hands & seals the day & year first before written.

Executed Before Us In duplicate.

J. N. Wall	Frank + Mortton, his mark
J. J. Burch, ordinary	C. H. Allen

Georgia } [558]
Elbert County } This Indenture, Made this the 7 day of December 1903, between Abe Foster & Mandy Foster, of said County, for & in behalf of their minor son John Foster, being of the age of 13 years, of the one part, and S. A. Hutchinson, of the County aforesaid, of the other part. Witnesseth: That the said Abe & Mandy Foster, as aforesaid, does by these presents bind out their said son John, of said County, as Apprentice to said S. A. Hutchinson in the trade or craft of Husbandry or as laborer upon the plantation of the said S. A. Hutchinson, to be taught the said trade or craft of Husbandry or laborer, & to live with, continue, & serve the said S. A. Hutchinson as an apprentice from the date hereof for & during the term of one year. During all of which time, said Abe & Mandy Foster, as aforesaid, doth Covenant with the said S. A. Hutchinson that the said John Foster shall well & faithfully demean him self as such faithful apprentice, observing fully the Command of the Said S. A. Hutchinson, & in all things deporting & behaving his self as a faithful Apprentice to the said S. A. Hutchinson, neither revealing his secrets, nor at any time neglecting or leaving the business of the said S. A. Hutchinson. And for & in Consideration of the service well & faithfully rendered by the said John Foster, of the first part, said S. A. Hutchinson, of the second part, doth covenant, promise, & agree to instruct his said apprentice, or otherwise cause him to be well & faithfully instructed, in the said trade or craft of Husbandry or laborer, and shall also allow, furnish, & provide his said Apprentice with meat &

drink & clothing during the said term, and all other necessaries meet & proper, in sickness & in health, and shall also, at the expiration of the said term, pay the Said Apprentice Ninety five $^{50}/_{100}$ Dollars. Now it is expressly understood that we promise to make good all lost time by said John Foster from any cause whatever. All interlinations made before signing.

Witness our hands & seals the day & year first before written.

Executed Before Us In Duplicate.
T. W. Baldwin
J. J. Burch, ordinary

Abe + Foster, his mark
Mandy + Foster, her mark
S. A. Hutchinson

Index

   ———
   Bill, 24
   Calvin, 114
   Sallie, 225
Adams
   E. T., 63
   Henry, 167
   M. F., 63, 64, 66
   Minnie, 167
   Rosa, 167
   T. L., 63, 64, 66, 88
   W. A., 18
   W. B., 18, 112
   William, 167
Alexander
   D. B., 41, 42, 52, 62, 84, 219, 227, 228, 231
   L. N., 39
   M. D., 79
Allen
   Alen, 204, 205
   Alfred, 37, 38
   Ben, 28, 29
   Beverly, 204, 205
   C. H., 60, 61, 81, 232, 233
   C. M., 103
   Carey, 204, 205
   Charles, 81
   Clove, 231
   Emanuel, 178, 179, 182
   Ernest, 58
   Erskin, 58
   Georgia, 28, 29
   John, 58
   Maria, 178, 179
   Mary, 231
   Mattie May, 178, 179
   McIntosh, 204, 205
   Oliver, 37, 38
   Oscar, 58
   Willis, 37, 38
Almond
   G. L. A., 189
   J. M., 131
Anderson
   W. F., 212
Andrews
   T. P., 167
Arnold, 28, 68
   J. Y., 36, 68
   McAlpin, 34, 35, 114, 208
   W. T., 43
Auld, 22
   Fred W., 23
   W. N., 22, 23
Ayers
   W. J., 19, 20
Baldwin
   T. W., 234
Banks
   Cynthia, 195
   Dick, 54, 55, 73, 74, 96, 97
   Harrison, 160, 161
   Henry, 219, 220
   Joe, 195
   John, 160
   Lizzi, 74
   Lizzie, 54, 55, 73, 74
   Missy, 196
   Missy Lizzie, 197
   Paul, 160
   Sam, 195

Will, 196, 197
Wm., 195, 196
Beasley
   J. A., 136, 137, 138, 141, 142, 187
Bell
   Ann, 21
   Anna, 21
   B. B., 212, 213
   E. J., 4, 5, 16, 17, 18, 20, 21, 160, 161, 162, 176, 177, 178, 201, 207, 208, 221
   E. W., 228
   Norma, 212, 213
   W., 228
   Willie, 21
Biggs
   T. D., 192
   Thos., 8
   Thos. D., 131, 132, 133
   Tom, 8
Black
   J. W., 139
Blackwell, 100, 122
   Abner, 99, 100
   Alexander, 100, 101
   Allen, 129, 130
   Ana, 130
   Annie, 130
   Charlotte, 16, 17, 188, 189
   D. R., 21
   Edmond, 221, 222
   George, 29, 30
   H. A., 100, 101
   Hodge, 226, 227
   J. A., 65
   J. H., 173, 174
   Jim, 130
   John, 188
   Jun, 130
   Lavonia, 16, 17
   Lizzie, 6, 100, 101, 180, 181
   Lou, 16, 17
   Lou Hannah, 16
   Lula, 130, 173, 174
   Mamie, 226, 227
   Mary, 100, 101
   Mattie, 6
   Milly, 6
   Minnie, 100, 101, 130
   Nathan, 16, 17
   Robert, 180, 181
   Sing, 29
   Singleton, 29, 30
   Vina, 99, 129, 130, 131
   W. H., 121, 122
   Will, 115, 116, 179, 180
   William, 119, 120
   Wm., 100, 101
Bond
   C. T., 26, 27, 47, 48, 49, 74, 120, 147, 148, 153, 154, 155
   G. T., 87
   George C., 207
   J. R. E., 200
   J. W., Jr., 94
   Jas. W., Jr., 93
   M. R., 184
   Roberta, 107
   Roda, 107
   Will, 107
Booth
   J. R., Jr., 192
Bowman
   Oz, 183
Brady
   J. A., 136
Braw
   Lu, 47
Brawner, 122, 166

Albert, 38
Alia, 5
Calvin, 34, 35, 114
Charlie, 199, 200
Elbert, 47, 193
Elias, 10, 38, 39
Eugene, 148, 149
George, 165
H. J., 173
Henry, 150, 151
Jep, 4, 33, 34, 91, 92, 150, 151, 159, 160, 211, 212
Jesse, 193
Jno., 122
Joe, 91
Joe H., 33
Joe Henry, 33, 34
John, 121
Lu, 47
Mandy, 5, 6
Mathew, 34, 114
Robert, 47
T., 195
Thomas, 4, 114
Thos., 114
Tom, 34
Vomus, 4
William, 121
Wm., 121, 122
Brewer
  H. J., 58
  S. S., 146, 229, 230
Brown, 69
  Bob, 211
  C. H., 85, 86
  Frank, 105
  Georgia, 105, 106
  H. J., 85
  J. C., 115, 116
  J. H., 109, 110
  J. J., 8, 9
  Jim, 46, 47
  Jno. C., 30, 56, 57, 85, 141, 163, 164
  John C., 29, 30, 36, 37, 56, 57, 85
  John M., 17
  Jut, 215
  L. M., 155, 156
  Lula, 73
  M. J., 107
  Peter, 201, 202
  S. S., 81, 82, 92, 108, 109, 110, 111, 122, 123
  T. J., 99, 105, 109, 110, 116, 144, 200, 203, 209, 215, 224
  T. W., 99
  W. J., 87, 88
  W. T., 103
  W. T. M., 91, 92, 103, 159, 160
Brownlee, 56, 129
  D. E., 55
  T. J., 53, 129
Bullard
  George, 166
  Henry, 127, 128
  Jessie, 127
  Sol, 165, 166
Burch
  J. J., 4, 5, 6, 7, 9, 10, 11, 12, 13, 14, 15, 16, 17, 18, 19, 20, 21, 24, 25, 26, 27, 28, 29, 30, 31, 32, 33, 34, 35, 36, 37, 38, 39, 40, 41, 42, 47, 52, 54, 55, 56, 57, 58, 61, 62, 63, 64, 65, 67, 68, 69, 70, 72, 73, 74, 75, 76, 80, 81, 82, 83, 84, 85, 86, 87, 88, 89, 90, 91, 92, 94, 95, 96, 97, 98, 99, 100, 101, 102, 103, 104, 105, 106, 107, 108, 109, 110, 111, 112, 113, 114,

115, 116, 117, 118, 119, 120,
121, 122, 123, 124, 125, 126,
127, 130, 131, 136, 137, 138,
140, 141, 142, 143, 144, 145,
146, 147, 148, 149, 150, 151,
152, 153, 154, 155, 156, 157,
158, 159, 160, 161, 162, 163,
164, 165, 166, 167, 168, 169,
170, 171, 172, 173, 174, 175,
176, 177, 178, 179, 180, 181,
182, 183, 184, 185, 186, 187,
188, 189, 190, 191, 193, 194,
195, 197, 198, 199, 200, 201,
202, 203, 204, 207, 208, 209,
210, 211, 214, 215, 217, 218,
219, 220, 221, 222, 223, 224,
225, 226, 227, 228, 229, 230,
231, 232, 233, 234
  T. S., Jr., 12
  W. J., 70
Burdell
  Delroe, 214, 215
Burden
  G. N., 25, 26, 175
Burdett
  William, 206, 207
  Wm., 207
Burris
  J. G., 78, 79
Burriss
  M., 93
Burton
  Jim, 109
  John, Jr., 42
  John, Sr., 42, 43
  Sue, 109, 110
Cade
  Carter, 69, 190
  Corine, 133, 134
  Emil, 190
  Frank, 69
  Henry, 133, 134
  Jane, 133, 134
  Jim, 69
  Ora, 133, 134
  Sallie, 133, 134
Caldwell
  G. W., 107
  Geo. W., 106
Calhoun
  Sam, 205, 206
  Stephen, 205, 206
  Winnie, 205, 206
Calloway
  Richard, 227, 228
Campbell
  T. J., 25, 35
Carrooth
  C. P., 33
Carruth
  C. P., 34
Carter
  Emil, 190
  R. P., 84, 203
  T. H., 97, 98
  Thomas H., 97
  Thos. H., 97
Cason
  E. A., 180
Cauthen
  Beckie, 62, 63
  H. W., 149
  J. A., 72, 118, 119, 149, 203
  W. M., 157
Chandler
  J. J., 57
Chapman
  John C., 27
  John C., Jr., 27
Chidd

C., 193
Christian
  Bishop, 139, 140
  Wash, 41, 42
  William, 139
  Wm., 140
Clark
  Alice, 225, 226
  Edmond, 181, 182
  Larry, 225, 226
Clement
  Reuben, 145
Cleveland
  A. J., 199
  J. W., 122
  Joe, 66, 67
  L. M., 66
  P. A., 71
  R. M., 14
  Stark, 66
Clinkscales
  J. A., 66, 67
Colbert
  Omire, 4
Collins
  Charlie, 213, 214
Conwell
  J. M., 187
Cummings
  Ann, 93
  Bill, 93
  Bud, 78, 79
  Henry, 78, 79
Curry
  Willis, 215
Daniel
  M. A., 18
  Will, 198
Davenport
  Eli, 209, 210

Ely, 209
Jackson, 209, 210
Davis
  A. P., 186
  Andrew Jackson, 194
  Ap, 194
  Elizabeth, 194
  Giles, 183, 184
  Jim, 194
  Joe, 194
  Loualla, 194
  Pearce, 40
  Reubin, 40
  Rose Tate, 45, 46
  Sallie, 194
  Seaborn, 194
  Tom, 186, 194
  Willie, 194
Deadwyler, 132
  Jack, 156, 191, 192
  Jesse, 131, 132
  Minerva, 132, 133
  Sam, 131, 132
Dean
  Ora, 71
  Stephen, 71, 72
Dickerson
  Ella, 57
  Lizzie, 57, 58
  Lullu, 57
  May, 57
  Sallie, 57
  Tinsley, 57
  Tom, 57
  Wade, 52, 57, 58
  Will, 52
  Willis, 57
Dickson
  C. J., 202, 203
Dixon

J. M., 129, 152, 205, 206
Dodd
  C. P., 75
Downer
  Adam, 181, 182
  Marsh, 176, 177, 218
  Mary, 75, 76
  W. H., 150, 151
  Whit, 181, 182
Du Bose
  J. D., 129
  Luther, 176, 177, 218
Dubose
  Edna, 55
  Emma, 56
  Jerry, 55, 56
  Luvina, 55, 56
Durrett, 90
  Georgia, 90, 91
  Irene, 90
  John, 90, 91
  Rose Mary, 90
Dye
  Fayet, 112
  Fayett, 111, 112
  Fayette, 149
  L. B., 225, 226
  W. N., 203
Earle
  C. E., 111, 112
Eberhardt, 42, 43, 44, 45, 46, 47, 49, 50, 51, 59, 60
  L. P., 43, 187, 188
Eberhart, 38, 39, 40, 41
  Alexander, 101, 102
  Allen, 8, 9, 36, 37
  Anbury, 26
  Ansberry, 10
  Ansbury, 25
  Asbel, 14, 15
  Asberry, 11, 12
  Asbury, 93, 94, 101, 102, 135, 136
  Bud, 102, 103, 135, 136, 144, 145
  Charley, 10, 101, 102, 135, 136, 137
  Corine, 133, 134, 225
  Henry, 133, 134, 225
  Jane, 133, 134
  Jess, 101
  Jesse, 101, 102
  Jessie, 14
  Jim, 25, 26, 135, 136, 137, 138, 187
  John, 36, 37
  Judge, 11, 135, 136, 137, 138
  Ora, 133, 134
  Sallie, 133, 134, 225
  York, 93, 94, 101, 102
Ector
  C. G., 203
  Capus, 202
  G. A., 203
  Georgia, 202
Edmonds
  Sam, 43, 44
Edward
  E. B., 100
  L. C., 48
Edwards
  Andrew, 204
  C. A., 78
  Elijah, 59, 60
  L. C., 49, 81, 141, 185
  Marcus, 204
Fambrough
  L. G., 30, 31, 44, 145
Faust
  Burl, 120
  James, 120

Favors
  John, 185, 186
Fleming
  Charlotte, 77, 112, 113
  Josie, 76, 77
  Jossie, 77
  Masouria, 77
  Misoura, 76
  Russel, 76, 113, 114
  W. L., 12
  Will, 76, 77, 112
Fortson
  Andrew, 92
  F. B., 40
  Francis, 200
  H. A., 19, 86, 167
  Ira, 151
  Jessie, 53
  Jim, 210, 211
  John, 69, 70
  L. M., 27
  Launs, 27
  M. E., 148
  Peter, 189, 190
  Ransom, 151, 152
  Richard, 200
  Robert, 92
  S. H., 191
  T. F., 152, 168, 169
  Thomas, 53, 54
  Tom, 151, 168, 169
  Wash, 169
  Washington, 168
  Willie, 92
  Wyley, 92
Foster
  Abe, 233, 234
  John, 233
  John Henry, 85
  Mandy, 85, 233, 234

  William, 85
Gaines
  Alice, 203
  Arthur, 70
  Francis, 70
  Georgia, 192, 193
  Green, 70, 71
  Henry, 203
  Herbert, 192
  Ira, 70
  J. H., 222
  Joe, 203
  Lois, 203
  Mollie, 70
  R. S., 14, 15, 23, 24
  S. E., 30
  T. S., 60
  W. S., 158
Gant
  J. C., 203
Gibbs
  Ed, 177, 178
Glanton
  J. T., 80
Glove
  I. D., 152
Goss
  B. F., 129, 152, 205, 206
  B. H., 32
  Dan, 125, 126
  Fannie, 128
  John, 128
  Oister, 128
  Oyster, 128
Gray
  Alexander, 152
  Elexander, 152
  Elie, 53
  Lindsay, 52, 53
  Lindsey, 152

241

Lindsy, 152
Linsy, 152
Green
  L. G., 224
  Luke, 224
Gresham
  Mark, 89, 90
  Sue, 89, 90
  Tame, 89, 90
Grimes
  John, 74, 75, 76
  W. S., 31, 32
Grogan, 182
  Geo. C., 175, 179, 182, 183, 224
  George C., 182, 218
  W. M., 133, 134, 183
Gunter
  Antonett, 7
  Isaac, 7
  Lottie, 7
  Rosa, 7
  Sallie, 7
  W. C., 102, 103, 144, 145
Haley, 94
  Ada, 142, 143
  G. W., 71
  John, 142, 143
  Lonnie, 94, 95
  Vohamie, 142, 143
Hall
  G. P., 53, 54
  T. B., 77, 78
Ham
  Harrison, 43
  John, 81, 82
  William, 81, 82
Hamlin
  H. D., 212
Hammond
  A. E., 197
  H. T., 112, 113, 114
  J. B., 185, 186
  J. E., 76, 77
  W. J., 176, 215
Harden
  J. G., 135
Harper
  A. O., 83
  J. P., 104
  J. W., 110
  J. W., Jr., 110
  John, 197
  Mat, 118, 119
  Mattie, 197
  Missy, 197
Harris
  C. P., 145
Haslett
  George, 98, 124, 137, 157, 161, 181, 201, 208, 230
Hatten
  Hugh, 108
  John Frank, 108
Hawes
  P. M., 88, 158
Hawkins
  Ann, 147, 148
  Bella, 18
  George, 147, 148
  Harve, 147, 148
  Isabella, 18, 147, 148
  John, 18
Haygood
  Fletcher, 22
  George, 22, 23
  Martha, 22, 23
Heard, 131
  Anna, 128, 129
  Ben Joe, 32, 146, 147, 170, 171
  Bill, 217, 218

C. M., 160
Charley, 95
E. B., 133, 134, 178, 179
Eugene, 201
Frank, 95
Gate, 32
Gete, 146, 147
J. L., 223
J. T., 204
Jannie L., 224
Jefferson, 215, 216
Jno. Henry, 170
Jno. T., 68, 116, 117, 210, 211
Joe, 32
John, 32
John Henry, 146, 147, 170
John T., 116
Jordan, 35, 36, 131
Lavonia, 32
Llewellyn, 215
Llewylling, 216
Oscar, 35
R. M., 13, 61, 108, 113, 114, 177
Seven, 166, 167
Simond, 35
Tom, 217, 218
William, 201
Henry
  W. B., 225
Herndon
  J. E., 6, 86, 195
  J. E., Jr., 86, 87
  Luther, 149, 150
  Willis, 36
Hester
  W. A., 63
  William, 39, 62
Hicks
  Ben, 121, 155, 156
  Ben H., 120, 121

Charley, 120, 121, 155
Jim, 155
John, 155
Higginbotham
  E. B., 119, 120
Hill, 129
  Allen, 129, 130
  Ana, 130
  Ann, 99, 100
  Annie, 130
  Clara, 172, 173
  Clifford, 191
  George, 191
  Isham, 172, 173
  Jim, 99, 100, 130, 191
  Jun, 130
  Lula, 99, 100, 130
  Minnie, 99, 100, 130
  Peter, 99, 100
  Sally, 191
  Tilda, 191
  Vina, 99, 100, 129, 130, 131
  Walter, 191
  Yancy, 129
Hilly
  J. M., 228
Holley
  Earley, 39
  Joe, 39
Howard
  A. E., 24
Hudgens
  D. F., 10
  J. C., 105, 106, 107, 123, 124, 170, 201, 202, 216, 217
  Jno. C., 105, 106, 169
  John C., 105, 123, 169
  R. E., 47, 120, 193, 198, 199
  W. M., 100, 101
Hudson

Abe, 61, 62, 83, 84
Ada, 83, 84
Charley, 61
Eliza Ann, 114, 115
Falcon, 175, 176
Falcon, Jr., 176
Hattie, 115
Isaac, 175, 176
Zanie, 115
Zannie, 86, 87
Huff
  Lella, 51
  Lula, 51, 94
  Ron, 51, 52
Humble
  John, 106, 107
  Mary, 106, 107
Hunt
  L. H., 138, 139
  Sam, 181, 182
Hutchinson
  S. A., 233, 234
Hutson
  Isaac, 7
Irvin
  W. H., 76
Irwin
  W. H., Jr., 186
Isam
  Armstead, 24
  Sam, 24
Isham
  Armstead, 30, 31
  Corn, 30
  Sallie, 30
  Sam, 30
Jackson
  Jno., 68
  John, 50, 51
  Sam, 13, 14

  Willie, 13, 14
Jones
  Andrew, 60, 61
  Barney, 60, 61
  Cary, 60, 61
  Eugene, 164, 165
  George, 133
  Georgia, 225
  Hattie, 212, 213
  J. B., Jr., 53, 79, 93
  J. B., Sr., 104, 156
  Jack, 164, 165
  M. R., 24
  Mary, 146
  W. G., 25
  W. G. B., 77
  W. J., 67, 68
  W. J. B., 76
  W. O., 64, 65, 75, 76, 124, 125, 126, 195, 196, 197, 212, 213, 214, 215, 224
  Wilborn, 24, 25
  Willie, 146
  Willis, 85, 86
  Willis G., 25
Kay
  Benj. H., 28
Kennebrew
  Clark, 168
Kerlin
  D. S., 188
  W. H., 149, 203
King
  J. W., 45
Latimer
  Jane, 225
Lumkin
  Geo. B., 133
Lumpkin
  Geo. B., 132

Lunsford
  G. A., 70, 71, 79, 80, 101, 102
  Geo. A., 9, 74, 75, 135, 136
  George, 12, 13
Magill
  Geo., 96
Martin
  Mary, 122, 123
Massey
  Mary, 88
  Robert, 88
Mathews
  A. J., 208, 209
  W. J., 186
Mattox, 16
  C. M., 93, 198
  Clark, 26, 27
  Early, 216, 217
  Felix, 64, 197
  Gilbert, 116, 117
  Green, 116
  Isham, 15
  Jacob, 15
  John, 216, 217
  Julian, 15, 16
  Laura, 208, 209
  Tom, 194, 195, 216, 217
  Wes, 216, 217
Maxwell
  George, 222, 223
  J. D., 19, 20
  J. H., 150
  Janie, 223
  Jannie, 224
  M. E., 80, 92, 104, 117, 118, 164, 165, 211
  M. H., 179, 180, 181
  Thomas, 81
  William, 19, 20, 81
McCalla, 52, 127, 128, 194

  Danis, 73, 74
  Dunsie, 55
  Ephraim, 97, 98
  J. W., 53, 57, 128, 152, 162, 166, 167, 174, 194, 204, 205, 206
  Jno. W., 52, 127, 129, 152, 161, 175, 194
  John W., 57, 58
  Martha, 97
McClain
  D. M., 141
  Dillard, 141
  Jordan, 141
  Loyed, 141
McGill
  George T., 106
McIntire
  James, 37
McIntosh
  Albert, 117, 118, 158, 159
  Alfred, 40, 41
  Elijah, 117, 118
  James, 56, 72, 73, 90, 95, 115, 117, 146, 159, 162, 167, 175, 194, 217, 220, 221, 224
  Jane, 40, 41
  Jas., 170
  Lige, 158, 159
  Peter, 158, 159
  Robert, 117
McKinley
  Lint, 178
McKinly
  Lint, 178
McLanahan
  D. L., 71, 72, 143, 144
  E. V., 41, 42, 88, 89
  G. H., 115, 190, 218
  Geo. H., 115

J. A., 61, 62, 84, 181, 182, 192, 193
J. J., 149, 150, 200
J. T., 182
M. A., 89, 90, 95
Mack, 69, 70
Mc, 70
Mewborn
  A. T., 11, 12
  J. H. H., 11, 12
Mewbourn
  M. F., 92
Miles
  J. Alan, 211
  J. Allen, Jr., 176
Moon
  Arthur, 28
  Freddie, 28
  Jack, 28
  Ollie, 28
Moore, 15, 16
  W. F., 15, 16
Morris, 126, 127
  Will, 126, 127
Morrison, 13, 175
  Amy, 21, 22
  Anderson, 175
  M. A., 175
  Moses, 21, 22
  Wiley, 12, 13
Mortton
  Frank, 232, 233
Moseby
  Junius, 10
Moss, 67
  Jackson, 67
  Orn, 121, 122
Motes
  N. M., 156
Neal

B. A., 10
Nelms
  J. J., 83, 84, 184, 185
  T. A., 94
Nickols
  Henry, 134, 135
  Matilda, 134, 135
Norman, 153
  E. B., 137
  G. P., 36, 55, 74, 97, 99, 105, 153
  Geo. P., 55, 73, 74, 96, 97, 98, 99, 105, 153
  George P., 96, 99, 104, 105
  H. P., 33, 34
  J. W., 32, 35, 36, 146, 147
  W. B. J., 231
Oglesby, 124
  A. L., 131, 132, 192
  Abda, 21, 29, 36, 39, 82, 95, 111, 114, 117, 118, 119, 120, 130, 131, 140, 142, 171, 183, 190, 213, 229
  Ada L., 131, 132, 133, 191, 192
  B. J., 125
  D. P., 172, 173, 178
  Martha, 228
  Sarah, 228
  Sophia, 228
  Walter, 124, 125
  Willie, 228
Olbon
  J. F., 10, 11
Oliver, 38, 39, 40, 41, 42, 43, 44, 45, 46, 47, 49, 50, 51, 59, 60
  A. S., 43, 156, 157, 158, 159, 170, 171, 172, 228, 229
  A. S., Jr., 43
  Sam L., 48, 49, 124, 125, 126, 127, 154, 155, 174, 196, 197
  Samuel L., 15, 16

Parker
　Henry, 84
　Lewis, 9
　William, 84
Parks
　Ann, 206, 207, 220, 221
　Anna, 219
　Dennis, 206
　Eddie, 206, 220
　John, 206, 221
　Lizzie, 206
　Richard, 206
　T. M., 193
　William Dennis, 219
　Willis, 206
Partain
　D. O., 232
Partin
　D. O., 96
Pass
　Edmond, 31
　William, 31, 32
Peyton
　Helen, 140
　Hellen, 140
　James, 140
　Jas., 140
Pressley
　Bettie, 161
　Cora, 161
　Fannie, 161, 162
　Frank, 161, 162
　George, 161
　Warren, 161
Pulliam
　J. M., 65, 66
　Jim, 73
　William, 44, 45
Ray
　John, 122, 123

Rena, 122, 123
Reaves
　Jas. F., 4
Rembert
　Robert, 113, 114
Rhodes
　G. B., 171, 172
Richardson
　Charley, 26
　Dora, 26, 27
Robson
　Steve, 88, 89
Rock
　Alex, 12
Roebuck
　Adam, 23, 24
　H. A., 204
　Jim, 23, 141, 142
Rogers
　Z. B., 23, 191
Rousey
　H. C., 73, 184
Rouzie
　T. F., 38
Ruck
　J. W., 38
　W. A., 197
Rucker
　Ada, 54
　Albert, 68
　Ben A., 68
　Benjn., 68
　Caroline, 56, 57, 163
　Charles, 64, 65, 67, 68
　Claiborn, 20, 21
　Fletcher, 22
　George, 54, 187, 188, 232
　Harriet, 54
　Hattie, 54
　Hettie, 48, 49

Hunter, 54
Hunter, Jr., 54
Ida, 5, 6
Ike, 56, 57, 163, 164
J. W., 25, 37, 38
Jeptha, 64, 65, 67
Lewellyn, 56, 57
Lizzie, 54
Minnie, 54
Nathaniel, 187, 188
Nathiel, 187
Ned, 232
Robert, 20, 87, 88
Samie, 54
Sarah, 47, 48
Sid, 158
Tinney, 64, 65, 67
Tinny, 67
Tinsey, 163, 164
Tinsley, 56, 57
W. A., 101, 102, 103, 165, 168, 169, 196, 207, 210, 211, 213, 215, 231, 232
W. P., 21
William P., 21, 22
Zennie, 87
Sanders
  W. M., 14
  Wm. M., 13
Scales
  Billie, 62
  George, 62
Seymore, 51
  A. A., 63, 64
  C. M., 82, 83, 88
  H. M., 51, 52
  J. G., 143, 217, 218
  J. H., 51, 139
  J. W., 139, 140
  O. J., 218

Owen J., 211
Shaw
  T. D., 143
Shon
  J. L., 89
Shumate
  A. M., 55, 163, 164
  T. M., 97
  W. A., 122
Smith
  A. F., 182, 183, 214, 215
  B. F., 219, 220, 227, 228
  Barnard F., 220
  Clarence, 82, 83
  George, 82, 83, 198, 199
  Joseph, 82, 83
  Sue Jett, 140
  W. J., 20
  W. T., 166
  William, 111
  Willie, 111
Spear
  George, 96
  Warren, 96
Spurlock
  Arthur, 64, 80
  Corry, 64
  Ephrie, 80
Stark
  Allen, 59
  Henry, 173
Starke
  Alice, 108, 109, 229, 230
  Anderson, 143, 144
  E. B., 128
  E. B., Sr., 202
  Luther, 108, 109
  Margaret, 176, 177, 218
  Robert, 143, 229, 230
  Sam, 17, 18

Stone
  Luther, 103, 162
  Marsh, 162
  Marshal, 103
Stovall
  A. S. J., 54, 72, 121, 148, 149, 209, 210, 222, 226, 227
  J. B., 222, 223
  J. H., 32, 91, 147, 151
  J. M., 78
Stowers
  Henry, 207, 208
  Paul, 207
Strange
  John Henry, 110
Summons
  J. W., 47
Swift
  J. Y., 21, 29, 100, 130, 134, 135, 220, 221, 225
  James Y., 21, 28
  Jas. Y., 21, 29, 131, 133, 134, 135
  Thos. M., 186
  W. A., 129, 130, 188, 189
Tate
  Doe, 75, 76
  Edna, 56
  Emma, 55
  Eugene, 145
  Fox, 174, 175
  Gordon, 45
  Jim, 174, 175
  Lewelling, 56
  Lewellyn, 55, 56
  Norma, 212, 213
  Sarah, 174, 175
  W. D., 178
  Z. A., Jr., 200
  Zimri, 199
Taylor

  C. P., 162
  G. C., 107
Thompson
  Annie, 169
  Clide, 63
  Clyde, 63
  Emily, 169, 170
  George, 123, 169
  Gordan, 65
  Harman, 123, 124
  Harrison, 169, 170
  Henry, 49, 50, 169
  Kye, 65
  Millard, 63, 64, 65, 66
  Ora, 63
  Rossie, 169
  W. H., 140
  William, 123, 169
Thornton
  B. H., 59
  Ben, 230, 231
  J. E., 43, 45, 46, 47, 50, 51, 59, 60, 68
  J. H., 6
  Jim, 79, 80
  Parker, 230, 231
Thunderburg
  Kate, 4, 5
Thurman
  A., 219
  Arthur, 219
Tinsley
  M. E., 58
Tinsly, 58
  Martha E., 58
Turner
  L. H., 123
Tutt
  W. D., Jr., 22, 95
Upshaw

Joe, 189
T. C., 64
Vail
  W. B., 50
Van Duzer
  J. C., 182
Vanduzer
  J. C., 52, 183
Vanpin
  J. W., 216
Vickery
  L. M., 138
W., 72
Wall
  J. N., 24, 145, 178, 198, 223, 226, 233
  King, 77, 78
  Mat, 184, 185
  R. E., 76, 77
  Sallie, 194, 195
  T. J., 76, 77
  Tommie, 77, 78
  Willis, 194, 195
Wallis, 125, 126, 127
  W. E., 125, 126, 127
Wansley
  H. C., 120
Washington
  General, 72
  William, 72
Webb
  Lucinda, 189, 190
Wharton
  James, 58

White
  Ann, 18
  Frank, 106
  George, 18, 98, 104, 105, 157
  Henry, 99, 153, 154, 155
  Ida, 153
  Mamie, 153, 154, 155
  Rosa, 153
  Sam, 98, 99, 104, 105, 153, 157
  Sol, 98
  Solomon, 153
  T. R., 135
  W. M., 99
  William, 98
Whorton
  J. W., 52
Wilhite
  J. L., 46
Wilker
  Collins, 172
  Jno., Jr., 171
  Judge, 228
Wilkins
  Henry, 120, 121
  Will, 138, 139
Willis
  R. M., 27
  T. A., 31, 40, 44, 47, 54, 69, 80
Worley
  Jos. N., 18
Worton
  Mattie, 208
Wyche
  M. H., 128

www.ingramcontent.com/pod-product-compliance
Lightning Source LLC
Chambersburg PA
CBHW020646300426
44112CB00007B/259